IMAGES
of America

KEW GARDENS

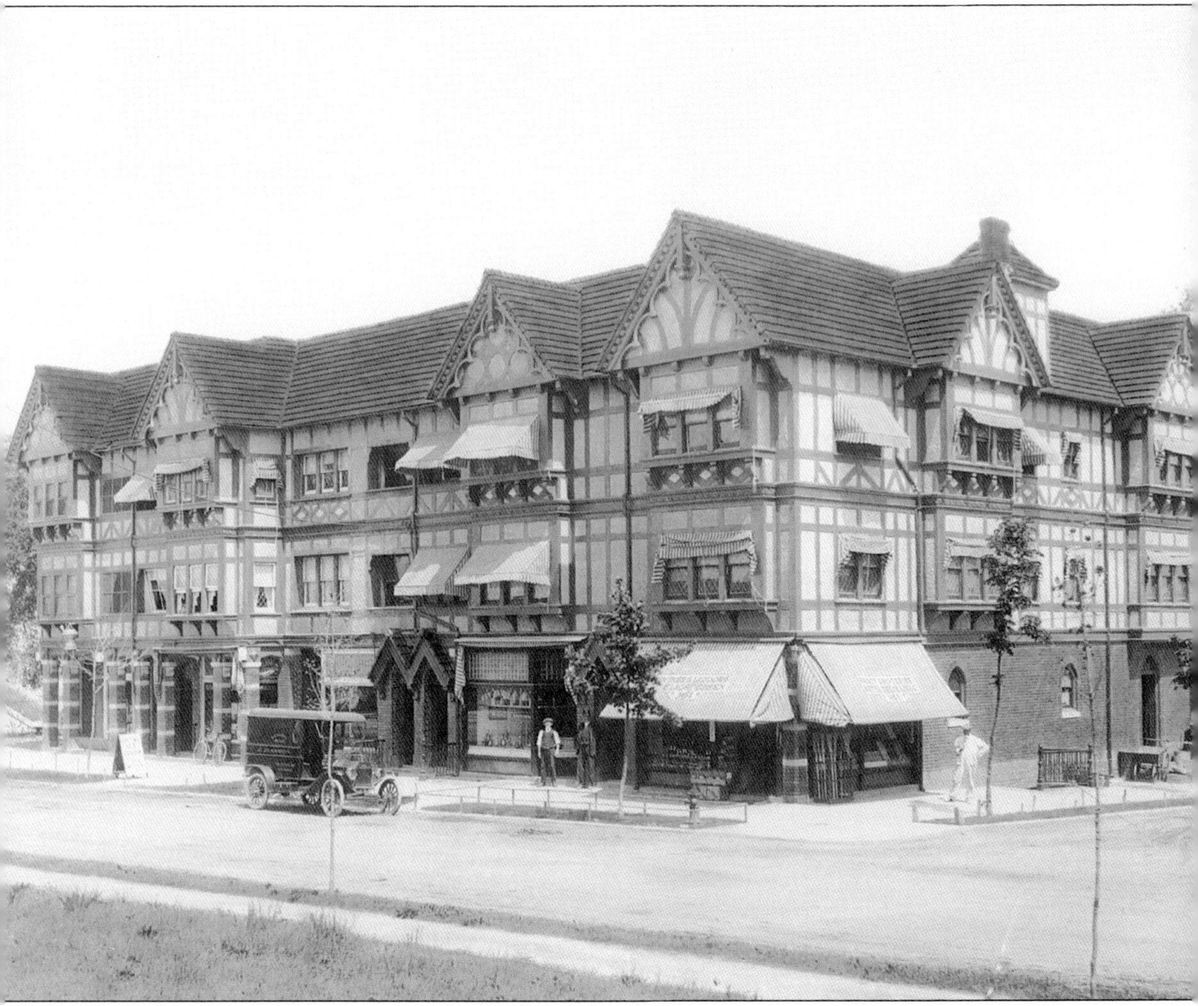

Shown here is the Homestead Building. The *New York Herald* reported the following on November 24, 1912: "Foundation work for a unique business block was begun last week at Kew Gardens, L.I., on a plot located at the corner of Lefferts Avenue and Cuthbert Place and will be completed on January 1, 1913." The corner shop with extended awnings became the first grocery store serving Kew Gardens. (Author's collection.)

On the Cover: This photograph shows Brevoort Street near Abingdon Road. The *New York Press* reported the following on May 3, 1914: "This spring will be the greatest building season the Kew development ever has known. New houses are being built in all sections and plans for many more completed last week. The prices of these houses range from $9,500 to $22,500, and are of the latest type." (Courtesy Bob Stonehill.)

IMAGES
of America

KEW GARDENS

Carl Ballenas with the Aquinas Honor Society
of the Immaculate Conception School

Foreword by Barry Lewis

ARCADIA
PUBLISHING

ISBN 978-1-4671-2072-3

Published by Arcadia Publishing
Charleston, South Carolina

Printed in the United States of America

Library of Congress Control Number: 2013941747

For all general information, please contact Arcadia Publishing:
Telephone 843-853-2070
Fax 843-853-0044
E-mail sales@arcadiapublishing.com
For customer service and orders:
Toll-Free 1-888-313-2665

Visit us on the Internet at www.arcadiapublishing.com

This book is dedicated to Joseph De May, the Josephine Foundation, and the Immaculate Conception School, all instrumental in nurturing the students of the Aquinas Honor Society.

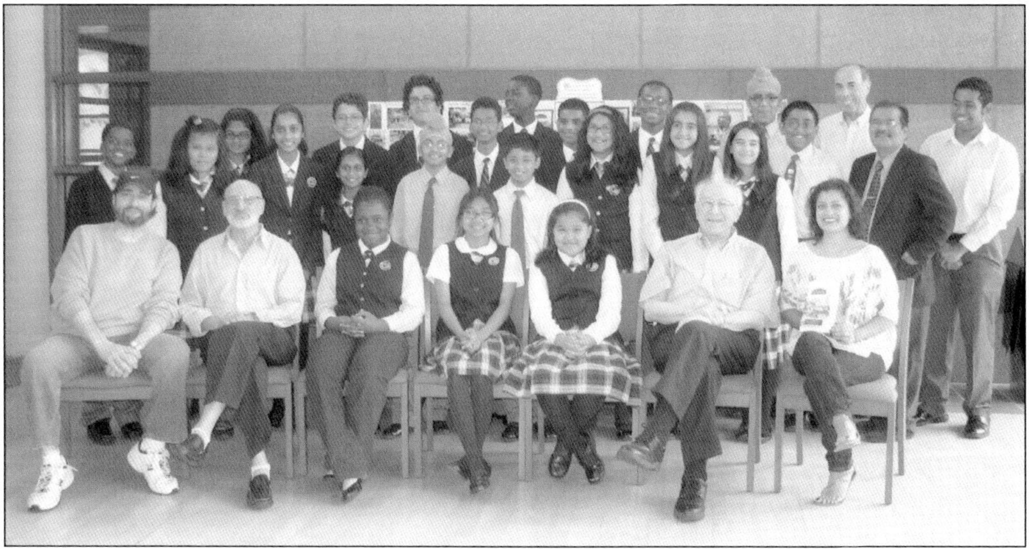

Contents

Foreword

Kew Gardens is part of American urban planning history. It came out of a generation that saw the downside of the modern industrial era: "city neighborhoods" composed of characterless row houses and tenements that spread out to infinity, no beautiful piazzas or squares, no town centers, and no parks or play areas to speak of. To counteract this architectural "anomie," innovative English architects in the 1870s dreamed up the idea of the "garden suburb," what today is called "the new urbanism."

The idea quickly spread to the States, and in New York City, an early version, Richmond Hill, began building up in the 1870s. By the 20th century, with the spread of fast mass transit, six more such planned communities rose in Queens: Kew Gardens, Forest Hills Gardens, Jackson Heights, Douglaston, Sunnyside, and Fresh Meadows. All, or most, brilliantly offered access to mass transit, so that residents did not *have* to have a car. The developments had a local "downtown" for shopping and entertainment, a community clubhouse for social gatherings, lectures, and classes, and community sports facilities to work off the stresses of the modern world. All of this was within walking distance of where people lived.

After World War II, Americans took to the car and went to the suburbs, considering neighborhoods like Kew Gardens to be too "old fashioned." But cycles play themselves out, and today's young America wants an urban experience, to live in a community that allows them to walk to the grocery store, the movie house, or a friend's for dinner. Had this country followed the examples of earlier New Urbanist neighborhoods like Kew Gardens, perhaps Americans today would not be stuck in traffic, consumed with road rage, and living a life that has eliminated the need for legs as mobility.

This book is a testament to the fact that a new, young generation is rediscovering the special qualities that have made, and continue to make, Kew Gardens a special example of living in a neighborhood that is both urban and green, spacious and compact, set apart and yet so much in the middle of New York City.

—Barry Lewis
Kew Gardens, New York

Acknowledgments

One cannot tell the rich story of Kew Gardens in 127 pages. So many fascinating, interesting, and extraordinary people, places, and events have influenced Kew Gardens that could not be included in this book, and we regret their being omitted. The following have contributed greatly to the making of this book: Carl Ballenas, Ron Marzlock, Gavriel Maman, Malini Singh McDonald, Joe De May, and Patrick Wing. The following Aquinas Honor Society students also contributed to this book: Varun Arjoonsingh, Tobi Ayeni, Temi Ayeni, Jason Bacalla, Bernadette Bismonte, Abigail Bossa, Carlos Carranza, Kaitlyn Castillo, Nathalie Castillo, Hazel Charcos, Munawar Choudhury, Neela Dookhie, Tori Dasraj, Anjali Deodat, Anuja Deodat, Jessica Doyle, Tiffany Espeut, Gabrielle Hollant, Gregory Hollant, Guillaume Hollant, Dylan Hoosein, Kyle Hoosein, Katelyn Hoosein, Rosemarie Hernandez, Mayka Johnson, Sultan Kaur, Arjun Kirkland, Amanda Lallemand, Nandita Mathura, Patrick Menchaca, Harvey Miguel, Kent Mira, Niya Mitru, Carmilia Moise, Ariel Narine, Kevin O'Neale, Johnathan Overton, Ryla Pasaoa, Anissa Phoolsawat, Kiana Powell, Kimberly Ramcharitar, Gabriella Ramlall, Andrew Ramdas, Phillip Ramdas, Julia Reese, Jason Remy, Jexel Jay Sabordo, Orlando Santiago, Sierra Santiago. Keyana Saunders, Gabrielle Singh, Agampreet Singh, Jasmilian Singh, Jorawar Singh, Carl Smith, Gaurav Srivastava, Ellaine Talusan, Gabriella Tamayo, and Esha Vohra.

During the making of this book, numerous individuals and institutions offered their invaluable services, such as the families of the authors, the Immaculate Conception faculty and staff, Principal Dorothea Breen, Andrew Koslosky and the Josephine Foundation, Barry Lewis, Judith Todman, and Eric Huber of the Archives at the Queens Borough Public Library, the Richmond Hill Historical Society, William Krooss, Nancy Cataldi, Bonnie Thompson Dixon and the Maple Grove Cemetery Association, The Friends of Maple Grove, Helene and Bob Stonehill, Jean Philippe Rancy, Alex Samaroo, Murray Berger, Sylvia Hack, Philippe Woolley and family, Enyi Lu, Lucy Ballenas, Dr. Carlos Ballenas, the Dr. Edgar Ballenas family, and the Dr. Nancy Baxter Ballenas family. A special note of gratitude to MTB and to Lawrence Waterhouse. Photographs in this book belong to the private collection of the author, unless otherwise noted.

INTRODUCTION

Kew Gardens and its older sister community of Richmond Hill were built by two generations of the Man family. Albon Platt Man, a successful New York lawyer, founded Richmond Hill, a Victorian-era village, in 1868, with his partner Edward Richmond, a noted landscape architect. According to his granddaughter, Elizabeth Man Sarcka, Albon's vision for a future community developed as follows: "It seems that grandfather Man, when driving in his buggy from Wall Street to his summer home, would pause to enjoy the sunny slope, which dropped gently southward form the 'backbone' of the island. Its well-kept farms and woodland were perfect for a rural community where city workers could escape from turmoil, and enjoy peaceful homes." This ideal—to create a tranquil, peaceful natural community far from the urban strangulation of congestion, noise, and confined spaces—would become instilled into the mind of his son, Alrick Hubble Man.

Albon's son also became a successful lawyer and would have the opportunity to fulfill his own vision of a tranquil rural community, a sister village to his father's Richmond Hill, when he developed the community of Kew Gardens at the advent of a new century, in 1910. Its ideals stayed strong for years, as is evident by this 1927 quote from Charles S. Cole, president of the Coloka Realty Company and one of the oldest residents of the village. "This beautiful residential section of 10,000 to 12,000 has had nearly all its growth in the last decade. The influx is not only from Manhattan, but from all parts of the country."

Over 100 years later, Kew Gardens has been witness to change and redevelopment. The terrain that would one day become Kew Gardens was the northern part of Richmond Hill. In 1896, the Mans developed the area into a renowned nine-hole golf course. By 1910, the Long Island Railroad rebuilt and electrified its Main Line. The Mans noted that the land was highly suitable for development and, quickly thereafter, the village of Kew Gardens was born. Many additional changes would occur in its century of existence.

One

From the Beginning

Influences of the Past

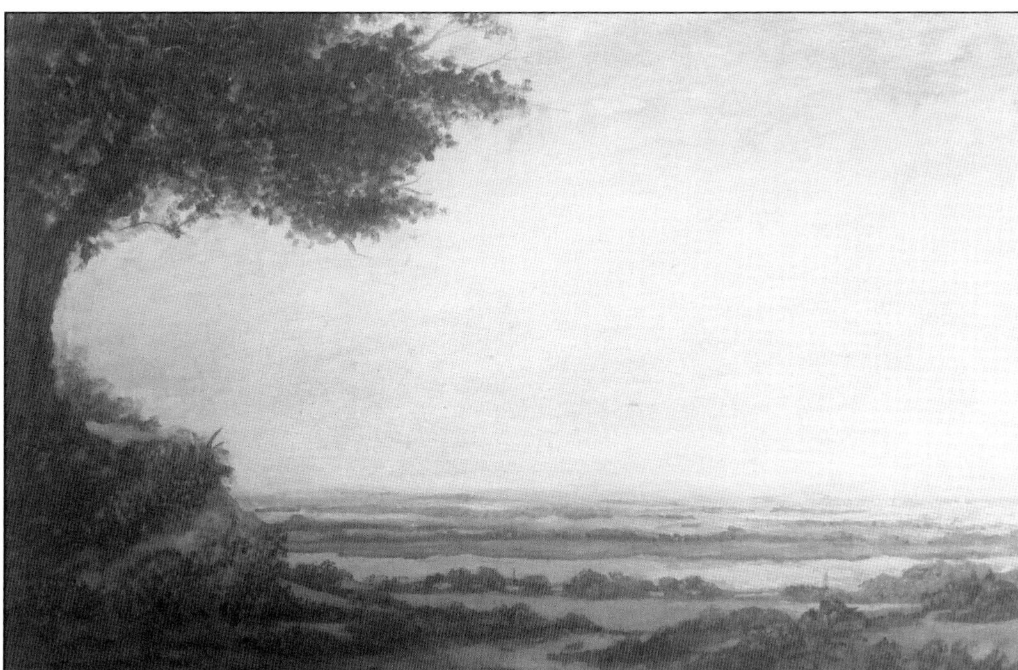

This 19th-century painting shows the "brow of the hill," which refers to the Terminal Moraine, the "Backbone of Long Island" created by glaciers 10,000 years ago. It was from this location that Albon Man had a vision to create the town of Richmond Hill, below this peak, in 1868. Decades later, his son Alrick would develop this hilly land into the town of Kew Gardens. Both communities were in the Jamaica Territory.

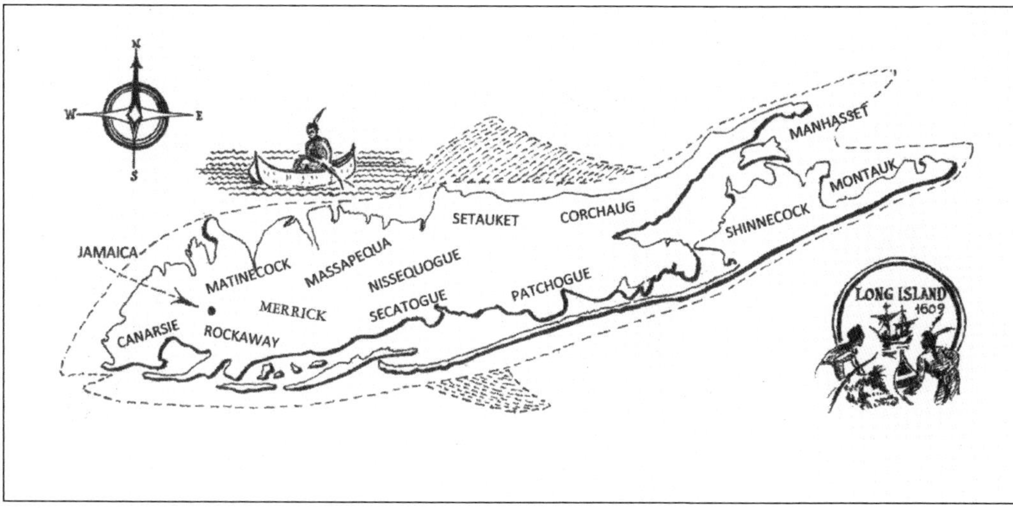

Tribes of indigenous people living on Long Island viewed the land in the shape of a fish and called it *Paumanok*, meaning "island that pays tribute." Powerful tribes in the surrounding areas forced the relatively peaceful Long Islanders to give tributes to avoid attacks. The people lived as hunters and fishermen, but some were farmers, raising beans and corn. Animals found there included deer, bear, raccoon, turkey, quail, partridge, beaver, and duck.

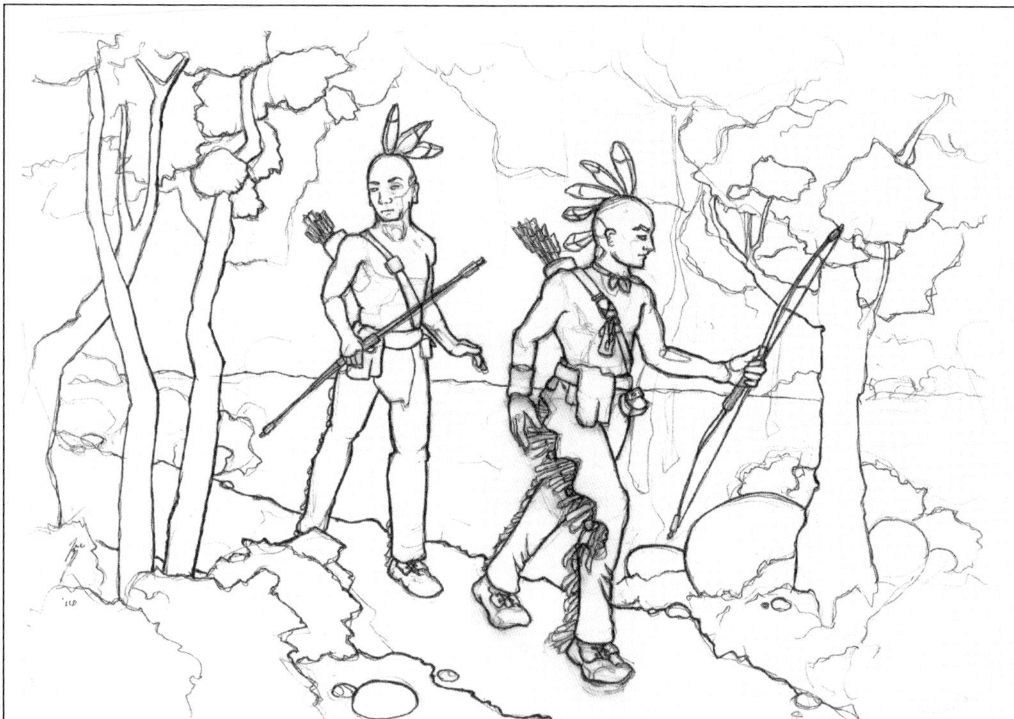

The tribes that would occupy what became the Jamaica Territory included the Canarsie and Rockaway. The indigenous tribes on Long Island used an antique trail that would one day become Jamaica Avenue. People from as far away as the Ohio River and Great Lakes used the trail to trade skins and furs for wampum, polished oblong shells strung on leather strings to form necklaces and belts

In 1609, the Dutch were the first Europeans to claim land in what is now New York. They started a settlement named New Amsterdam in 1625 at the southern tip of what is now Manhattan. The western portion of Long Island was also settled by the Dutch. In 1656, a group of English settlers petitioned Gov. Peter Stuyvesant (shown here) for permission to form a settlement in this Long Island area.

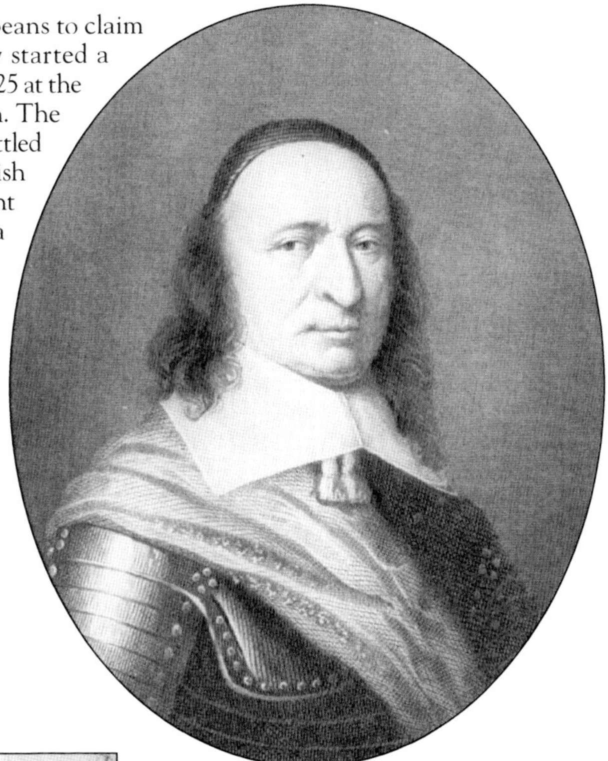

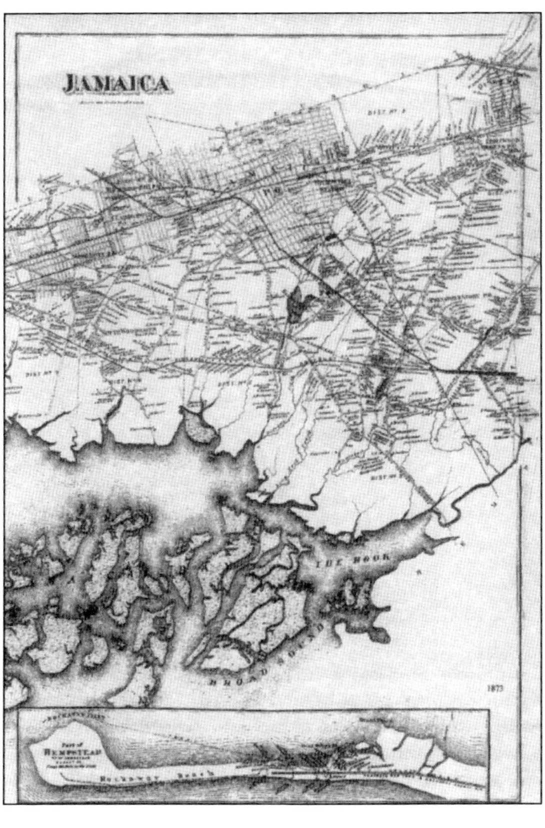

A charter was granted on March 21, 1656, for the area originally named Rusdorp, Dutch for "quiet village." New Amsterdam became New York in 1664 with the English conquest. Rusdorp became Jamaica (an indigenous word meaning "place of the beavers"). In 1683, the British divided the province of New York into counties, one of which was Queens. The Jamaica Territory in Queens County would be the location for Richmond Hill and Kew Gardens.

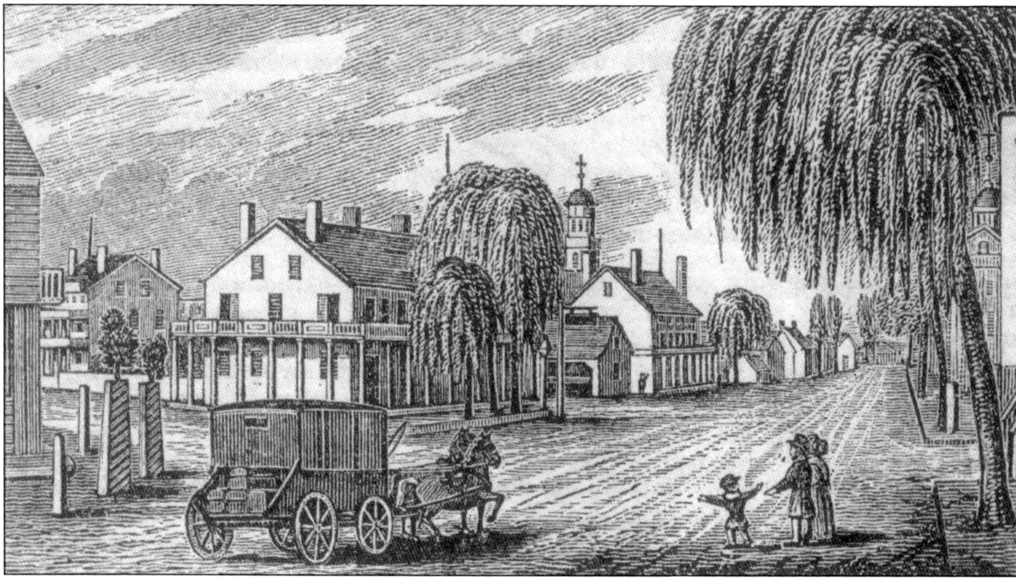

This 1841 engraving of Jamaica looks west on Jamaica Avenue from the Parsons Boulevard intersection. Beyond the horse-drawn coach is the Queens Head Tavern, where George Washington stayed in 1790. On the right, partially hidden by the tree, is Grace Church. It was erected in 1822, and destroyed by fire in 1861. Across the road is the steeple of the Dutch Reform church of 1833, lost to a fire in 1857.

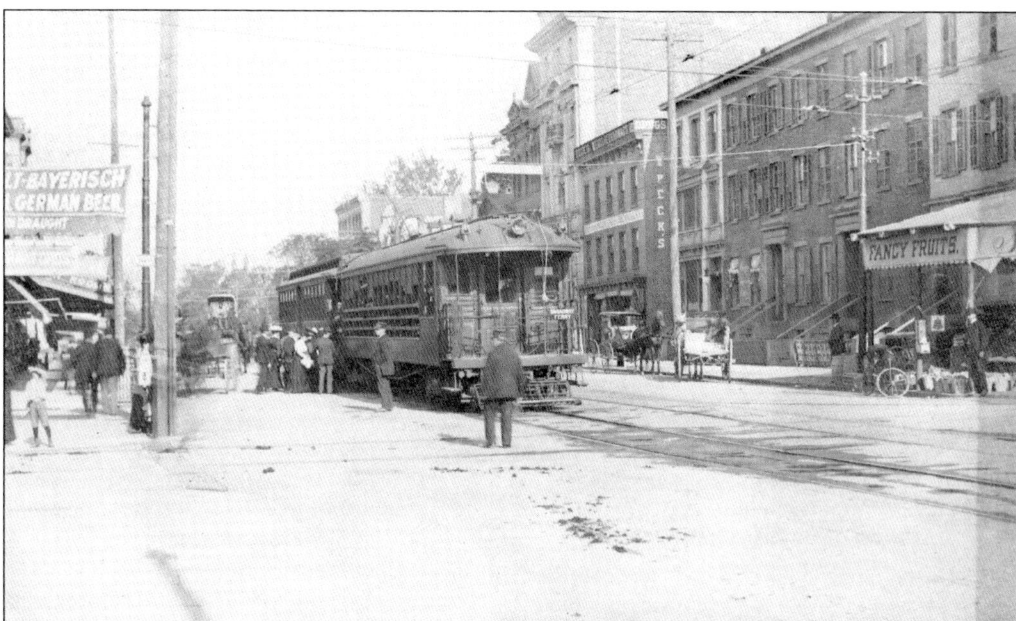

Walt Whitman wrote, "The infinitude of Jamaica stores and public houses allows an inference much which is the truth, viz.: that farmers, travelers, marketmen, and other passengers on the turnpike through the village give it all its trade and retail business." Whitman, a poet, essayist, journalist, and humanist, lived in Jamaica and worked as a typesetter for the *Long Island Farmer* newspaper in 1839. (Courtesy Bob Stonehill.)

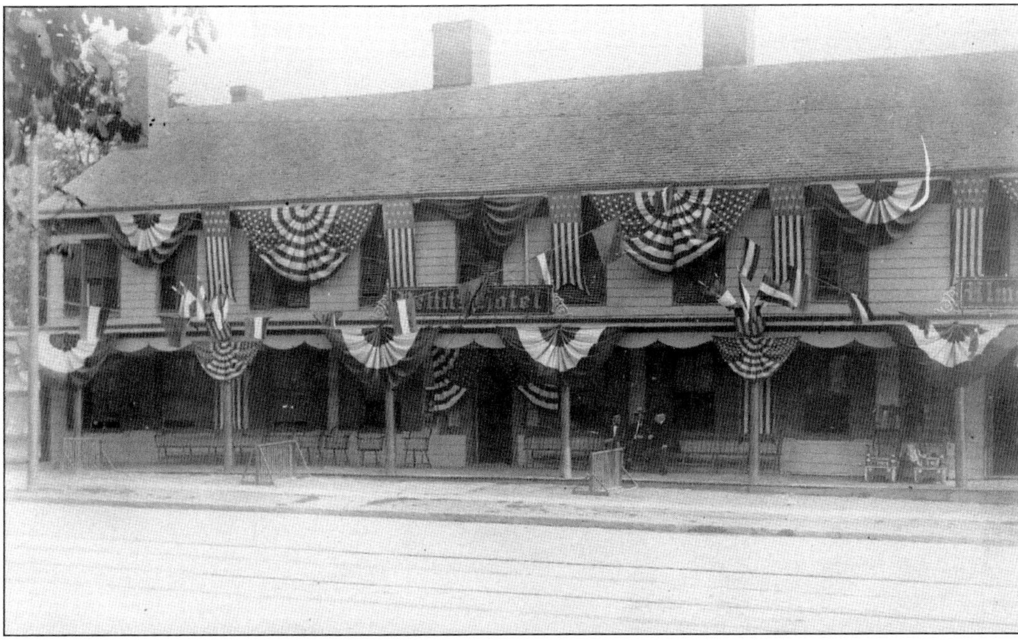

According to the *New York Times* of July 21, 1900, "Pettit's Tavern, on Jamaica Avenue is one of Long Island's oldest road houses. George Washington slept here in 1790, calling it a 'pretty good and decent house.' Known first as Queens Head, Thomas Rochford kept the tavern with an elegant tea garden." It was torn down in 1906, and the Joseph P. Addabbo Federal Building occupies the site today. (Courtesy Bob Stonehill.)

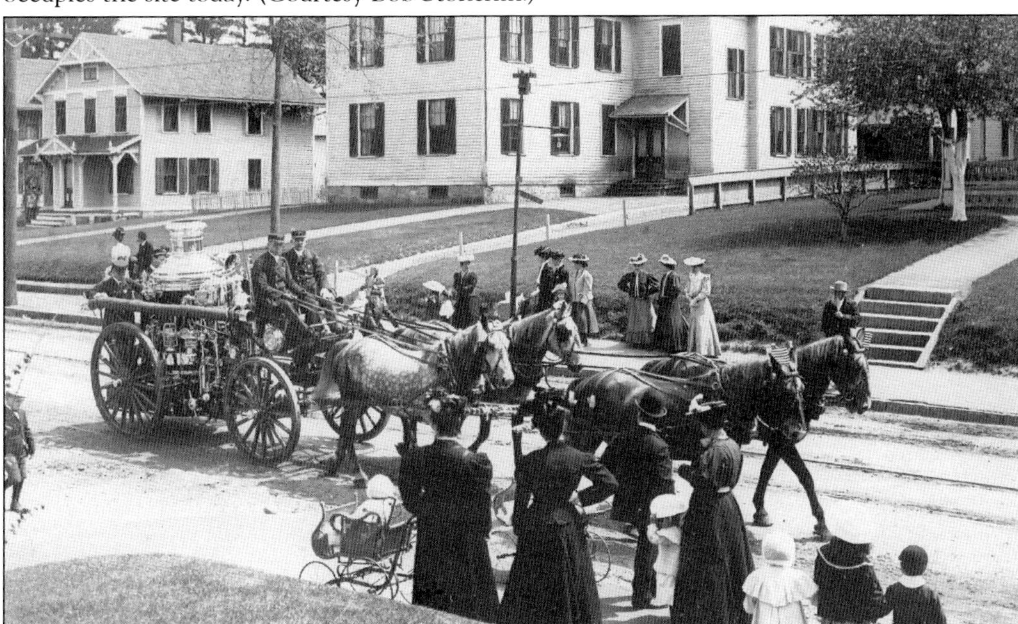

Citizens of Jamaica watch a parade in the early 1900s. A fire engine is drawn by a team of four horses. In 1797, James Waters, owner of a fire engine, petitioned for the better extinguishing of fires. Proprietors of a fire engine in Jamaica were authorized to form an organization of three to five trustees, who would choose 13 volunteer firemen. (Courtesy Bob Stonehill.)

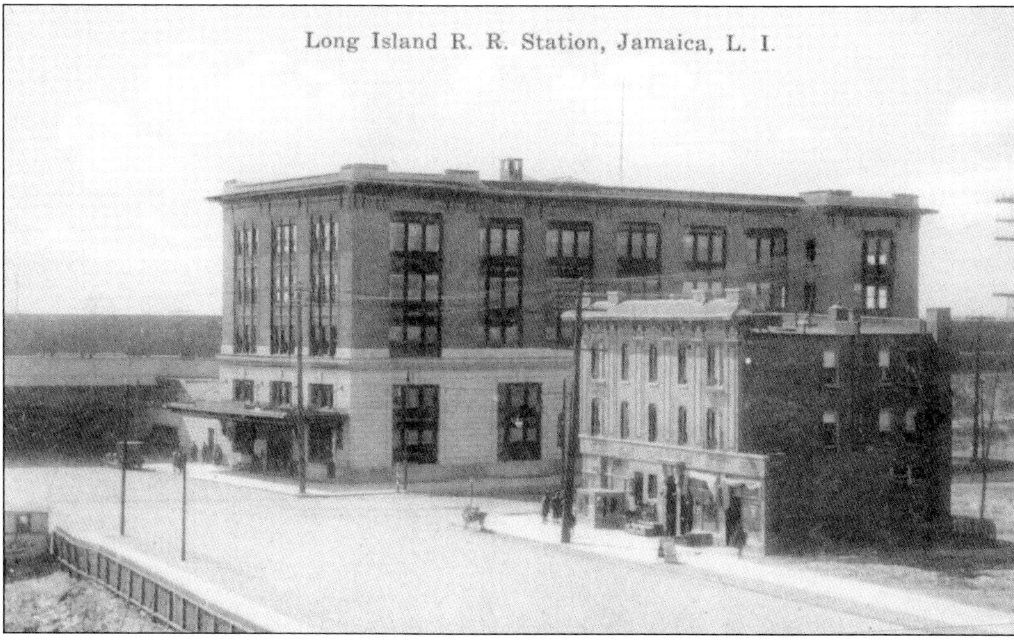

The Brooklyn & Jamaica Railroad, the first railroad on Long Island, incorporated in 1832. Completed on April 18, 1836, it ran from the East River to Jamaica. The original Jamaica depot was built in 1836. A second was built nearby at the South Side Railroad and was called Jamaica Beaver Street Station. Both stations were razed between 1912 and 1913, and a new station, pictured here, was erected at Sutphin Boulevard.

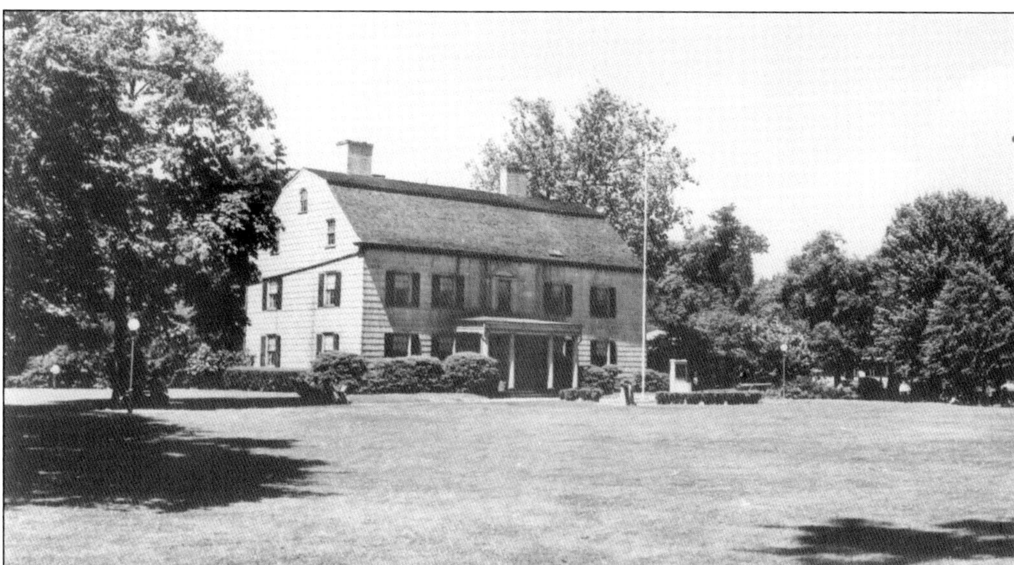

The King Manor House was the Jamaica home of lawyer Rufus King. He moved there in 1806, purchasing a 90-acre farm. Rufus was a delegate at the 1787 Constitutional Convention. He helped draft and signed the Constitution and was elected to the New York State Senate. He was also an ambassador to England and to the court of King George III. He spoke passionately against slavery decades before the Emancipation Proclamation.

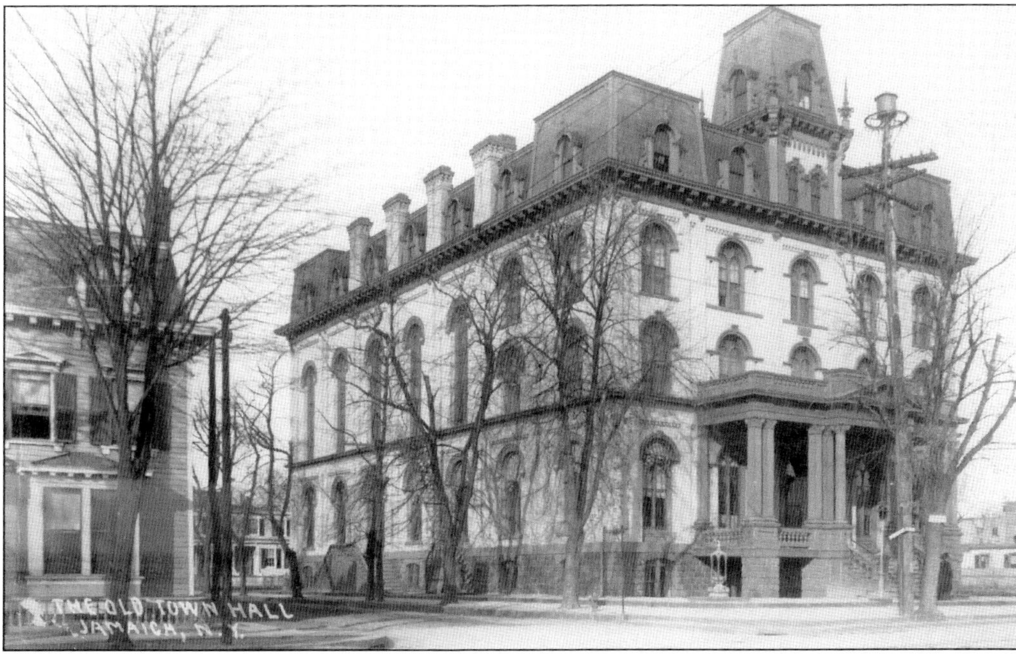

The Jamaica Town Hall was erected in 1868. It served as a courthouse, opera house, and jail and included meeting rooms for various clubs. After the 1898 consolidation of the five boroughs, it became the municipal courthouse, sheriff's office, and traffic court. Noted reformer, journalist, and author Jacob Riis lectured here in 1888. In 1894, the Women's Suffrage New York State Constitutional Convention was held here, with Susan B. Anthony as speaker.

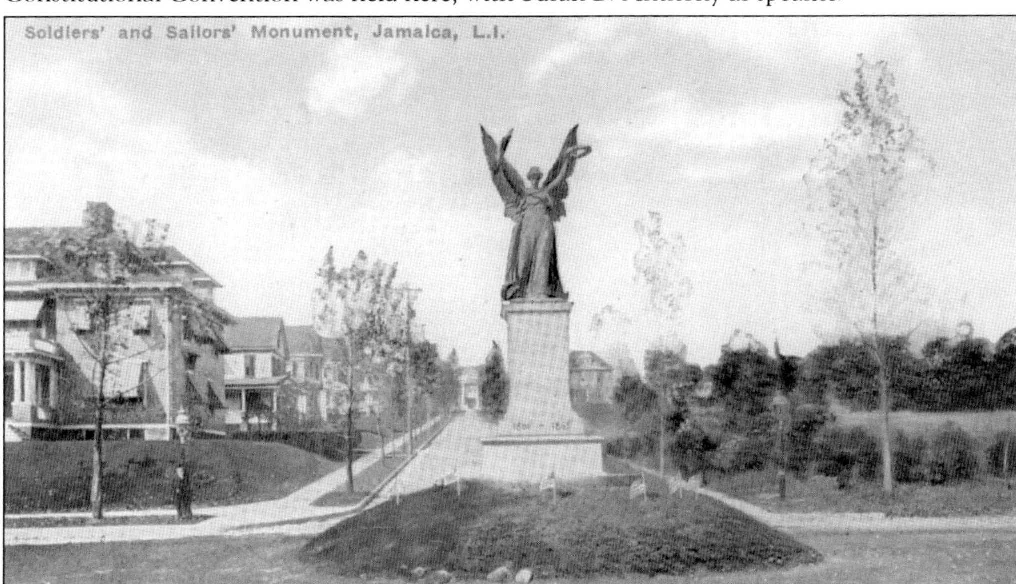

Designed by F. Wellington Ruckstuhl, the Soldiers and Sailors Civil War Monument depicts Victory alighting from the clouds. She holds a palm branch and a laurel crown, symbolizing fame and immortality for the soldiers of Jamaica who died for their country. Originally erected at Hillside Avenue and Merrick Boulevard and unveiled in 1896, the monument was moved in 1960 to 175th Street.

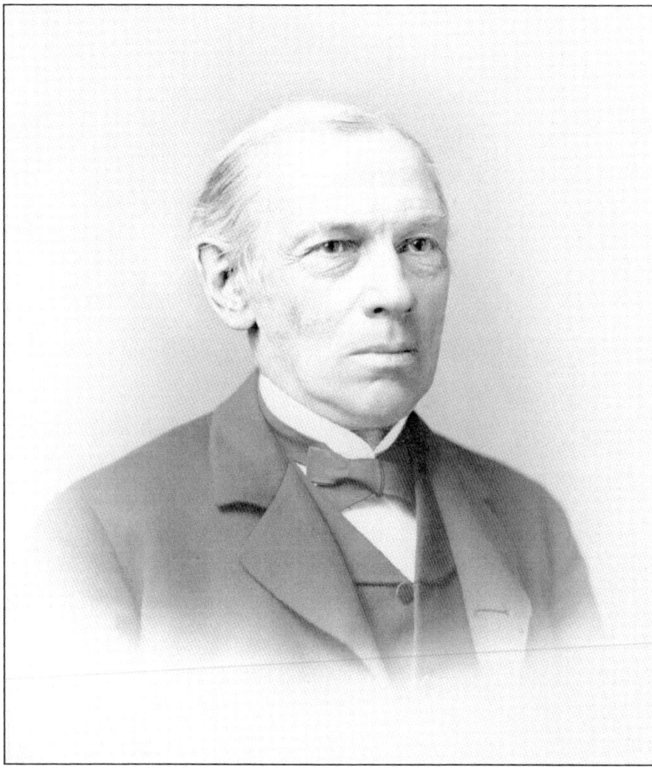

Albon Platt Man (1810–1891) was born in Constable, New York, and became a lawyer, admitted to the bar in 1832. He formed a partnership, Man & Parsons, in 1863 with his sons William and Henry H. Man. Albon would create Richmond Hill, a community one mile west of the Town of Jamaica in the Jamaica Territory.

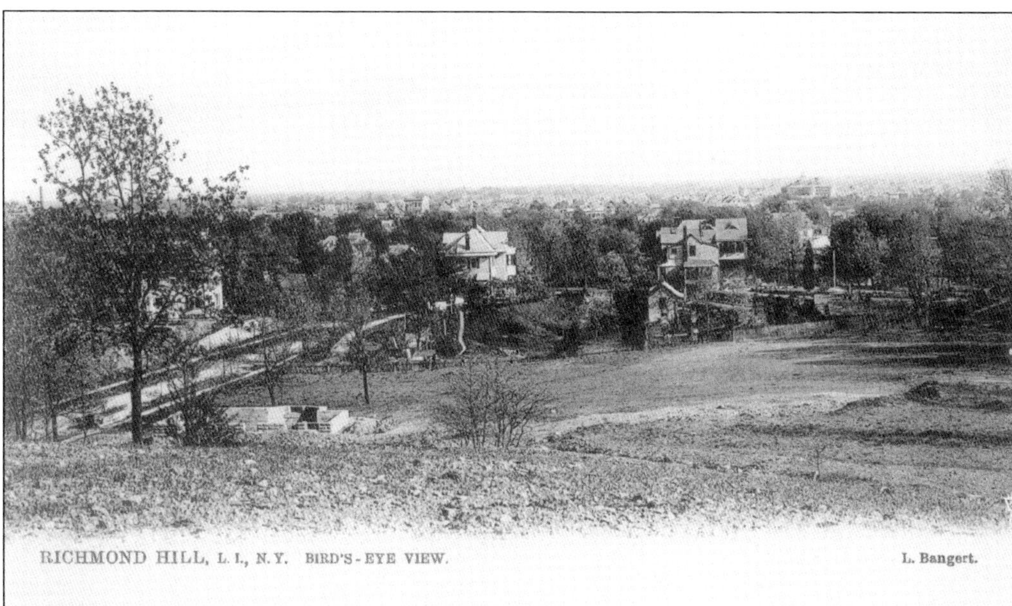

This is an early 1900s view of Richmond Hill from the "Brow of the Hill." Elizabeth Man Sarka said of Albon in 1976, "It seems that grandfather Man, when in his buggy from Wall Street to his summer home, would pause to enjoy the sunny slope, which dropped gently southward form the 'backbone' of the Island. Its well kept farms and woodland were perfect for a rural community where city workers could escape from turmoil, and enjoy peaceful homes."

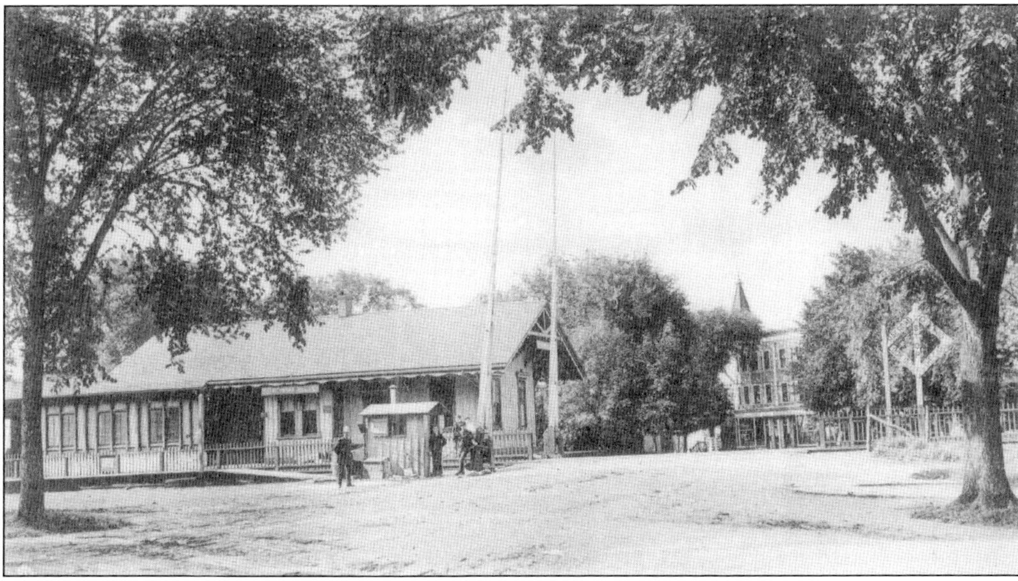

The Richmond Hill train depot is seen here in 1906. In the *New York Times* of November 27, 1932, Albon's great-grandson spoke on the naming of the town: "Albon Man was attracted there because his family lived in Richmond Hill, a suburb of Surrey, outside of London, England. The favorable character of the land in Richmond Hill, with its trees and gently rolling hills, was characteristic of his former home."

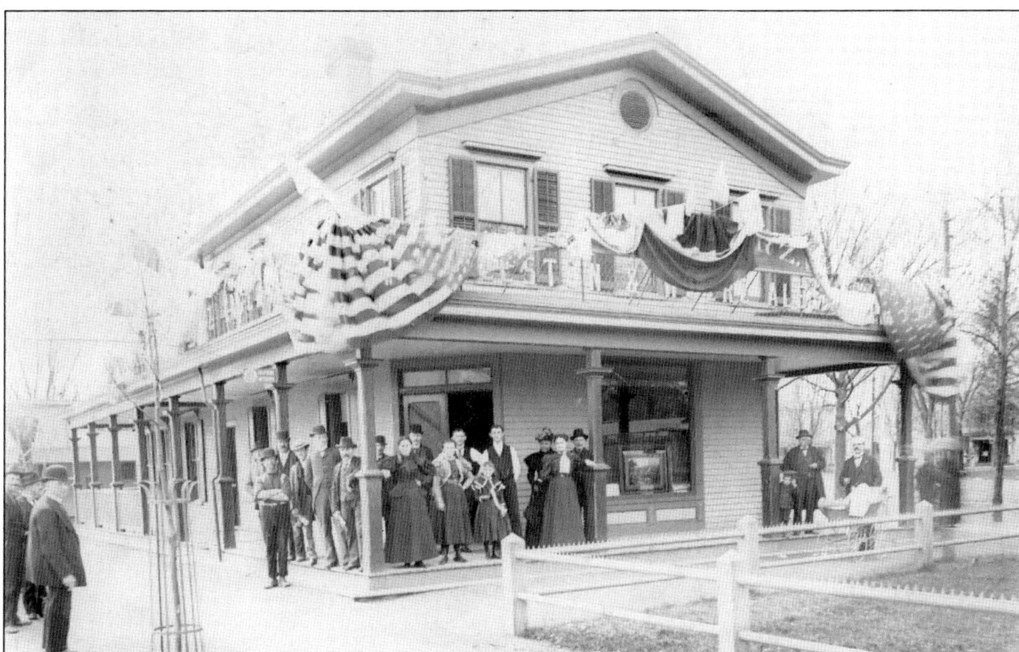

In 1868, Charles Paulson purchased a triangular plot of land on Jamaica Avenue from the Bergen Farm. He erected this building and rented it to Jacob Van Wicklen, who opened the first grocery store and post office serving the town of Richmond Hill. The establishment changed venues many times and served as a hotel, roadhouse, saloon, and restaurant. By the 1920s, it became known as the famed Triangle Hofbrau Haus.

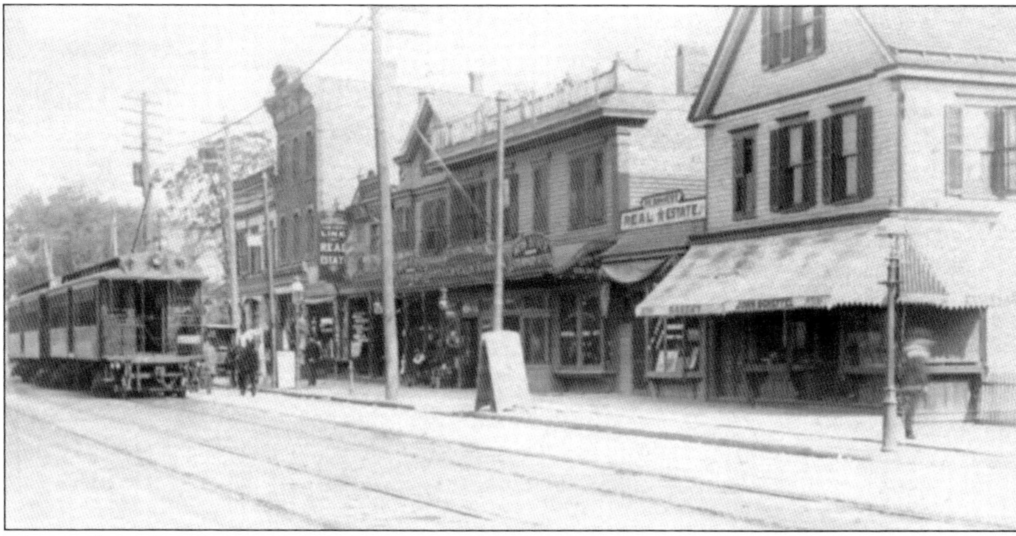

This trolley is heading west through Richmond Hill along Jamaica Avenue. The corner building, behind the trolley, stands at the Lefferts Boulevard intersection. The building on the far right is at the 118th Street intersection. According to a 1909 article in the *Richmond Hill Record*, "The change from the old horse motive power to electrical trolleys and the improvements in electricity have all worked together for the advantage of this locality."

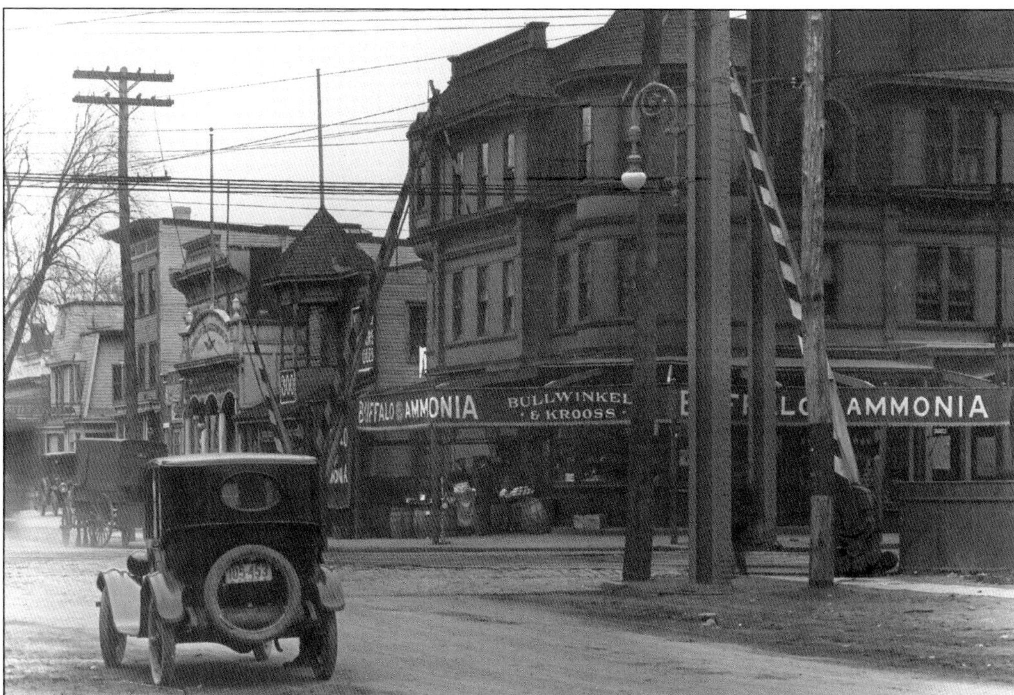

A car travels north on Lefferts Boulevard, across Jamaica Avenue. The corner store, Bullwinkel & Krooss, opened in 1910. According to noted Richmond Hill historian William Krooss, "This store had several horses and wagons from which deliveries were made. It was an old-time establishment which had a pot bellied stove used for warmth during winter, and local patrons would assemble there on Saturday nights and roast chestnuts."

In 1897, Capt. Thomas Baldwin (seated at left) sits with fellow policemen. The wooden police station was located on 118th Street. According to the *Richmond Hill Record* of August 5, 1909, "Fat Cops on Deck. But for them police building would have sailed away. Twelve Hundred pounds of plain patrolman saved the station from sailing away in Monday's storm." The next day, an angry resident wrote the editor, "We have no fat cops in Richmond Hill!"

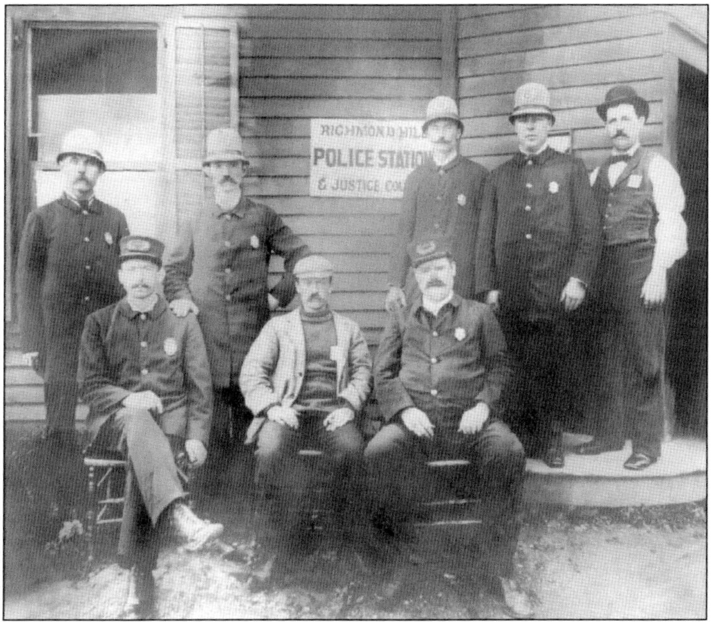

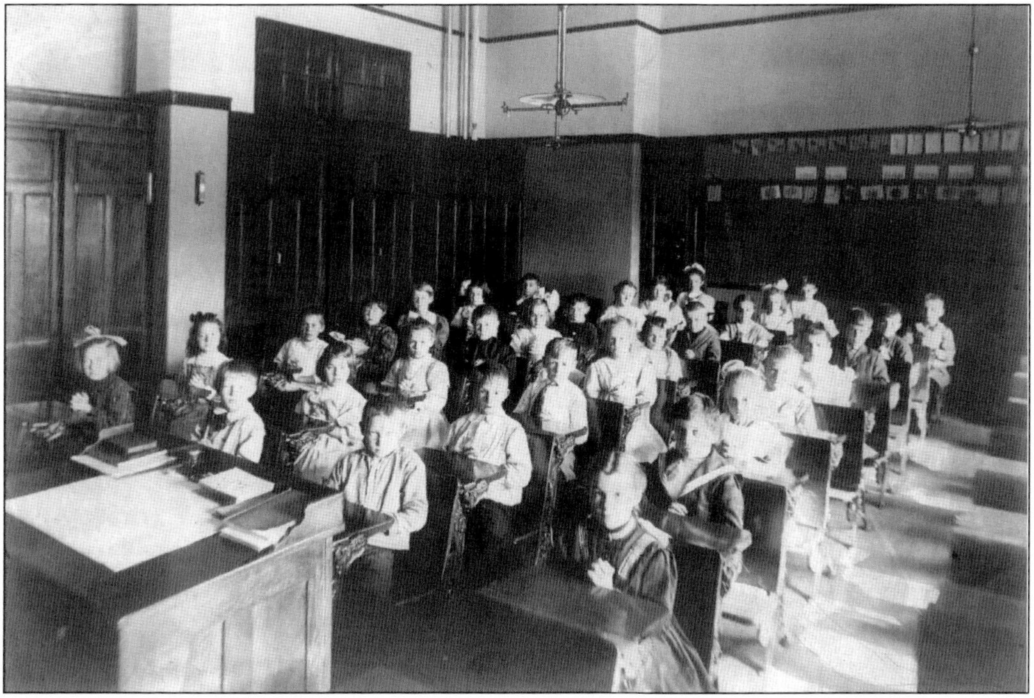

Students of P.S. 90 sit for a portrait in 1910. The first Richmond Hill school building, a wooden structure on Lefferts Boulevard, just north of Hillside Avenue, was erected in 1872. As the population grew, more schools were built: the Johnson Avenue School (P.S. 51) in 1891, P.S. 54 and P.S. 56 in 1894, P.S. 66 in 1898, and P.S. 90 in 1909.

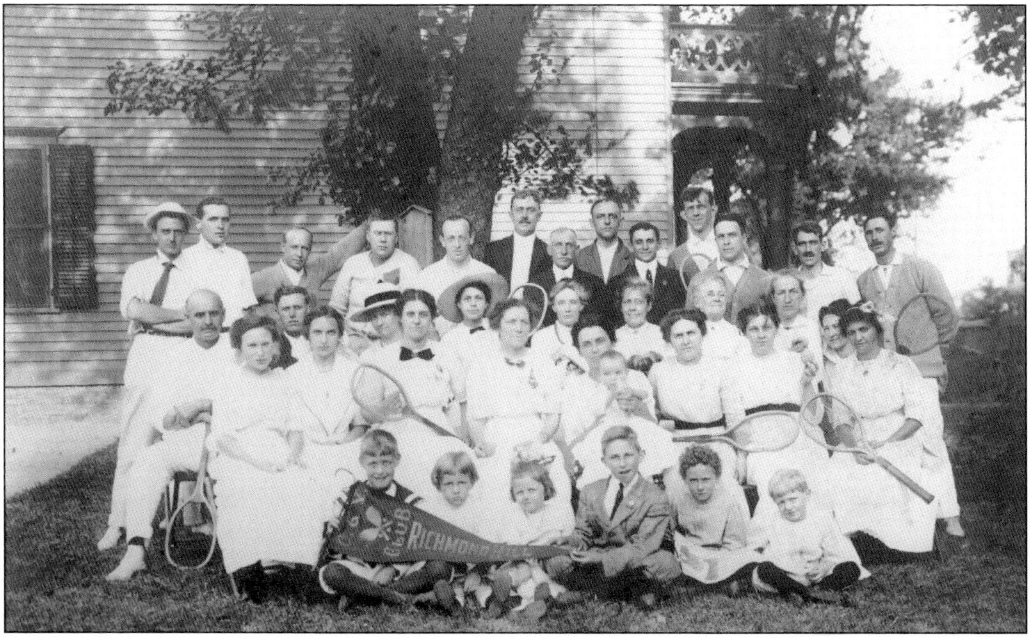

According to the *Daily Star* of May 2, 1911, "Chickens Cause Richmond Hill Tennis Club to Disband. A quarrel between Edward Dillmeier and Rufus Smith over chickens have caused the disbandment of club. Both have properties back to back and are club members. Dillmeiers owns the tennis court, leased by the club. Smith complained about the noise of Dillmeier's chickens. Dillmeier's refuses to lease the courts unless the Smith Family resigns. They refused!"

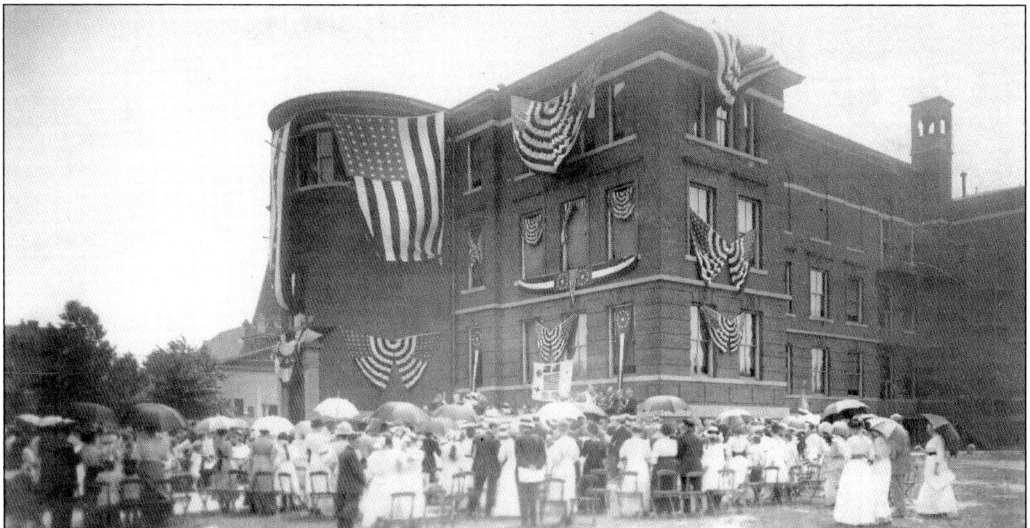

A patriotic celebration is held at Richmond Hill High School on 114th Street. The school was built in 1900, and its first principal was Isaac Newton Failor. The 1900 school annual reported: "On April 11, our splendid new building was dedicated. Appropriate exercises were held. The Assembly was prettily decorated with palms and flowering plants. A large audience was present. On the platform were seated many well-known citizens interested in educational matters." (Courtesy Bob Stonehill.)

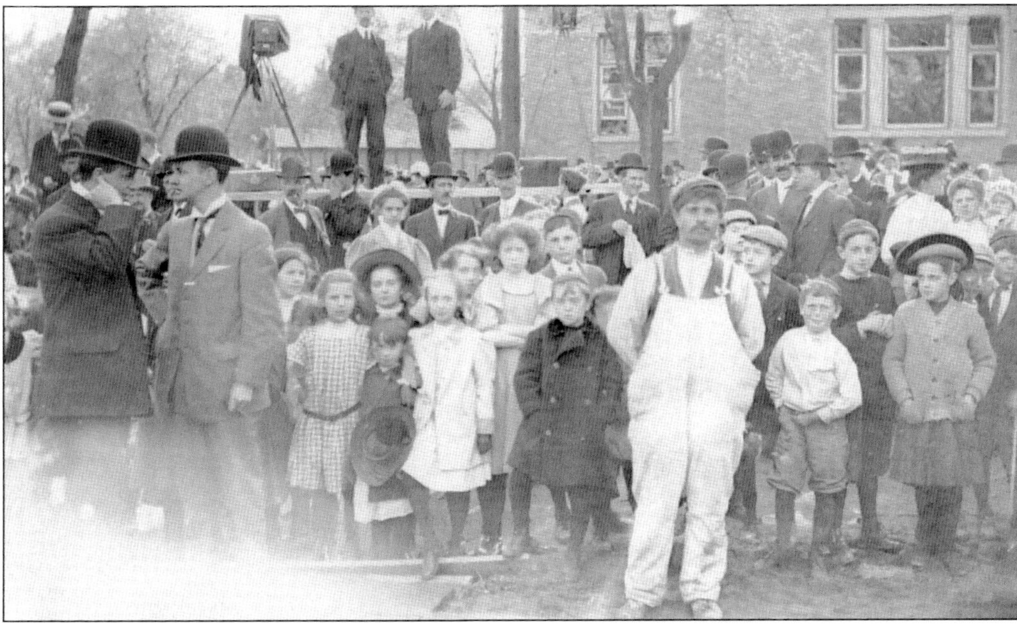

Richmond Hill citizens gather in front of the 1905 Richmond Hill Library on Lefferts Boulevard to watch the cornerstone laying of the Republican Club House in 1908. Designed by architect Henry Haugaard in the Classical Revival style, the building served as the Republican Party headquarters. During both world wars, it was used as a canteen for soldiers and sailors. It is the first official New York City landmark in Richmond Hill. (Courtesy Bob Stonehill.)

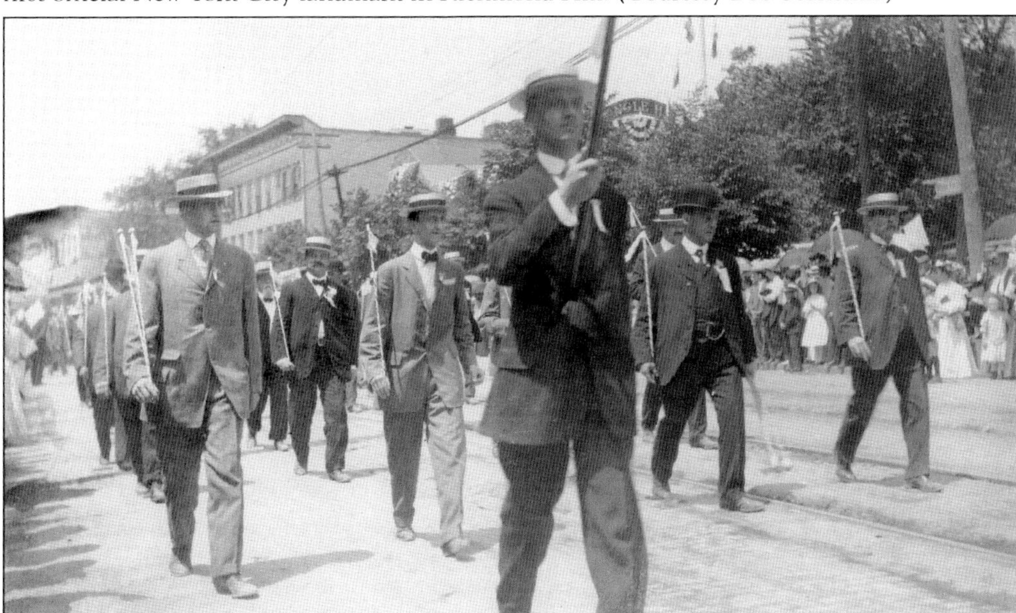

A group of marchers walks down Jamaica Avenue. The bunted arch is the Triangle Hofbrau Haus. One of the biggest Richmond Hill events took place in 1903, when Pres. Theodore Roosevelt spoke there. The president stopped at the train depot, which was decorated with flags and streamers. Over 2,000 people gathered, including 300 children, all carrying flags. The president greeted the people amid cheering and flag-waving. (Courtesy Bob Stonehill.)

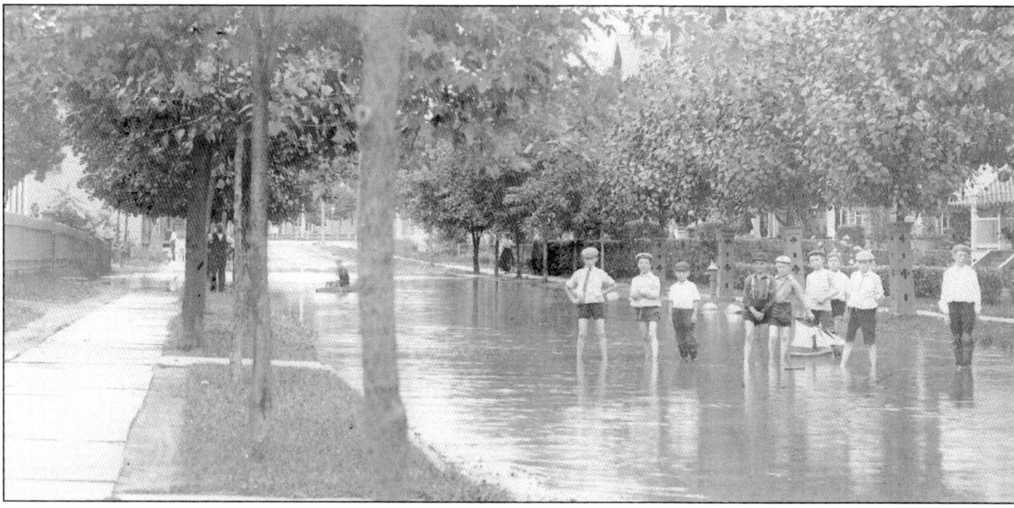

Heavy rains in Richmond Hill created large "lakes" before sewers were installed. According to the *Richmond Hill Record* of October 10, 1913: "An effort is being made to hold a political meeting on the borders of one of the great lakes. There's a dandy one at Lefferts and another on Johnson Avenue [118th Street] and one on Briggs [117th Street]." Shown here is the Johnson "lake" facing the police station. (Courtesy Bob Stonehill.)

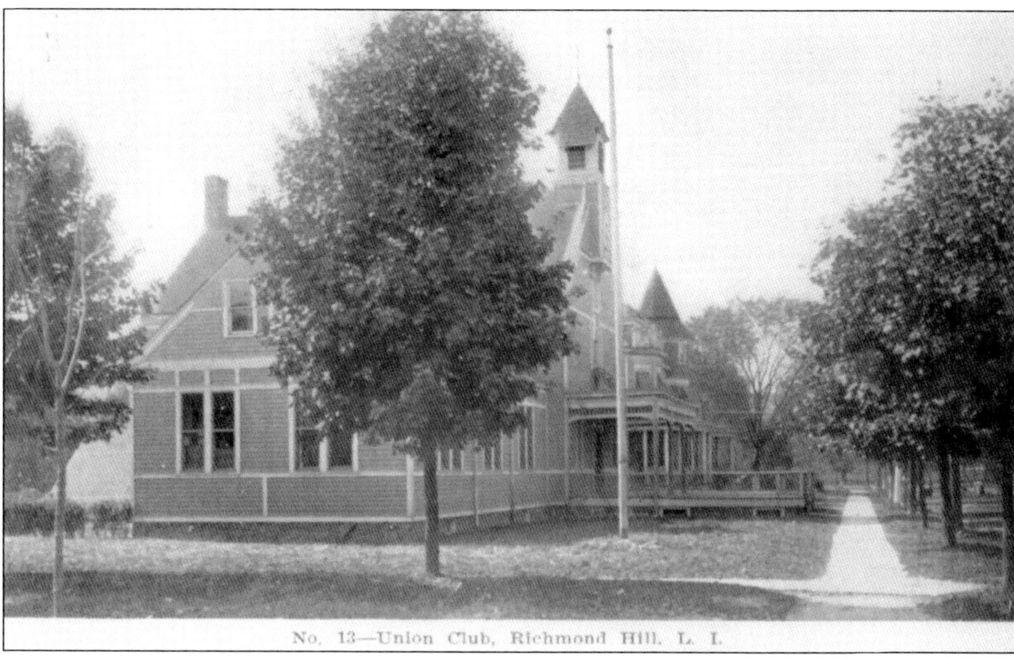

The first Richmond Hill schoolhouse was built in 1872 on Lefferts Boulevard. When a larger brick school was built in 1892, the old schoolhouse was moved to Hillside Avenue (pictured here) and became the Richmond Hill Clubhouse. When Kew Gardens was created, the early meetings of the Kew Gardens Country Club began here in 1910. Jamaica was the mother village, Richmond Hill the daughter village, and Kew Gardens became the granddaughter.

Two

Transformation

Becoming a New Community

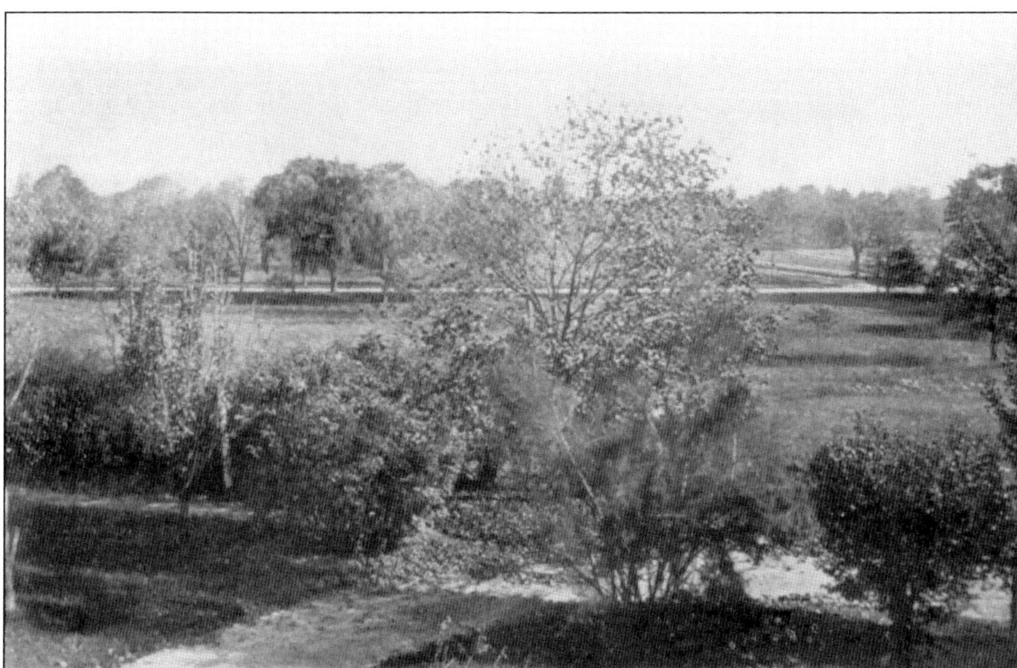

When Kew Gardens was developed in the northern section of Richmond Hill, streets that were identified in postcards as being in Richmond Hill were relabeled to show that they were now in the new community. New streets were laid out and named. In the distance in this photograph is the newly cut Church Street (118th Street) in the Kew Gardens section. It intersects the old Division Avenue (Eighty-fourth Avenue) on the right.

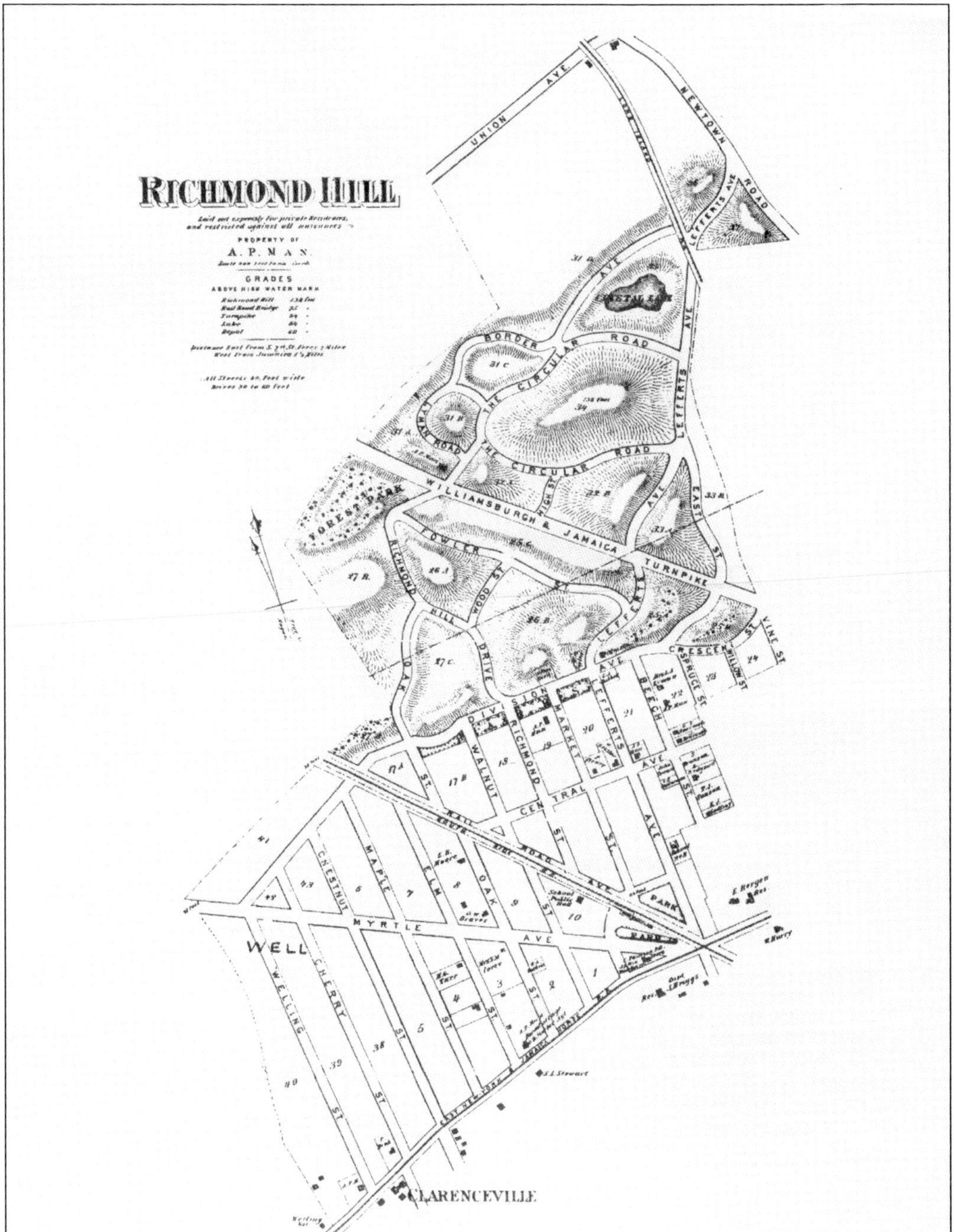

This is the earliest Richmond Hill map, dated 1873. Richmond Hill developed on the flat plain below Division Avenue (Eighty-fourth Avenue). The northern hilly area, left in its natural state, was used for picnics and hiking. Rowing, fishing, and ice-skating were enjoyed in the glacial ponds. North of the Williamsburgh and Jamaica Turnpike (Metropolitan Avenue) was the site of the Richmond Hill Golf Course. This entire northern section of Richmond Hill would become Kew Gardens.

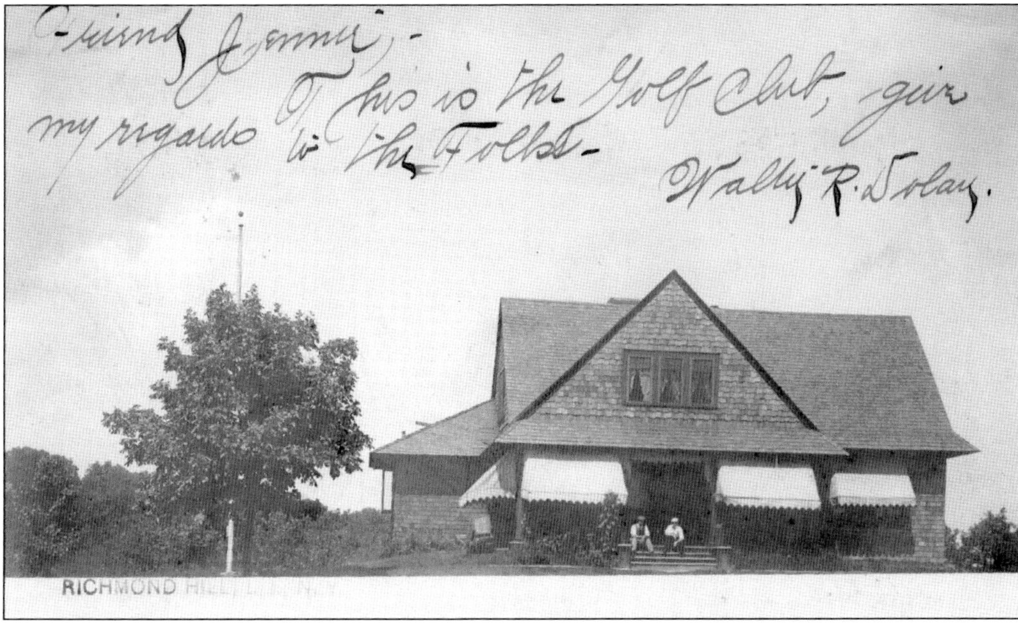

For years, members and friends of the Man family used the northern part of their estate as a golf course. On April 3, 1896, the Richmond Hill Golf Club was organized. During the summer, the course was overhauled, and a clubhouse (pictured here) was built. The *Brooklyn Daily Eagle* of April 25, 1897, stated, "The club house commands a view of the greater part of the course with Flushing and Jamaica Bays in the distance."

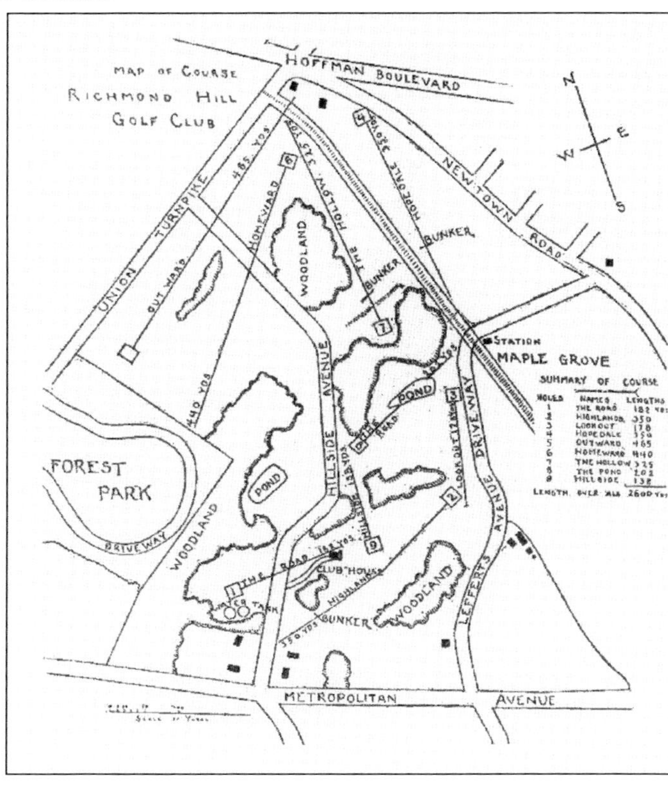

This 1907 illustration shows the Richmond Hill Golf Club's nine holes. The glacial pond near the Maple Grove Station was known as Crystal Lake and served as a golf course hazard. Hoffman Boulevard on the north is now called Queens Boulevard. The borders were Newtown Road (Kew Gardens Road), Metropolitan Avenue, Union Turnpike, and Lefferts Avenue (Boulevard).

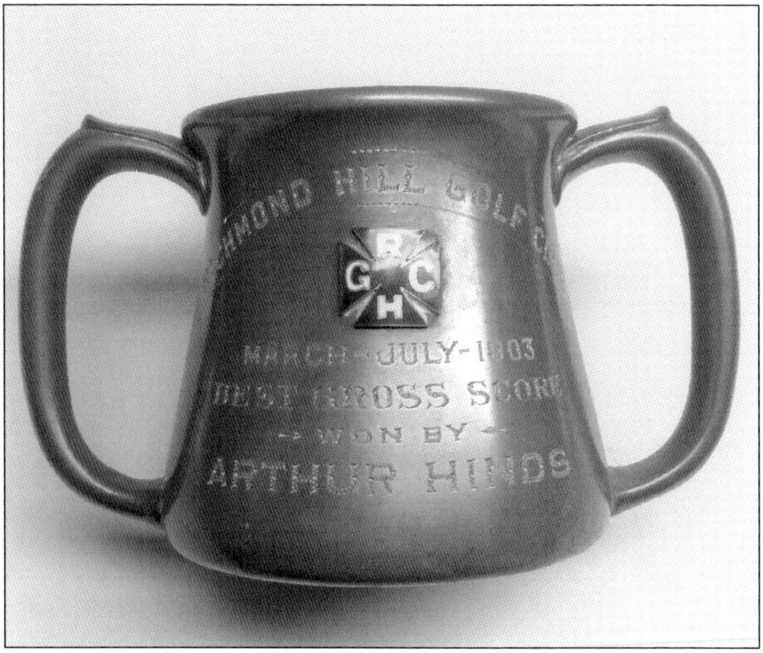

In 1903, the Richmond Hill Golf Club presented this cup to Arthur Hinds for "Best Gross Score." The *Brooklyn Daily Eagle* reported on April 25, 1897, "The course is an interesting and tricky one of a markedly sporting character. It is laid out over and around a series of hills and knolls which, intersected though they be by valleys and ravines, help form the ridge that serves as Long Island's backbone."

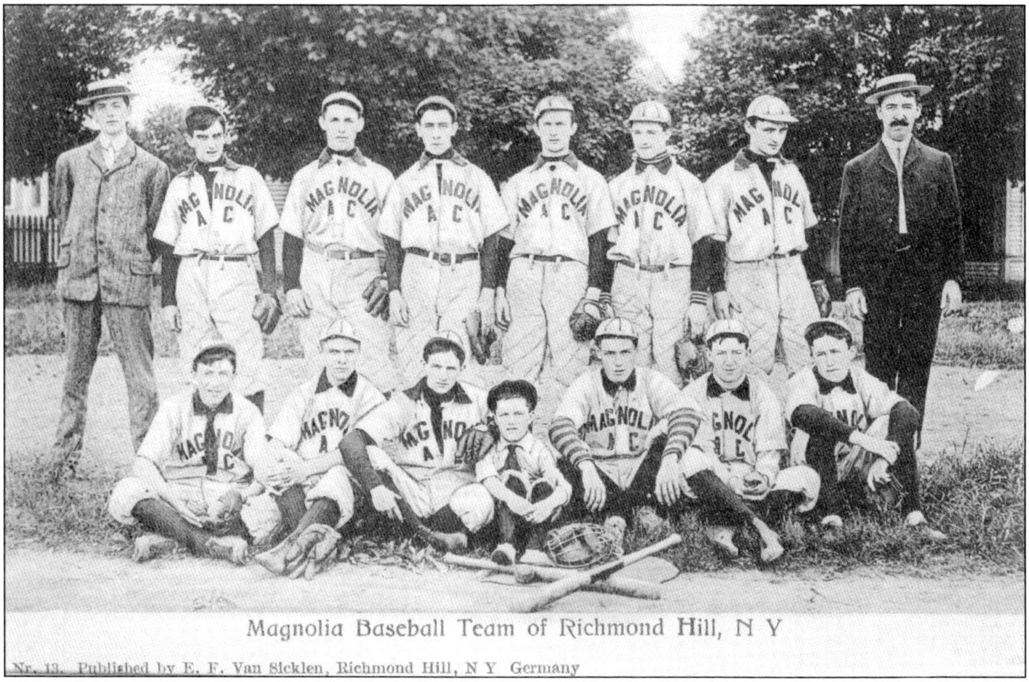

This is a postcard of the Magnolia baseball team of Richmond Hill. Bess Parsley reported the following in the *Kew-Forest Life* on December 21, 1929: "One of my early recollections is the Fourth of July fireworks display at the golf club. People came up from Richmond Hill. One year there was a baseball game, where the players wore their wives gowns. I can vividly remember some of our leading citizens running to base in trailing and entangled skirts."

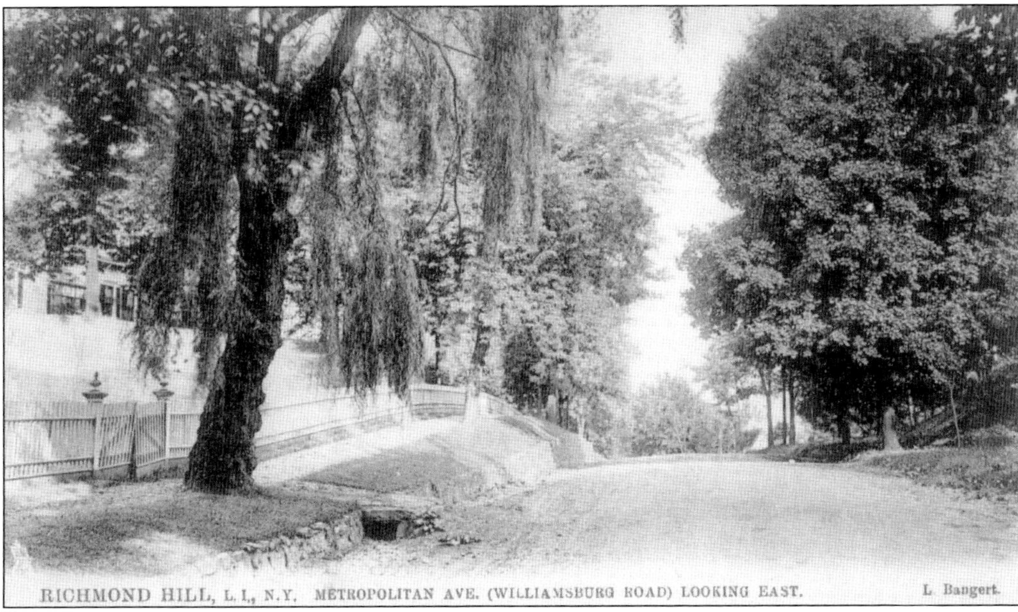

Originally called the Wiliamsburgh and Jamaica Turnpike, this road connected the towns of Williamsburg in Brooklyn and Jamaica in Queens. This photograph is looking east toward Lefferts Boulevard. Its name was later changed to Metropolitan Avenue. It was on this road in 1868 that Albon Man, noting the vistas to the south, envisioned the town of Richmond Hill, leaving his son Alrick to develop the northern hilly terrain into Kew Gardens.

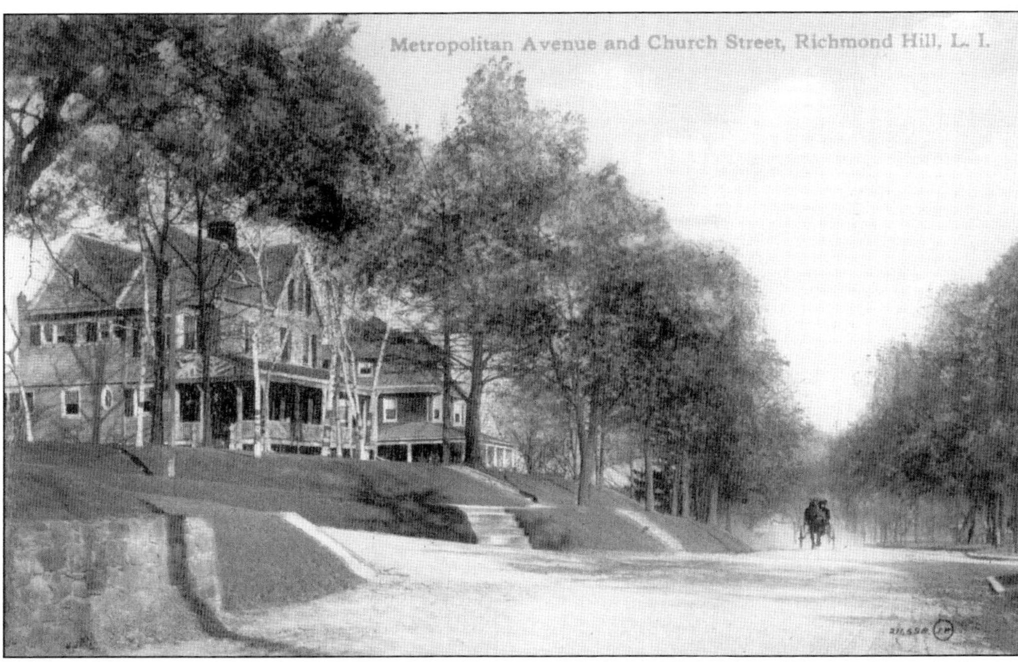

A horse and buggy travels west on Metropolitan Avenue at the Church Street (118th Street) intersection. According to the *Long Island Democrat* of July 26, 1870, "Richmond Hill contains about 250 acres of land, lying at an elevated grade, well drained and perfectly healthy, restricted against nuisances and easily accessible by various roads."

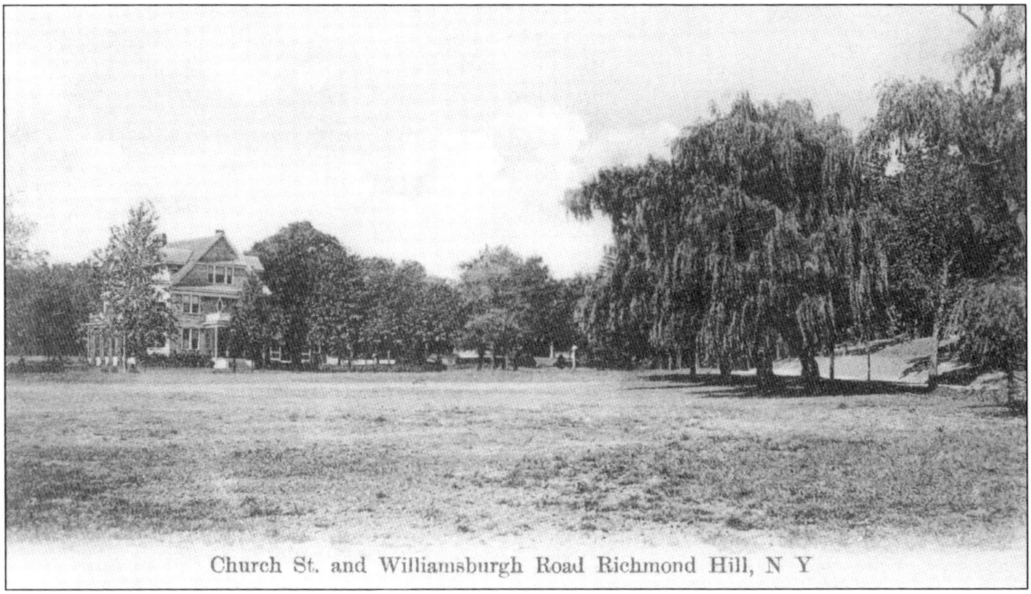

In this postcard, Williamsburgh Road (Metropolitan Avenue), visible here on the right, veers west and intersects Church Street (118th Street). The Richmond Hill Golf Course is located to the right. The *Richmond Hill Record* reported on December 19, 1903, "When asked what are the particular advantages of living in Richmond Hill, we point to our churches, schools, excellent public library, fine golf links, and the many spots, where boys can play ball and skate to their hearts content."

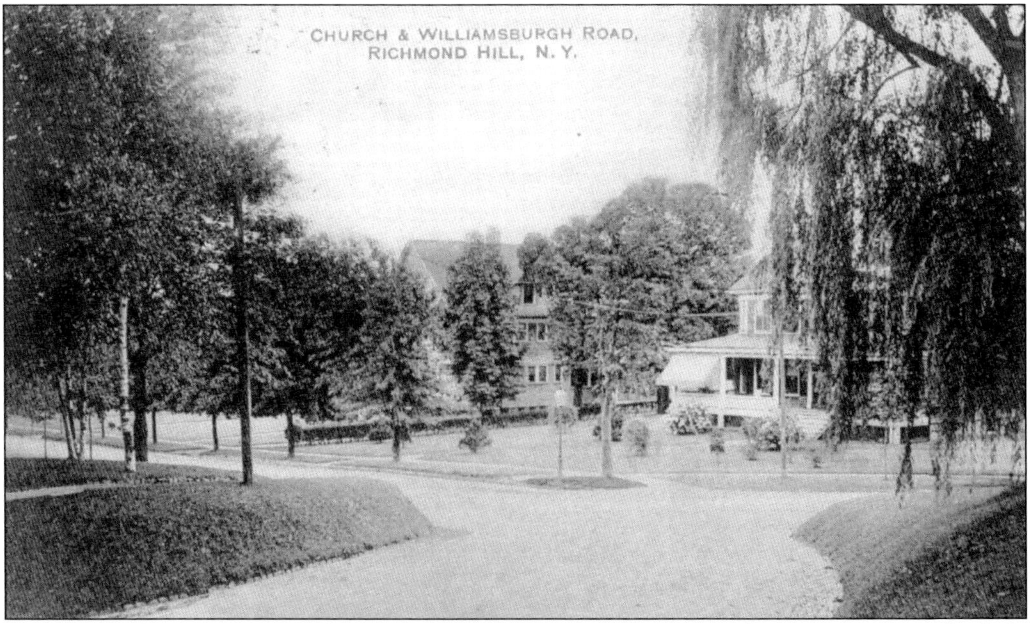

This south-facing photograph shows Church Street (118th Street) as it curves to the left, where it intersects Metropolitan Avenue. According to the 1905 *Industrial Recorder*, "Rich in sylvan wealth and with a peculiar charm which is especially attractive to families of culture and refinement, Richmond Hill is at once one of the most beautiful and convenient suburban sections of the metropolis."

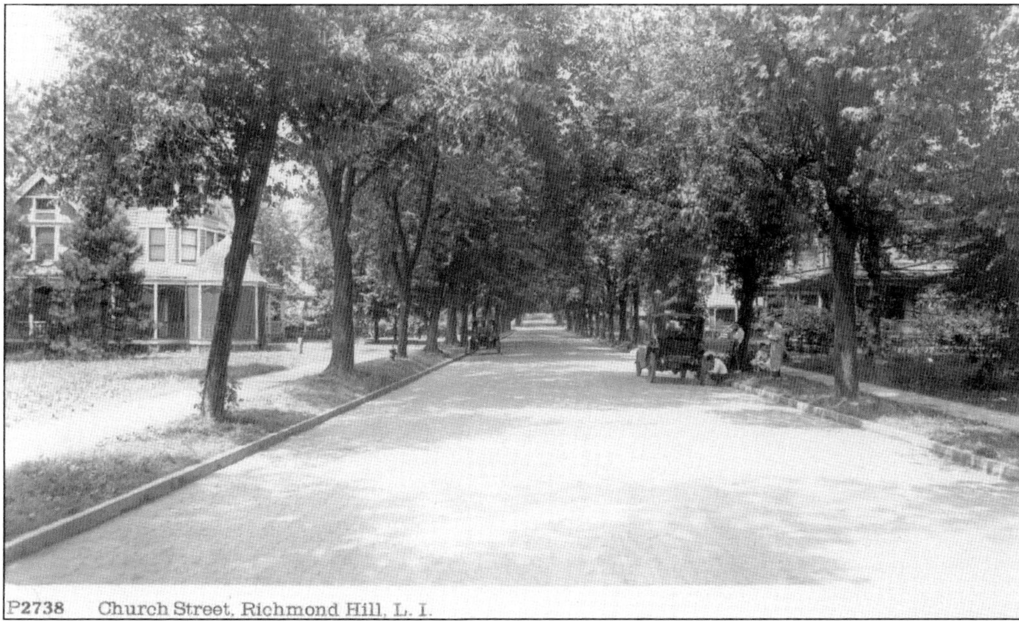

This is Church Street (118th Street) looking north from Hillside Avenue. Alrick Man and his family lived farther north on this street. When he moved in, the house was in Richmond Hill, but its location was changed to Kew Gardens when he developed this area. Albon Platt Man III wrote in his 1913 diary, "Yesterday roses, geraniums, chrysanthemums, dandelions and other flowers were blooming, but this morning was a 'black frost,' that ushers in our real winter."

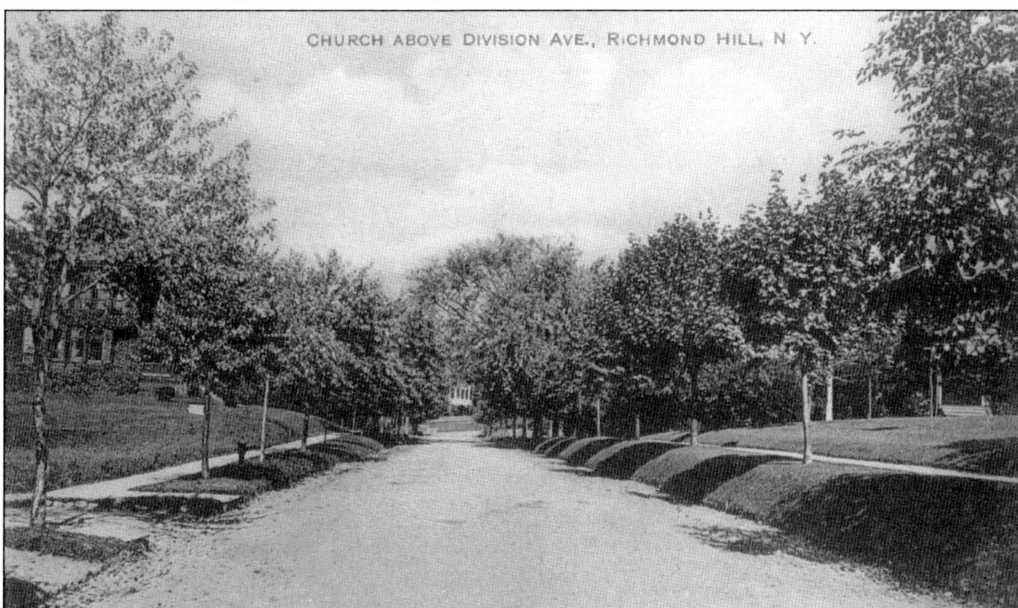

This north-facing photograph shows Church Street (118th Street), running to Metropolitan Avenue. The Alrick Man house is on the right, hidden by trees. According to the *Industrial Recorder* in 1905: "On the higher ground are many fine residences which command a view of the ocean, distance about nine miles. The broad and well kept lawns and trees embowered streets and avenues give a beautiful park-like effect and the section around it is rich in Sylvan scenery."

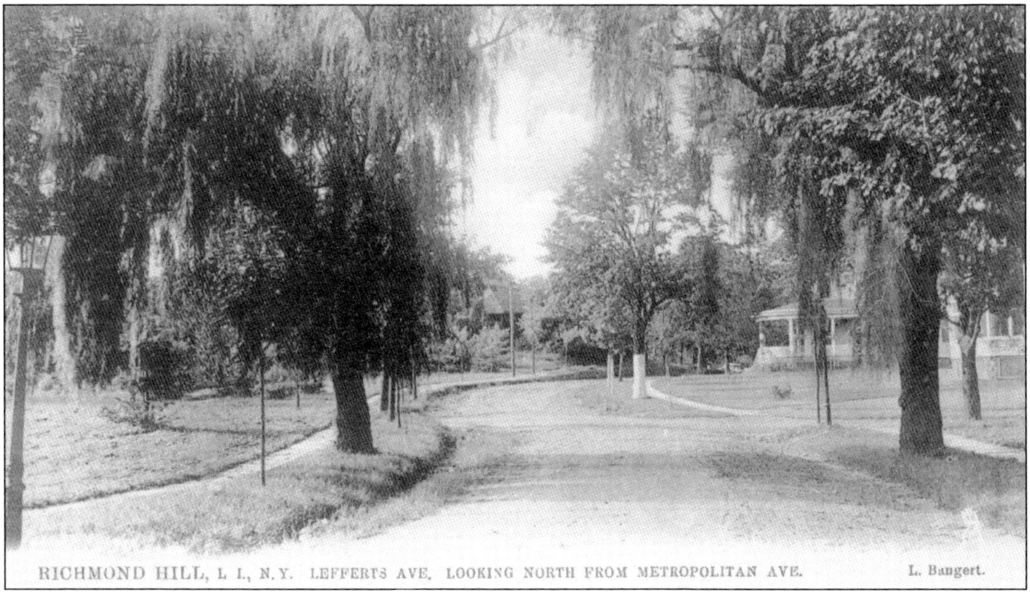

Here, Lefferts Avenue (Boulevard) is running north toward the future location of Kew Gardens. Lefferts was named for the Lefferts family, which owned a farm to the south. On June 29, 1868, Man and his business partner, Edward Richmond, bought the 200-acre Lefferts farmland for $59,944.80 in order to create a garden community.

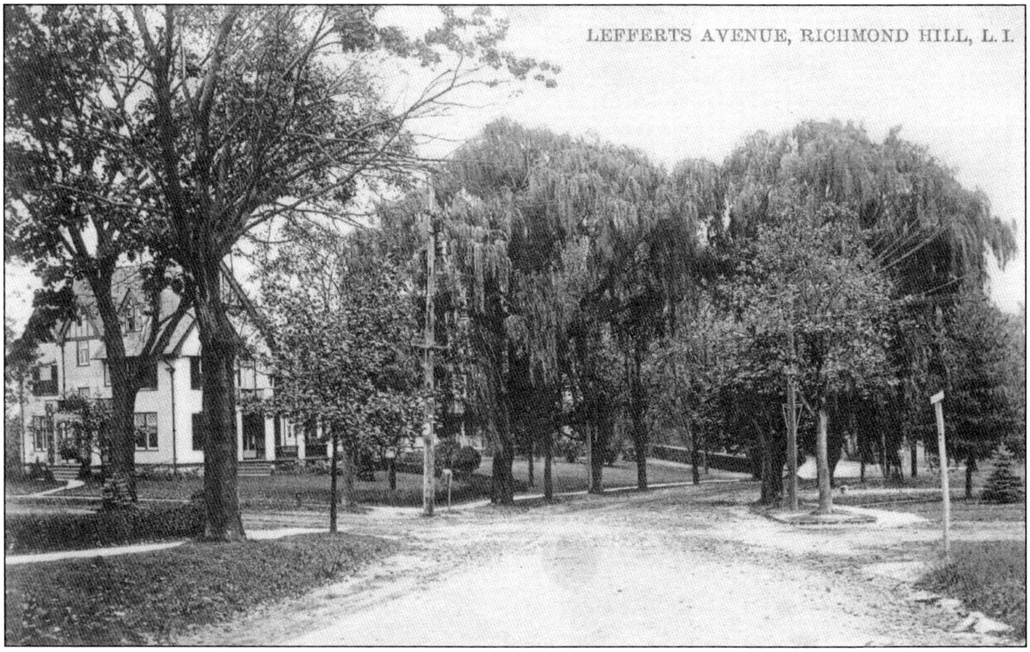

In this photograph, looking south, Lefferts Avenue runs toward the Metropolitan Avenue intersection. According to the *Richmond Hill Record* of April 20, 1907: "Richmond Hill is the Mecca for those who buy and sell real estate. It is the Mecca not because there are bargains to be had, but because it is felt it is a land of opportunity." The following year, Alrick Man began his vision for a new community, Kew Gardens.

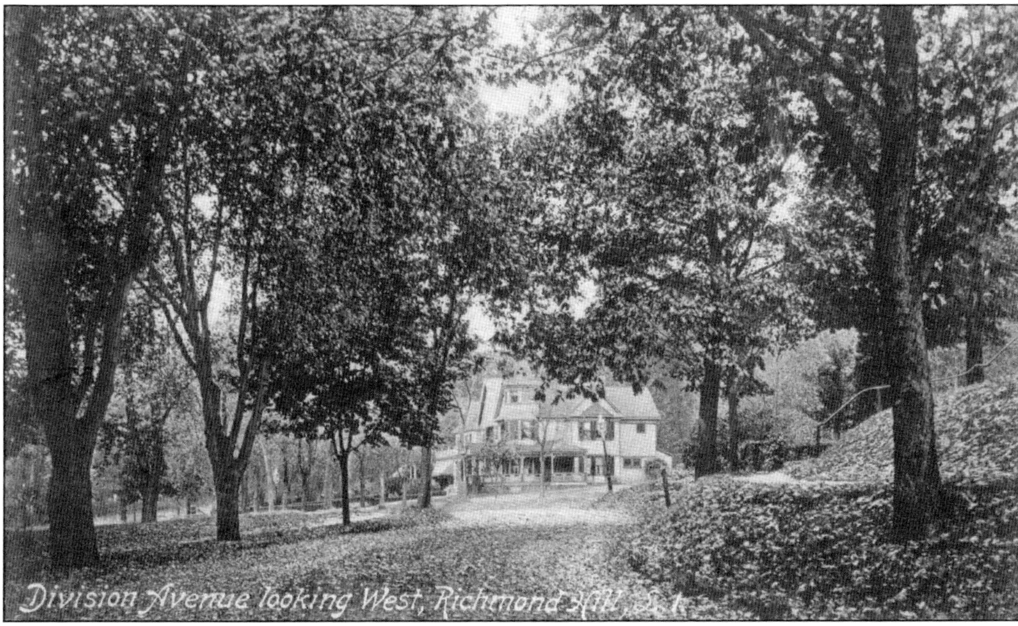

Division Avenue (Eighty-fourth Avenue) is seen here, looking west. According to the *Richmond Hill Record* of June 27, 1913: "A real and lasting foundation had been laid to build up a town of fine homes, wide streets with beautiful trees giving them shade and coolness. Last but not least, a community of real homes where the tired city worker can find rest and where his wife and children can live in peace and quiet."

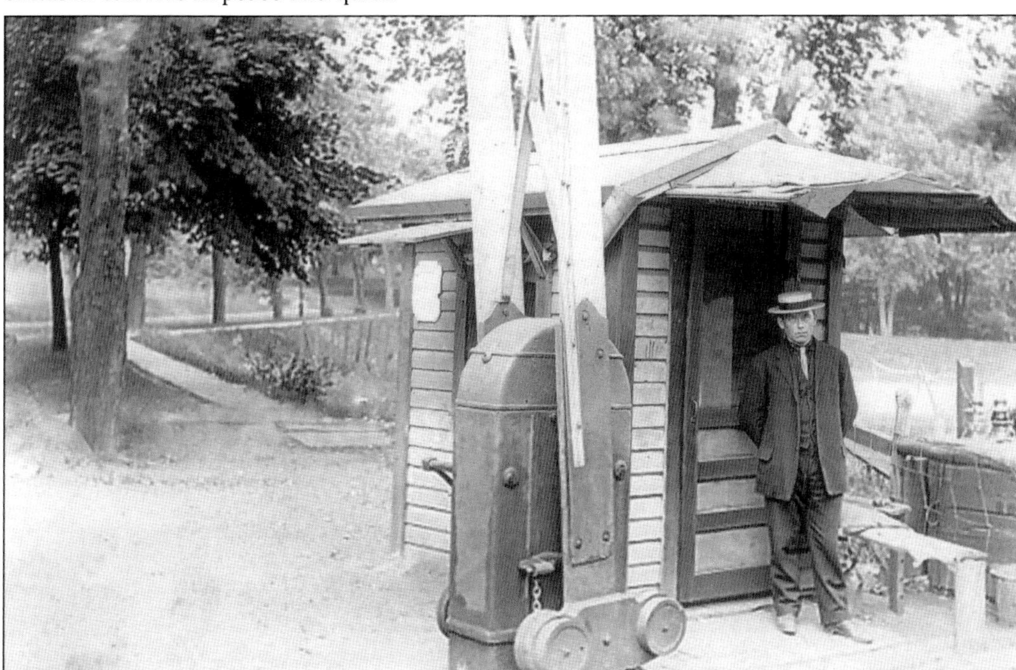

This is the railroad crossing on Division Avenue (Eighty-fourth Avenue) between Maple Street (113th Street) and Elm Street (114th Street). Barely visible to the right of the crossing guard attendant are the Richmond Hill Tennis Courts.

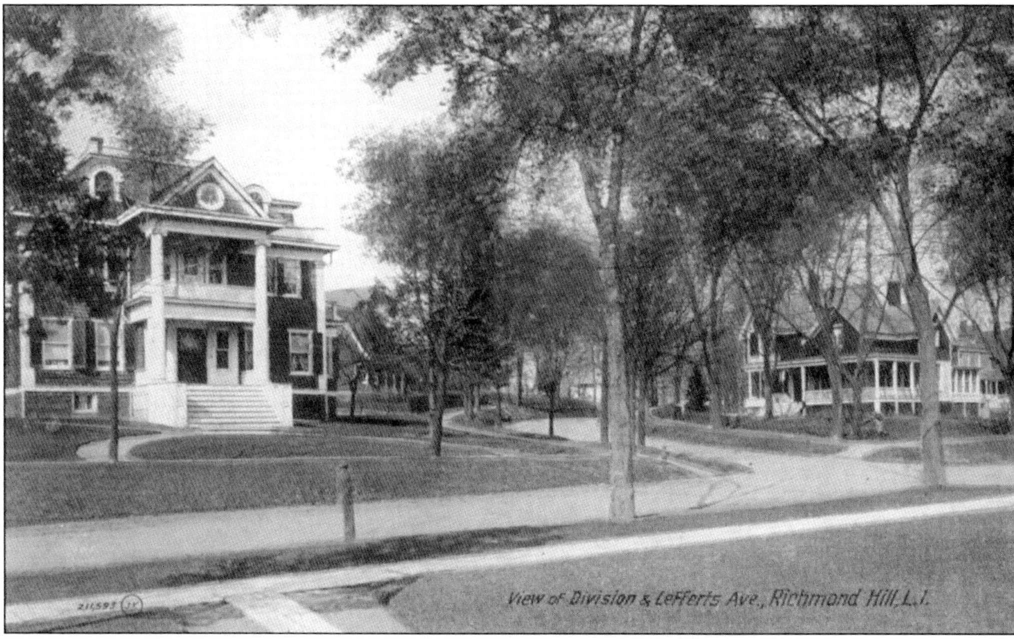

Stately mansions stand proudly on Division Avenue (Eighty-fourth Avenue), which intersects Lefferts Boulevard on the right as it curves north. As reported in the *Long Island Democrat* on September 23, 1884: "Carpenters are now demanding $2.75 and $3 per day for their daily toll. Even at such wages there are none out of employment, and people are compelled to go to the city for help."

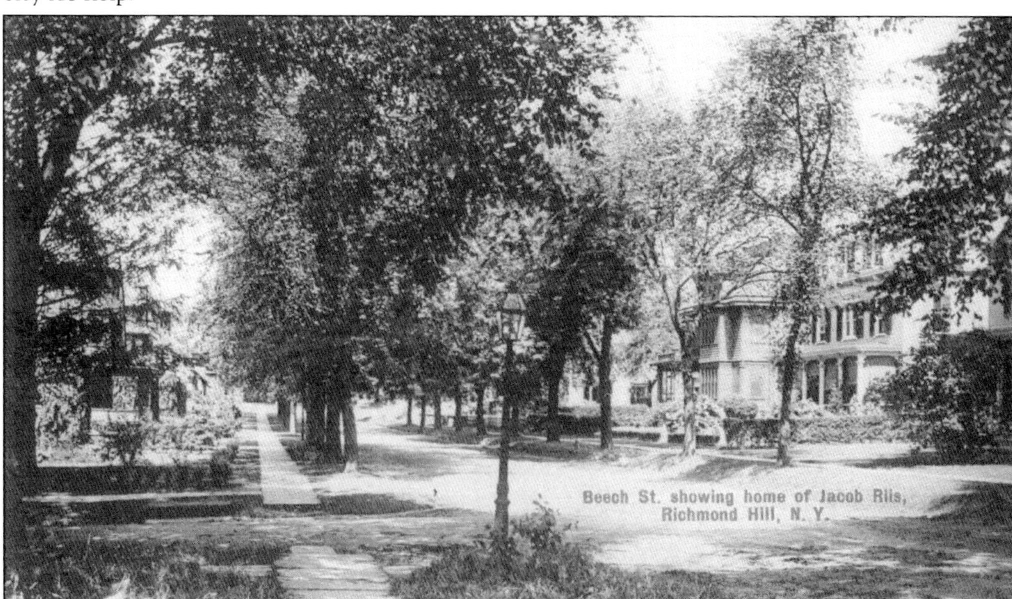

This postcard notes that Jacob Riis, the reformer, reporter, and author, lived on Beech Street (120th Street). Upon his first visit to the area, Riis wrote in his autobiography, *The Making of an American*, "I came upon Richmond Hill and thought it was the most beautiful spot I had ever seen." He moved his family to Richmond Hill and lived there for nearly 30 years. This section of Richmond Hill is now Kew Gardens.

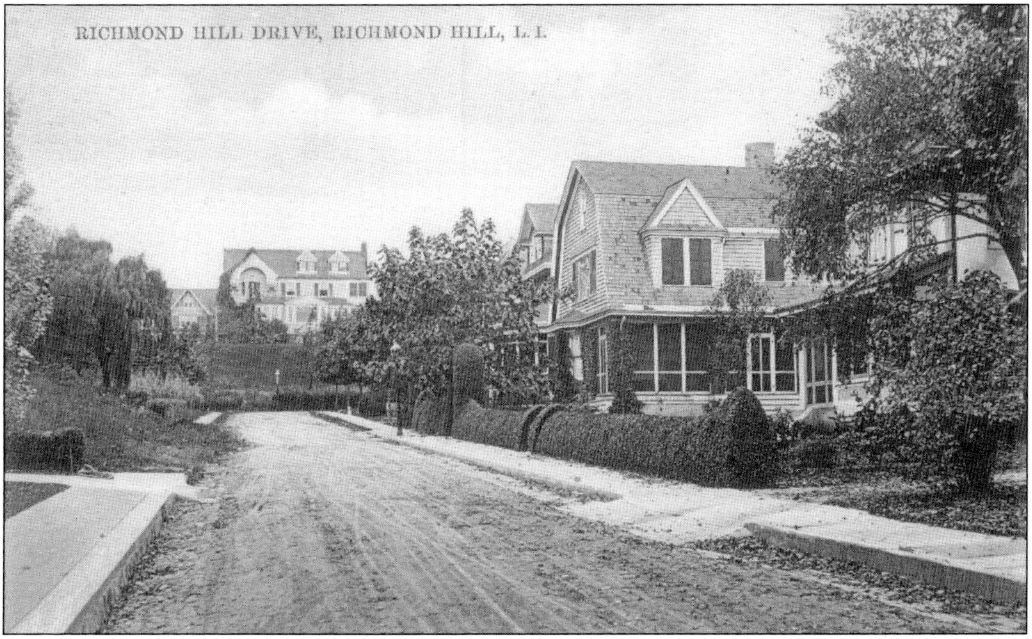

In 1886, Kimball and Wisedell designed a large residence at the top of a hill for the wife of Lt. William Cowles in Richmond Hill. Lieutenant Cowles was the deputy commander of the Brooklyn Navy Yard. His wife, the oldest daughter of Sen. Allen Thurman of Ohio, was known as a bit of an eccentric. The $30,000 Cowles residence, two and one-half stories tall, was constructed of masonry and clapboard.

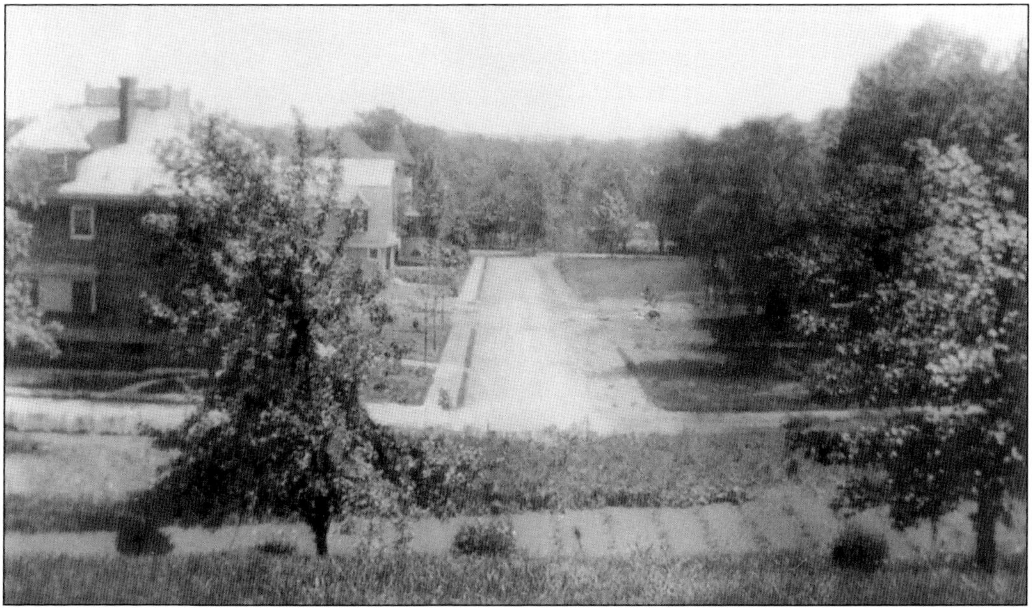

This view is from the Cowles house, looking south on Richmond Hill Drive (117th Street). To take advantage of the great views, the house was given a large, glassed-in porch. Lieutenant Cowles was often away on military duty. His wife filed for divorce in 1889, on the grounds of neglect. In 1897, William Cowles married Anna Roosevelt, sister of Theodore Roosevelt. Later, Cowles became a decorated admiral in the Spanish-American War.

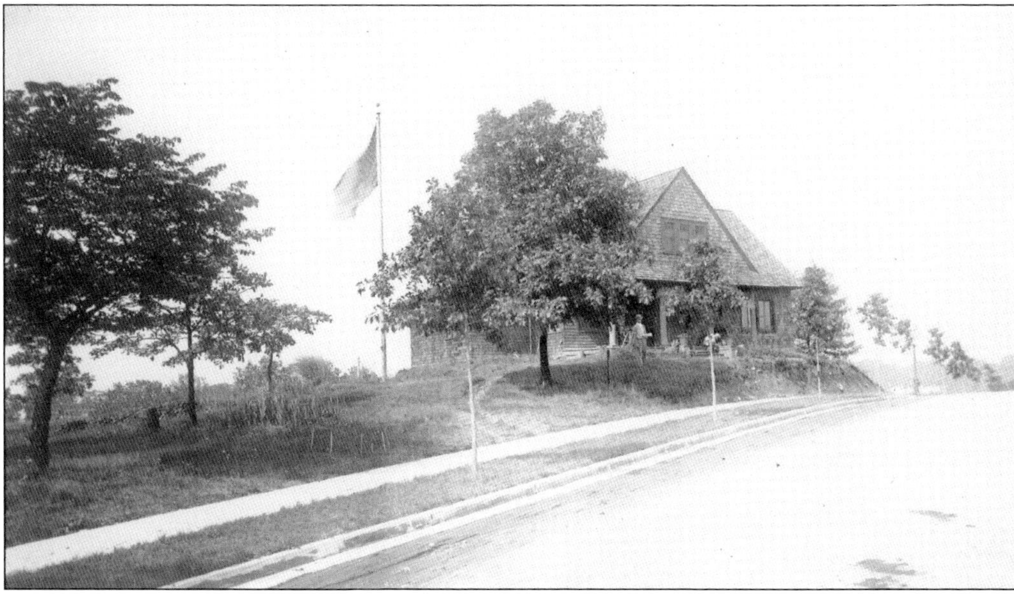

By 1908, the golf course closed when the Man estate sold a portion of the course to the railroad, which then moved the tracks, cutting the links in half. The *Brooklyn Daily Eagle* stated on April 29, 1908, "Alrick Man has commenced cutting streets through the portion of the golf links, and handsome residences are being erected." The golf house shown here was moved next to Audley Street.

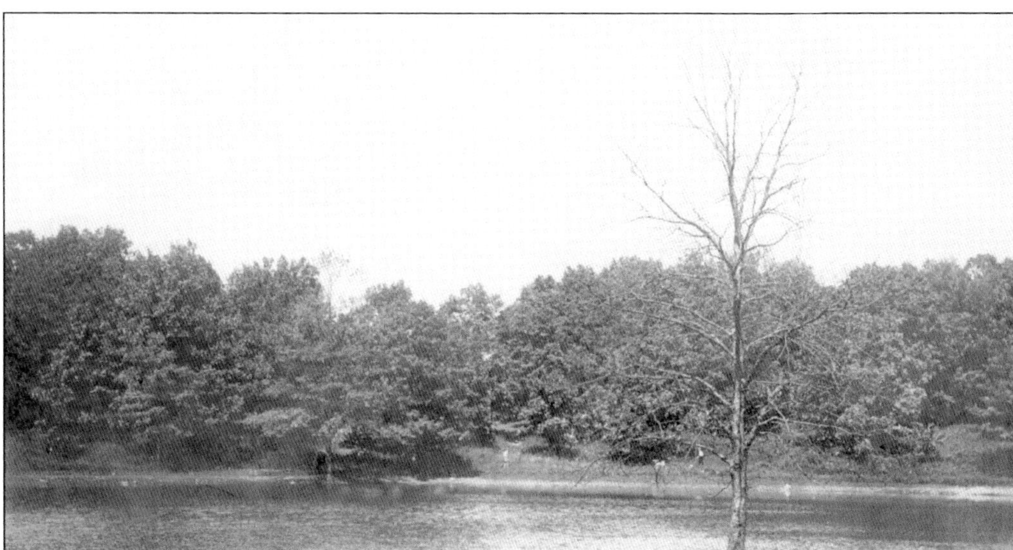

This is Crystal Lake, on the Richmond Hill Golf Course. According to the *Richmond Hill Record* of August 22, 1908, a group of 10 young girls from Brooklyn caused a scene when they took a swim minus suits, "The bathers attracted the attention of a photographer. With his camera in focus, one of the bathers screamed 'Girls! A photographer.' He took to his heels, but it was too late. He and his light summer suit were plastered with mud."

Three

Kew Gardens

The Early Development

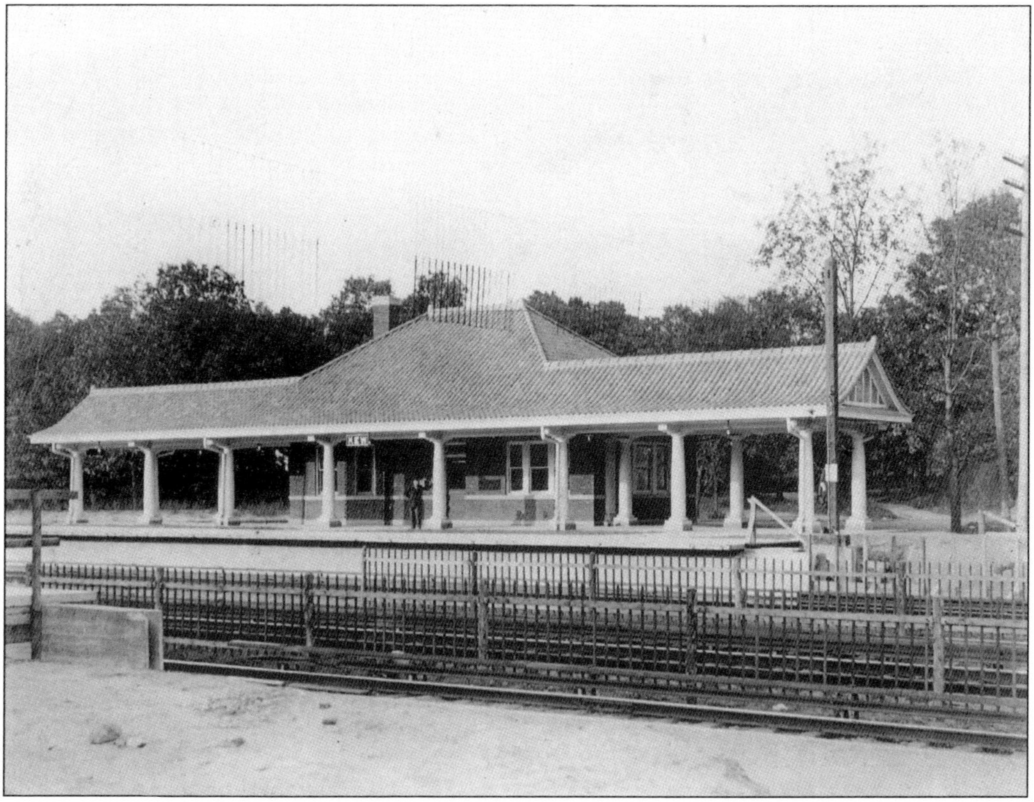

Kew Station was built on the former Richmond Hill Golf Course. The *Richmond Hill Record* of July 23, 1910, outlined recent changes and discussed a mystery: "Residents of Richmond Hill walking through Lefferts Avenue toward Maple Grove Cemetery are amazed! Wonderful changes and improvements! New streets and fine residences, the new railroad bridge and double tracks, the handsome new Long Island Railroad station. But what do these three large gold letters, 'KEW' on the station building mean? What do they stand for?"

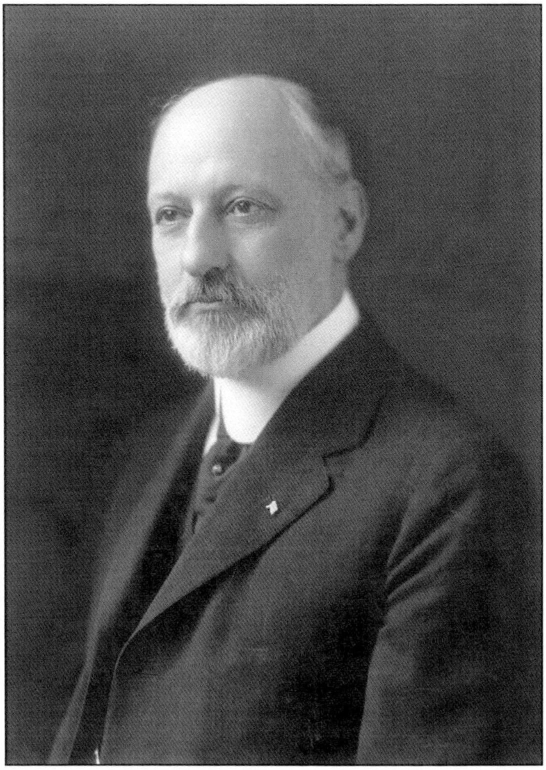

This is Alrick Hubble Man, son of Richmond Hill founder Albon Man. In 1908, Alrick began developing the northern portion of Richmond Hill into a town he named Kew. As reported in the *Richmond Hill Record* on July 23, 1910, "Kew is named after the town of Kew, England, where one of the most famous and beautiful botanical gardens is located. Kew, England, adjoins Richmond Hill, England, after which our own town is named, hence the appropriateness of the name."

Alrick moved his family to Richmond Hill into this grand house on Church Street (118th Street). He was very involved in the interests of both Richmond Hill and Kew Gardens. In 1895, Clarenceville, Morris Park, and Richmond Hill merged into the Village of Richmond Hill. Alrick was elected its first president. In 1912, he became president of the Kew Gardens Corporation, a position he held until his death.

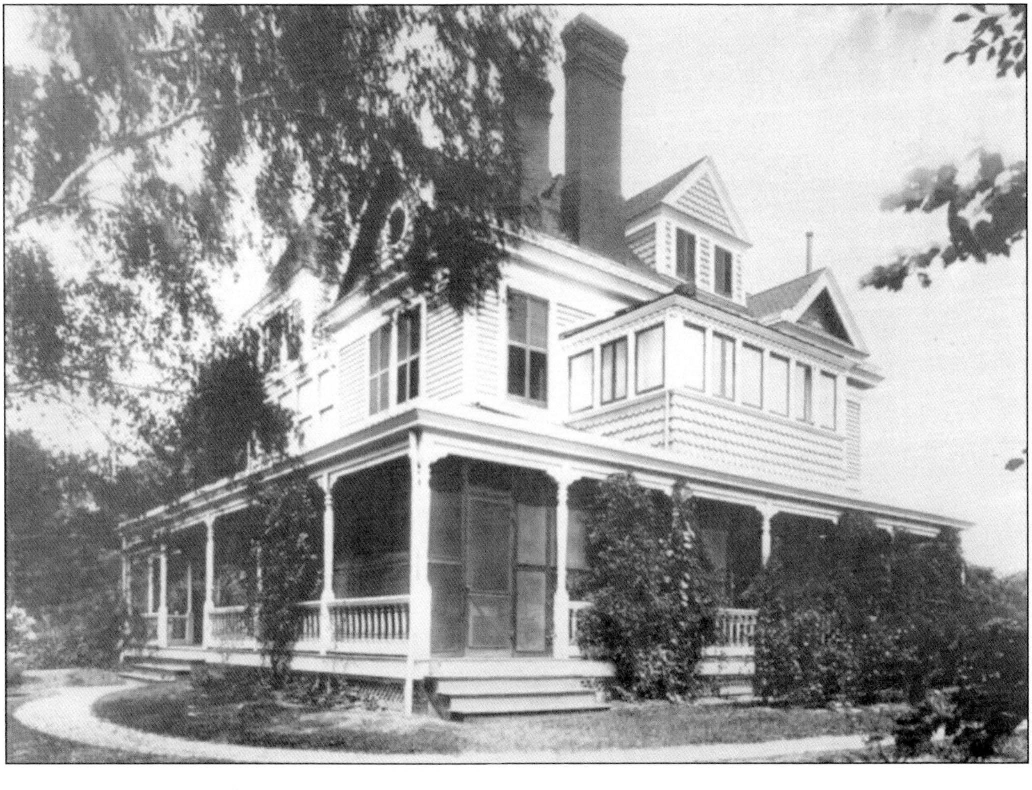

Kew Gardens was founded on a ridge of hills called the terminal moraine, which was created by glacial debris from the last ice age. The slow-moving glacier gathered and deposited soil and massive boulders, helping to shape the hilly terrain. The glacier stopped here, and the cascade of melting ice caused a torrential flood of water to the Atlantic Ocean, creating the southern flat plain that lies south of it.

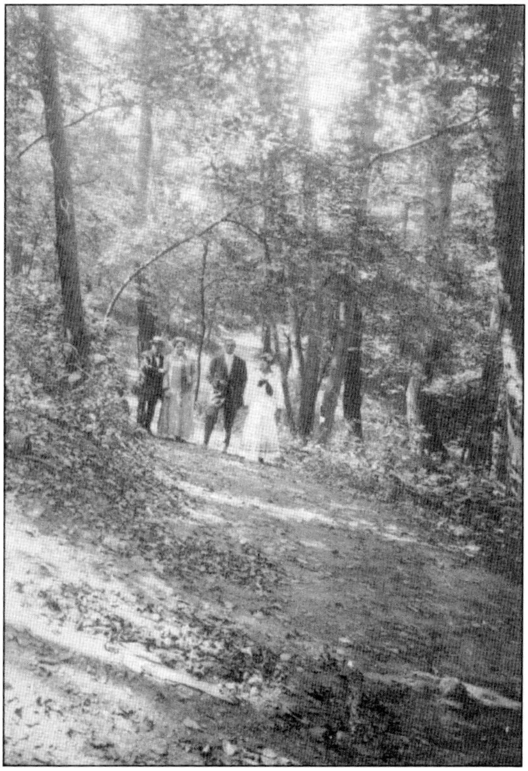

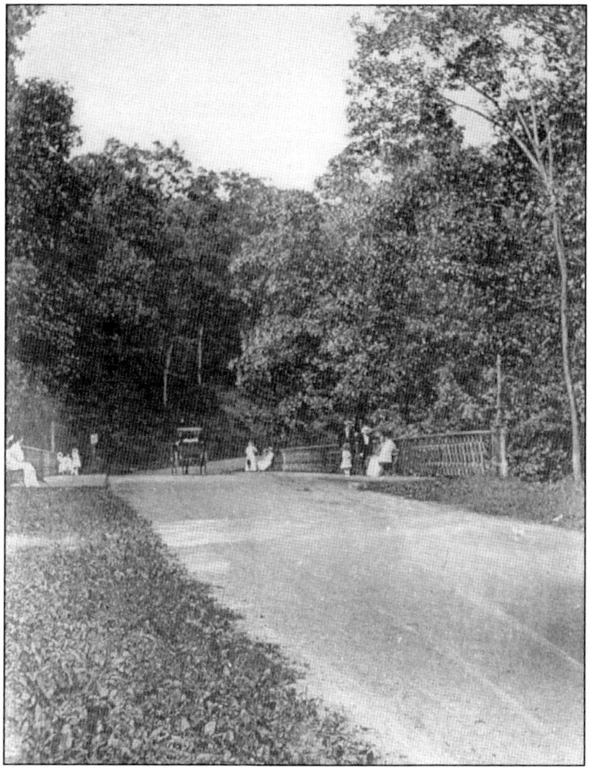

The southern plain became Richmond Hill, which was developed in 1868. The hilly terrain to the north, covered with dense lush forests, was known for its natural beauty and commanding views. It was used by the inhabitants of Richmond Hill and other local residents for hiking, hunting, and picnicking. The glacial ponds were used for fishing, swimming, and ice-skating in the winter. By 1908, the transformation of this area into Kew Gardens had begun.

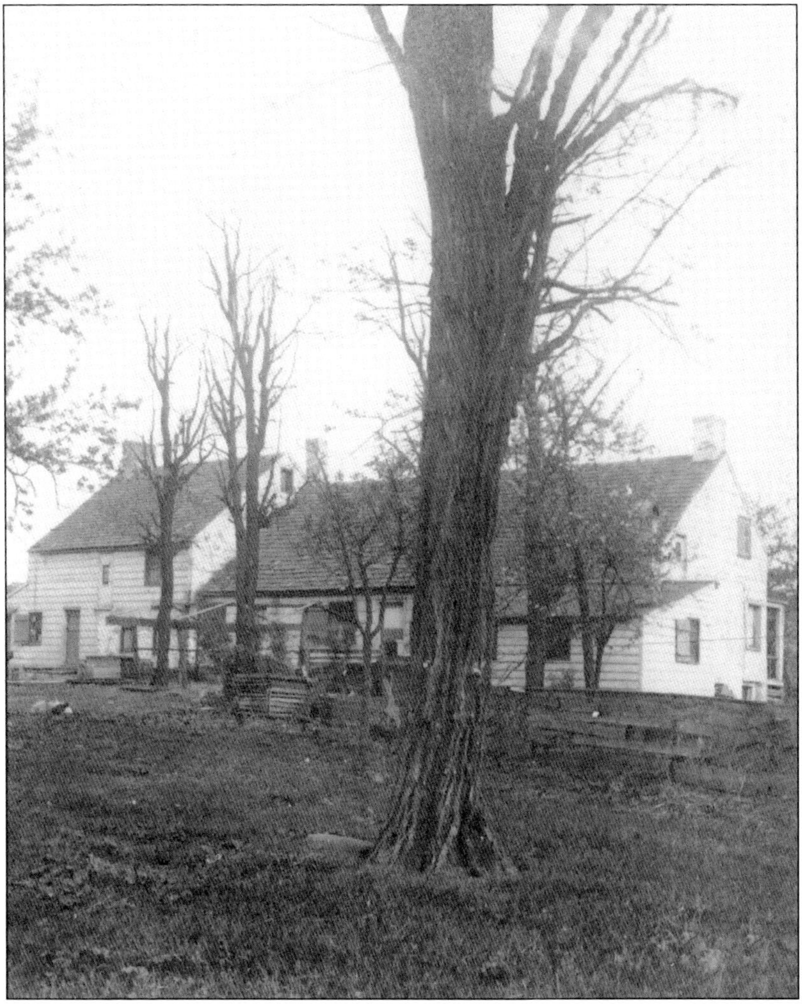

Some parts of Kew Gardens were also farmland, including the area east of today's Queens Boulevard. The Queens County Criminal Court House and New York City House of Detention are on land that used to be part of the Timothy Jackson Farm. His farmhouse is shown in this late-1880s photograph.

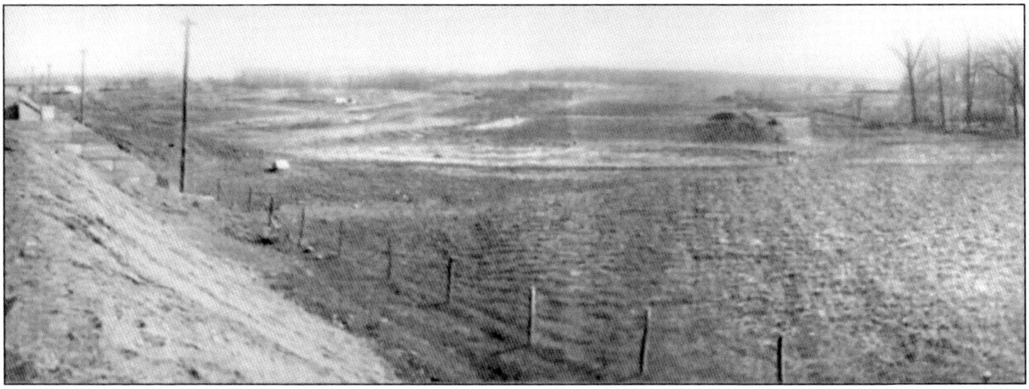

This photograph shows the Foulke farmland, where Station Square, Forest Hills, was erected. This view is to the south, toward Kew Gardens. The *Long Island Daily Press* reported on January 4, 1936: "Sarah Bolmer was the daughter of Daniel Cooper Foulk and born on the farm her father purchased in 1851, which took in the land lying along what is now Burns Street, as far as Station Square in Forest Hills, and 20 acres in Kew Gardens." (Courtesy of Nicholas Hirshon.)

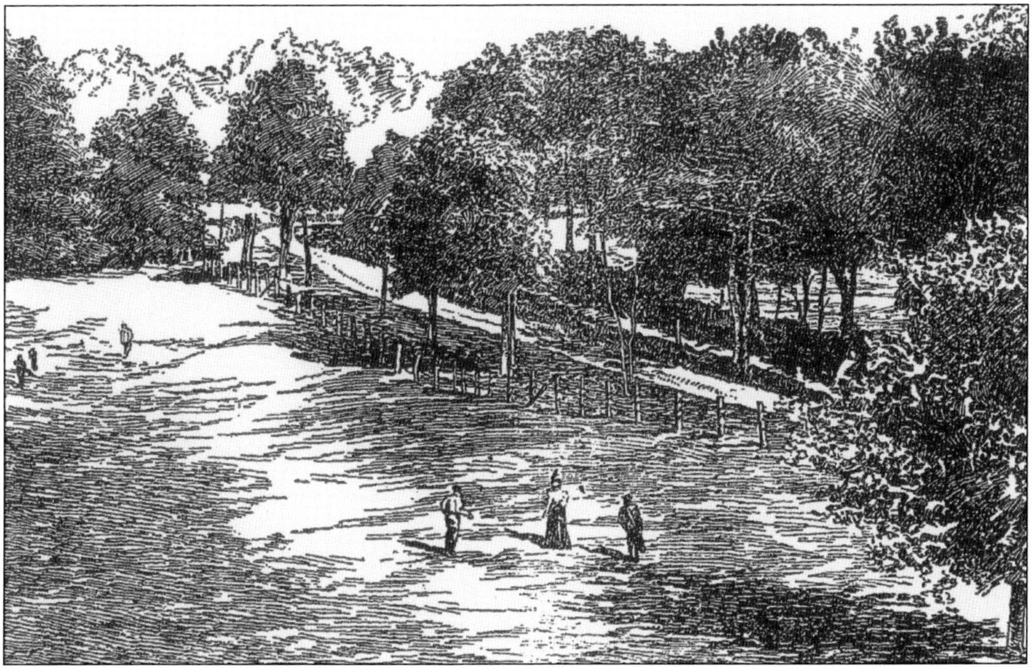

A major portion of Kew Gardens was built upon the nine-hole Richmond Hill Golf Club course. In this 1899 engraving of the ninth hole, Lefferts Boulevard is on the right. Beyond the trees is the Maple Grove Station. To the left, out of view, was Crystal Lake. According to the *Brooklyn Daily Eagle* of April 25, 1897, "The ninth hole is 170 yards from the teeing ground. Trees to the right and left punish a crooked drive."

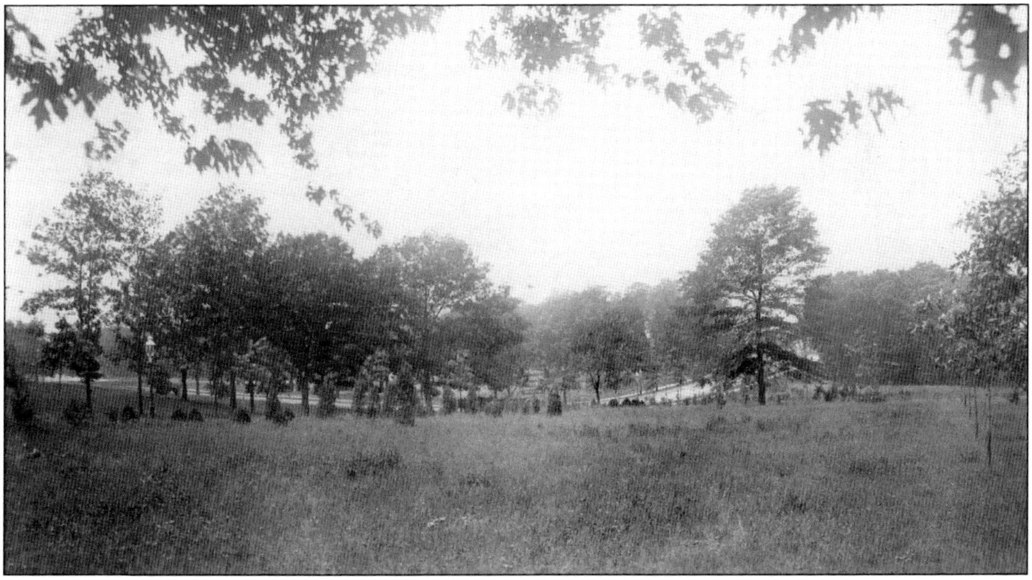

The transformation into Kew Gardens began in 1906, with the closing of the golf course. Crystal Lake was drained, and the Long Island Rail Road tracks were moved south, passing through the former golf course. According to the *Brooklyn Daily Eagle* of August 29, 1908, "Alrick H. Man has commenced cutting streets through the golf links." This photograph was taken from the newly made Grenfell Street at Audley Street, at what was once the golf course.

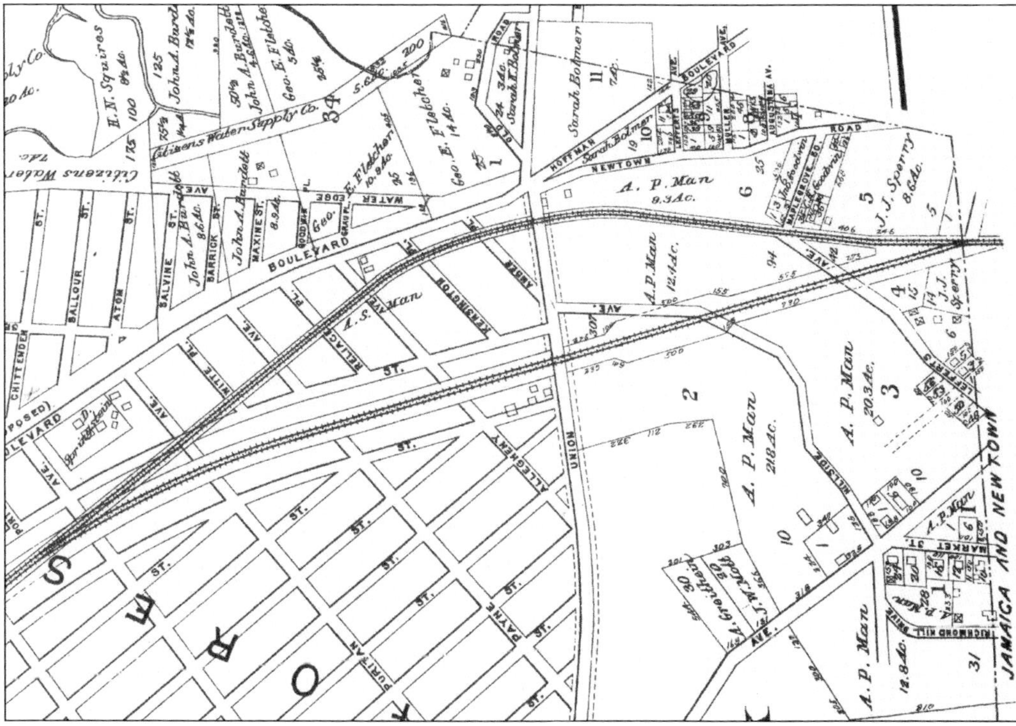

This 1908 map shows both old and new routes of the railroad tracks. The older, curved tracks were straightened and moved farther south, as shown here. The old Maple Grove Station was also moved farther south and a new one built upon the now-drained Crystal Lake. The small, old wooden station would become the Kew Gardens office, and a new station was built next to it and became the Kew Station.

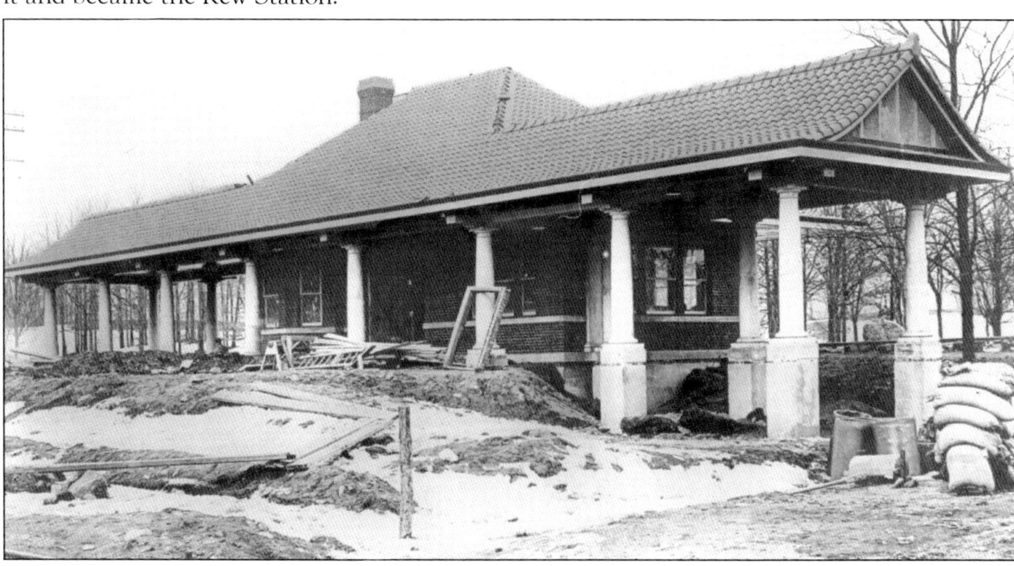

According to the *Richmond Hill Record* of August 14, 1909, "The new railroad station—a brick and cement affair—is about finished and will prove of great benefit to travelers on the new line." This photograph shows the construction of the new Kew Station, with terra-cotta tiles on the roof. The column supports were dug deep into the ground. (Courtesy Ron Marzlock.)

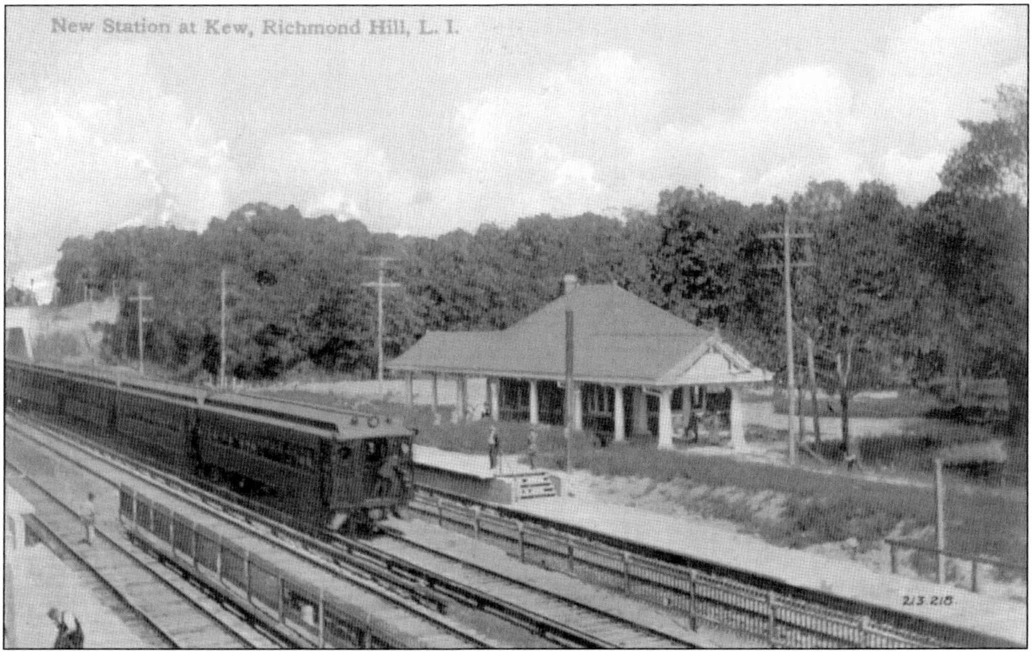

Early newspapers referred to the new development as North Richmond Hill. Then, a sign appeared at the station, three letters in gold: "KEW." This caused some confusion, as reported in the *Richmond Hill Record* on July 23, 1910: "KEW! KEW! To weary willies it may sound like stew. But it's only the new name for North Richmond Hill North. Surely that insignificant word cannot be a new name for such dignified surroundings?"

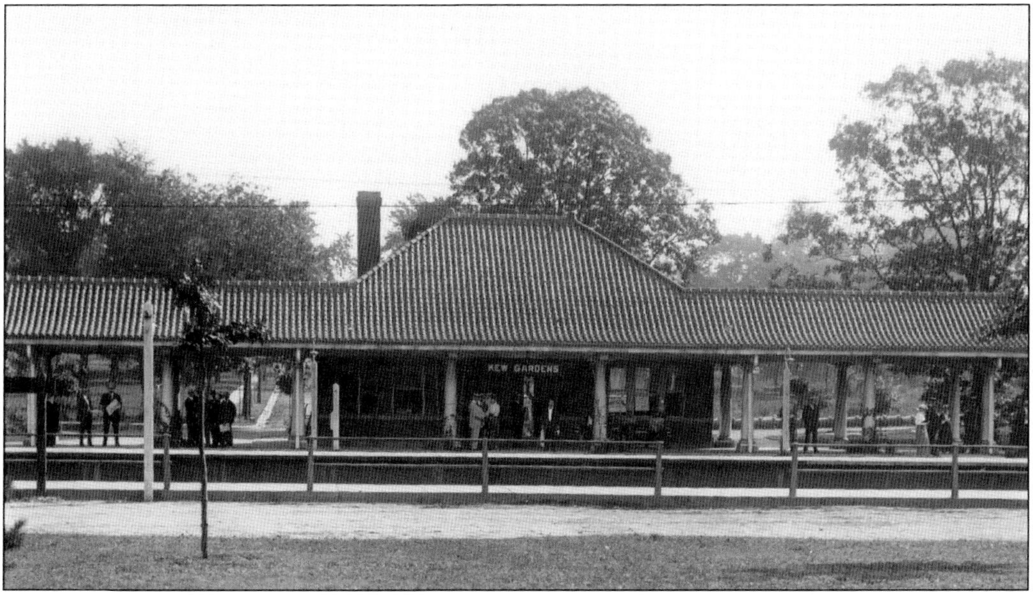

This is an early photograph of the new Kew Gardens Station. After the confusion with the Kew name, a new sign went up: "Kew Gardens." Clarification was found in local papers. "Kew" was the name of the town adjoining the town of Richmond Hill in England. Both American towns owe their names to Albon and Alrick Man, who wished to honor their ancestral home. (Courtesy Bob Stonehill.)

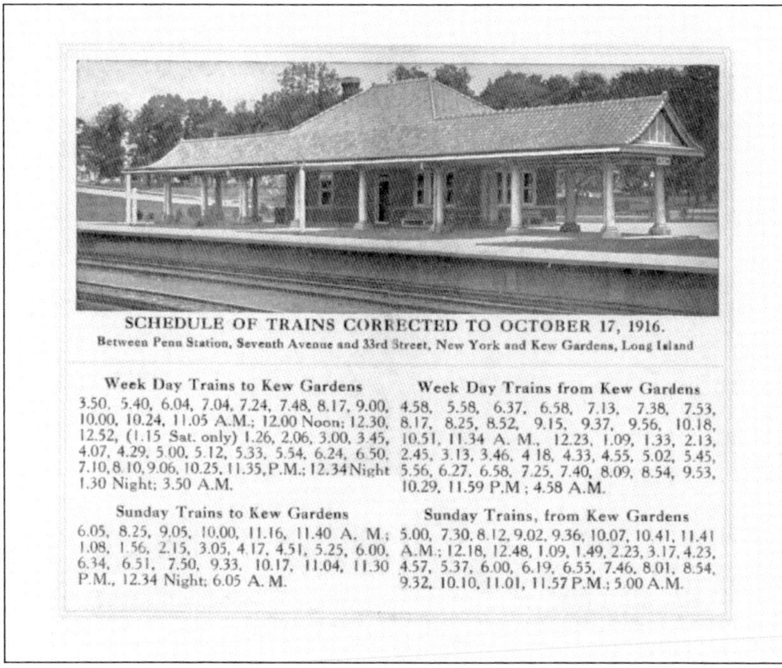

SCHEDULE OF TRAINS CORRECTED TO OCTOBER 17, 1916.

Between Penn Station, Seventh Avenue and 33rd Street, New York and Kew Gardens, Long Island

Week Day Trains to Kew Gardens

3.50, 5.40, 6.04, 7.04, 7.24, 7.48, 8.17, 9.00, 10.00, 10.24, 11.05 A.M.; 12.00 Noon; 12.30, 12.52, (1.15 Sat. only) 1.26, 2.06, 3.00, 3.45, 4.07, 4.29, 5.00, 5.12, 5.33, 5.54, 6.24, 6.50, 7.10, 8.10, 9.06, 10.25, 11.35, P.M.; 12.34 Night 1.30 Night; 3.50 A.M.

Week Day Trains from Kew Gardens

4.58, 5.58, 6.37, 6.58, 7.13, 7.38, 7.53, 8.17, 8.25, 8.52, 9.15, 9.37, 9.56, 10.18, 10.51, 11.34 A. M., 12.23, 1.09, 1.33, 2.13, 2.45, 3.13, 3.46, 4 18, 4.33, 4.55, 5.02, 5.45, 5.56, 6.27, 6.58, 7.25, 7.40, 8.09, 8.54, 9.53, 10.29, 11.59 P.M ; 4.58 A.M.

Sunday Trains to Kew Gardens

6.05, 8.25, 9.05, 10.00, 11.16, 11.40 A. M.; 1.08, 1.56, 2.15, 3.05, 4.17, 4.51, 5.25, 6.00, 6.34, 6.51, 7.50, 9.33, 10.17, 11.04, 11.30 P.M., 12.34 Night; 6.05 A. M.

Sunday Trains, from Kew Gardens

5.00, 7.30, 8.12, 9.02, 9.36, 10.07, 10.41, 11.41 A.M.; 12.18, 12.48, 1.09, 1.49, 2.23, 3.17, 4.23, 4.57, 5.37, 6.00, 6.19, 6.55, 7.46, 8.01, 8.54, 9.32, 10.10, 11.01, 11.57 P.M.; 5.00 A.M.

This is a 1916 train schedule. As reported in the *Richmond Hill Record* on July 23, 1910: "Residents of Richmond Hill in the vicinity of the new station, which was just electrified from Jamaica to Long Island City, are signing a petition to be presented to the management of the railroad, requesting that the electric trains stop at what is now known as Kew Station."

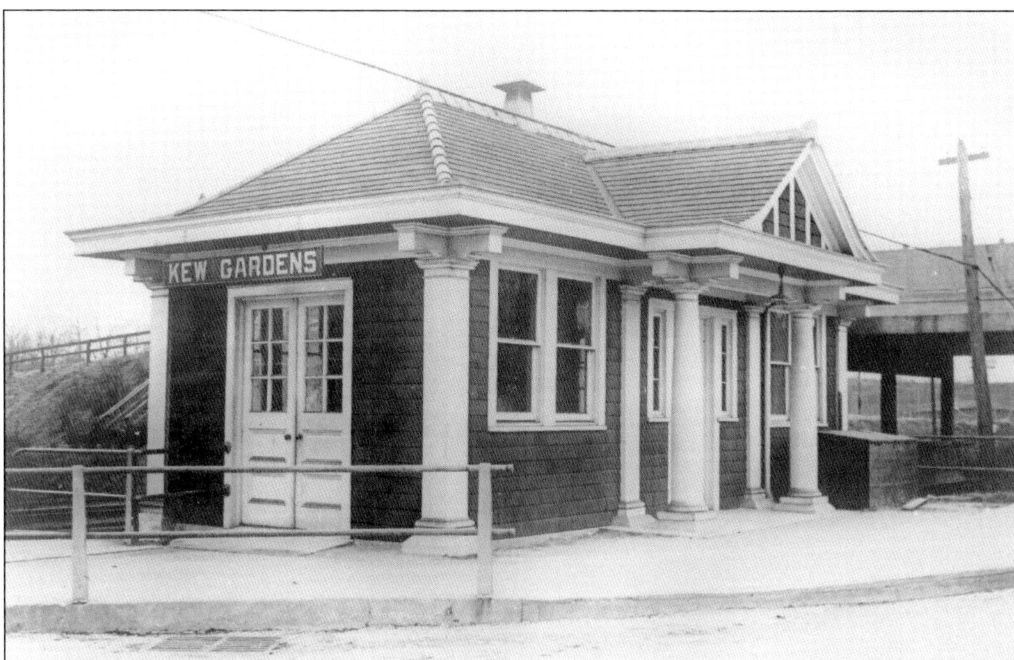

The Kew Gardens waiting room was built across from the Kew Gardens Station. Located on the eastbound platform, it was used by residents waiting for trains going to Long Island. The waiting room was torn down in the late 1970s. The Lefferts Avenue (Boulevard) overpass (visible in the background) was just a simple bridge, and the stores later found on either side had not yet been built.

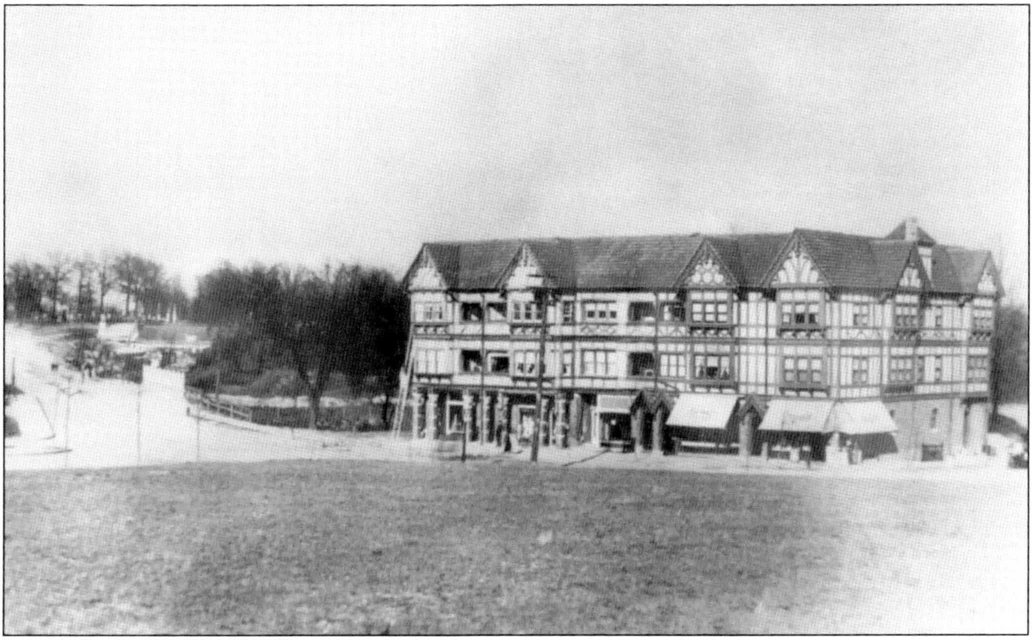

A c. 1930 manuscript in the files of Alrick H. Man reads, "The Railroad Company erected the fine bridges which carry the streets across its lines." The narrow Lefferts Avenue (Boulevard) bridge over the train tracks is seen at left. At the top of the hill is the administration building of Maple Grove Cemetery. The Homestead Building (pictured above) was the center of the early Kew Gardens business section.

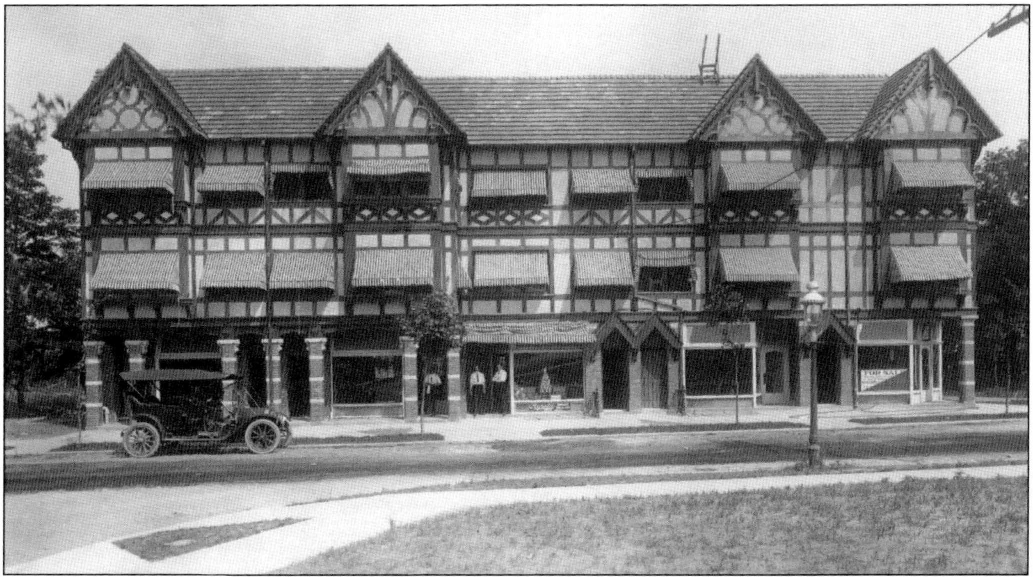

The *New York Herald* reported on November 24, 1912: "Foundation work for a unique business block was begun last week, on a plot located at the corner of Lefferts Avenue and Cuthbert Place and will be completed on January 1. Alfred E. Barlow is the architect. The large number of new houses erected at Kew Gardens has increased the demand for building stores of all kind." (Courtesy Robert Stonehill.)

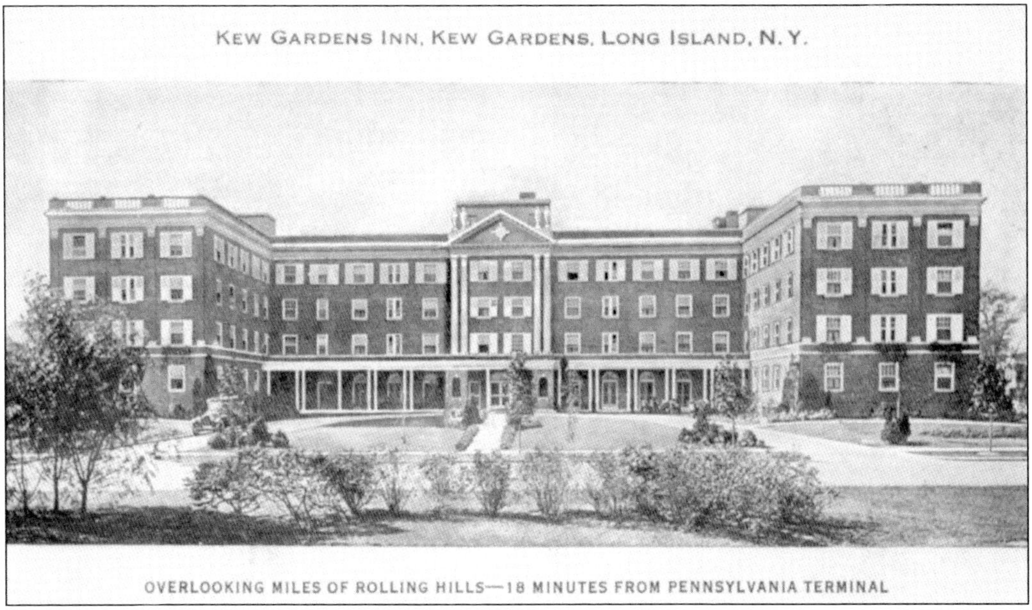

"Kew Gardens Inn, a traditional hotel, opened last week," reported the *New York Herald* on May 30, 1920. The inn, built by Alrick Man, was originally intended to be a veteran's hospital, but the deal with the governmernt fell through. In 1939, Alrick's son, Alrick Man Jr., renamed it the Kew Gardens Hotel and remodeled it in time for the world's fair. It was located at Queens Boulevard and Union Turnpike.

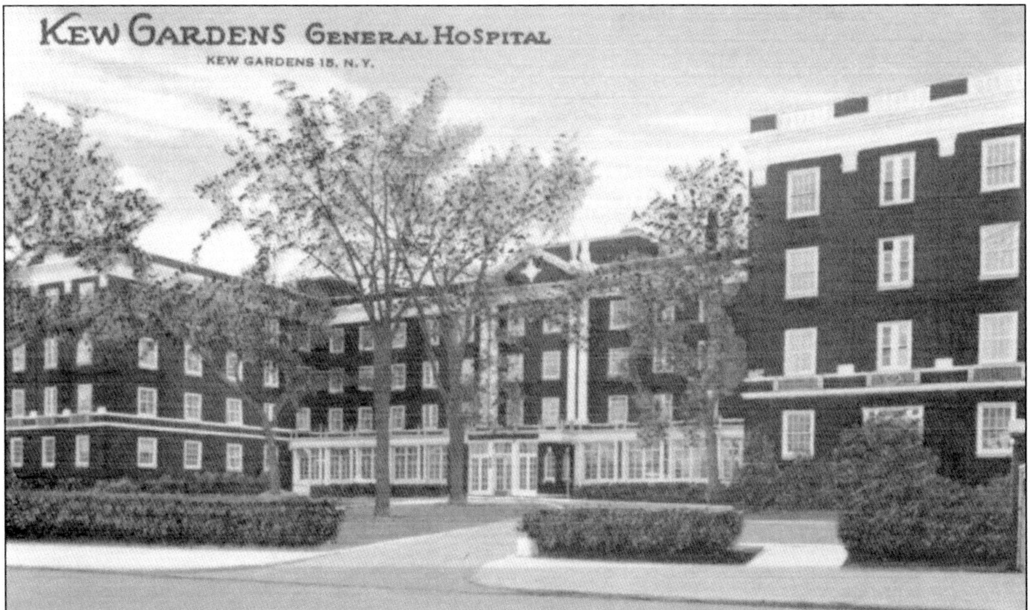

The *Long Island Daily Press* reported on December 24, 1940: "The Kew Gardens Hotel will close its doors January 1 and reopen in February as the Kew Gardens General Hospital. The new hospital will be a strictly private institution with 280 beds including a maternity ward and operating rooms." It served the community until 1978 and was demolished in 1982. It was replaced by the Crossroads Building.

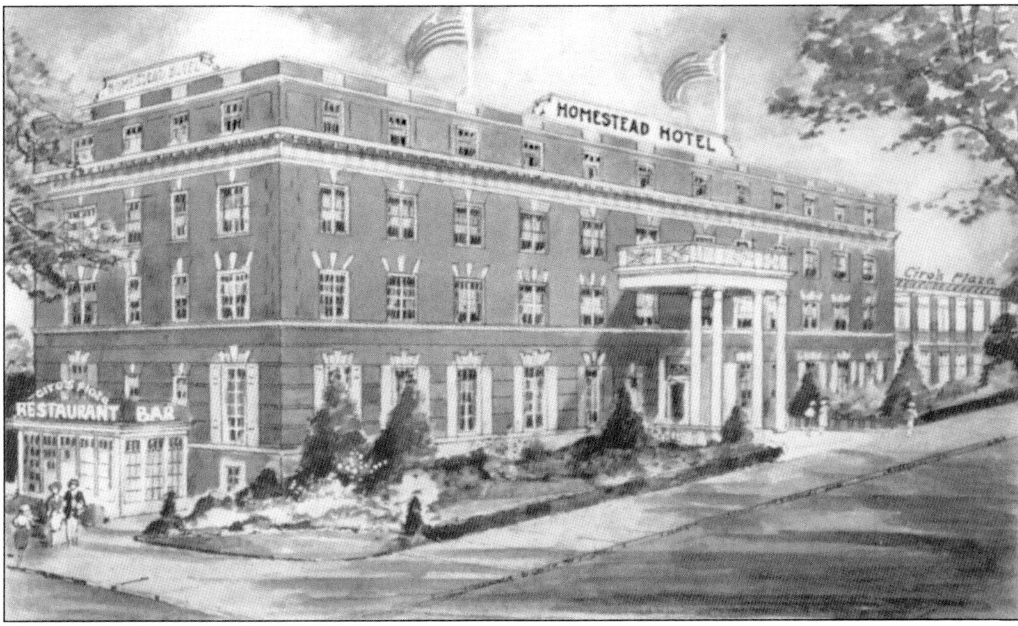

The Homestead Hotel stands on Grenfell Street. An article in the *Richmond Hill Record* of October 26, 1928, reads as follows: "The Homestead was opened in Kew Gardens a short time ago. The Homestead is intended primarily for a residential clientele, but ample accommodations are provided for transient patronage. The hotel is of four-story construction and follows the architecture of Colonial days. The hotel contains 120 rooms arranged in suites of one, two and three."

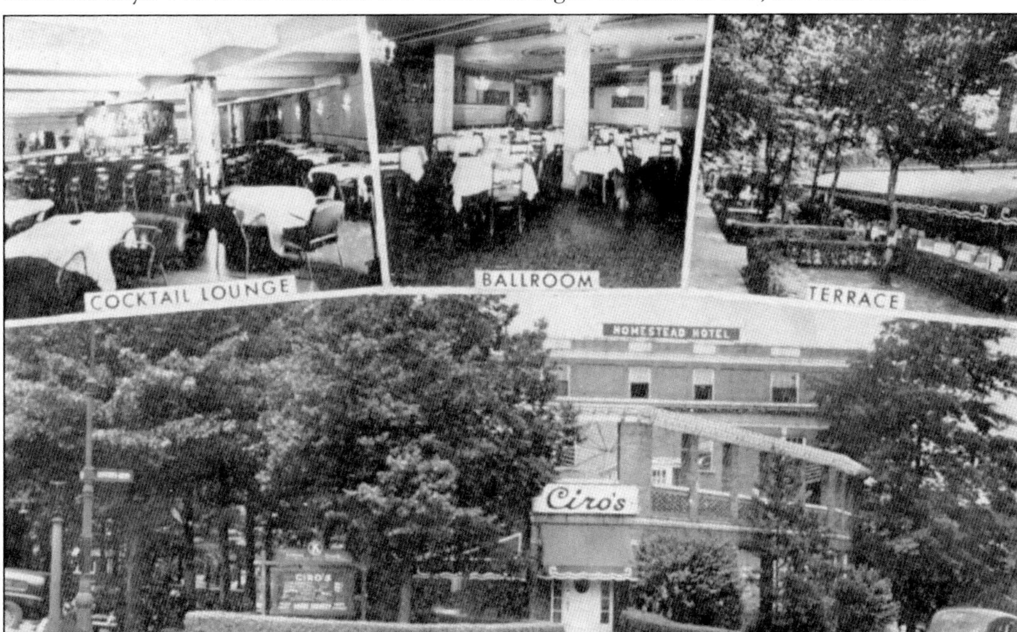

Ciro's Night Club was located in the Homestead Hotel and opened in 1940. It offered big-band music and an outdoor terrace for dinner and dancing. The *Brooklyn Daily Eagle* of April 5, 1940, called Ciro's the "newest night spot on the island . . . in the Homestead Hotel, Kew Gardens." A headliner at Ciro's for many years was Sleepy Hall and His Orchestra.

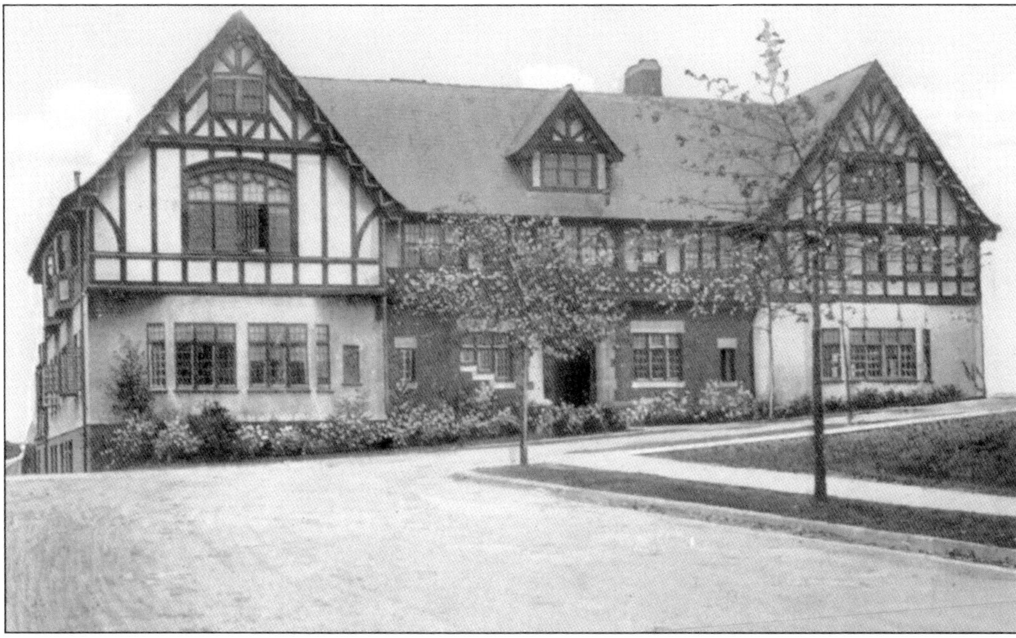

The Kew Gardens Country Club, a Tudor Gothic structure, stood at the corner of Austin Street and Lefferts Avenue, where the Kew Gardens Cinemas stands today. The birth of this club occurred in Richmond Hill at the old schoolhouse on Hillside Avenue that was transformed into a clubhouse. Many activities were planned at that early location until the Kew Gardens Club was opened in 1917.

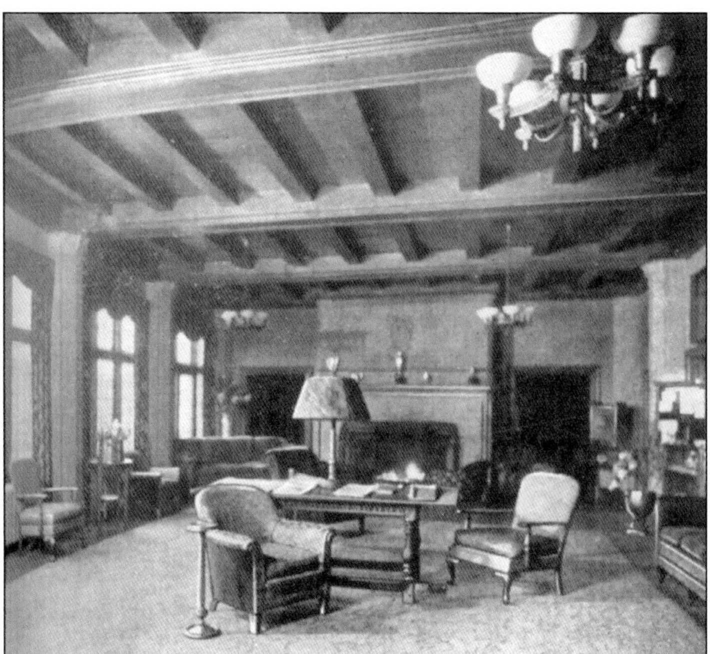

The clubhouse, designed by Nathaniel Vickers, became the focal point for the social life for both communities. The *Richmond Hill Record* of February 9, 1917, said of the club: "It is designed to appeal to the lovers of athletics. Its athletic facilities include 15 turf and dirt tennis courts, a squash court, putting green, shower baths, locker rooms, billiard tables and a bowling alley that is considered the finest in Queens Borough." (Courtesy QBPL Archives Periodical Collection.)

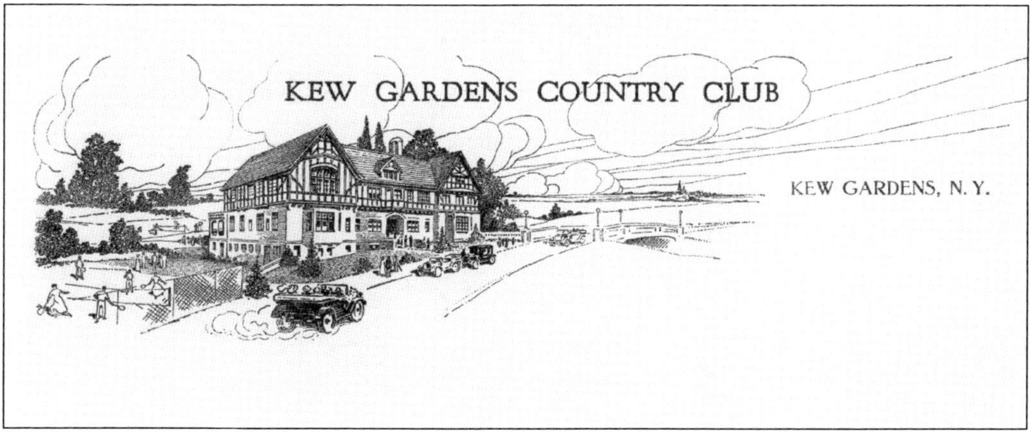

The *Richmond Hill Record* described the club on February 9, 1917: "The club's athletic activities will be centered on tennis. One of the most attractive features of the clubhouse is the extensive veranda which extends across the entire south front of the building. One need not necessarily be of a romantic trend of mind to imagine the picture when a radiant beauty sits here enthroned on a 'tournament' afternoon in May or September." Shown here is the club's letterhead.

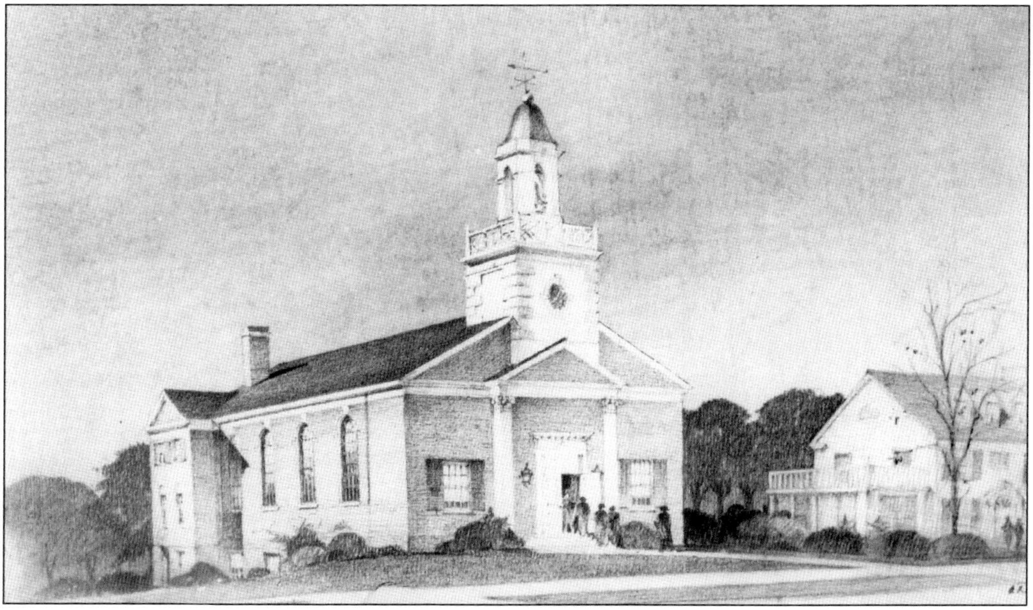

First Church of Kew Gardens held its first meeting in private residences starting in 1925. In 1926, the church chose Rev. Alexander Wouters as its first pastor. On December 2, 1928, the church was dedicated. It was located at the corner of Kew Gardens Road and Lefferts Avenue. The architect Hobart Upjohn designed a Colonial-style edifice. The bell was cast in 1843 and given as a gift to Dr. Wouters for the new building.

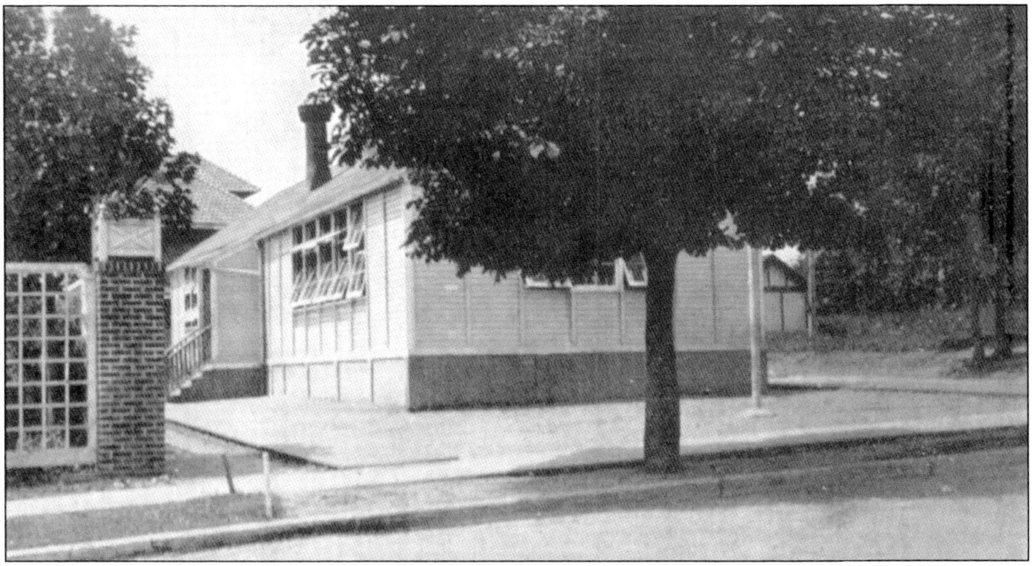

Before the large brick P.S. 99 was erected, the first school building was a small, portable, wooden schoolhouse located on Cuthbert Road one-half block east of Lefferts Avenue. As reported in the *Richmond Hill Record* on October 1, 1915: "Protest was made against the attempt of the school authorities to force children who have been going to Public School 54 to attend sessions in the new two-room portable school in Kew Gardens."

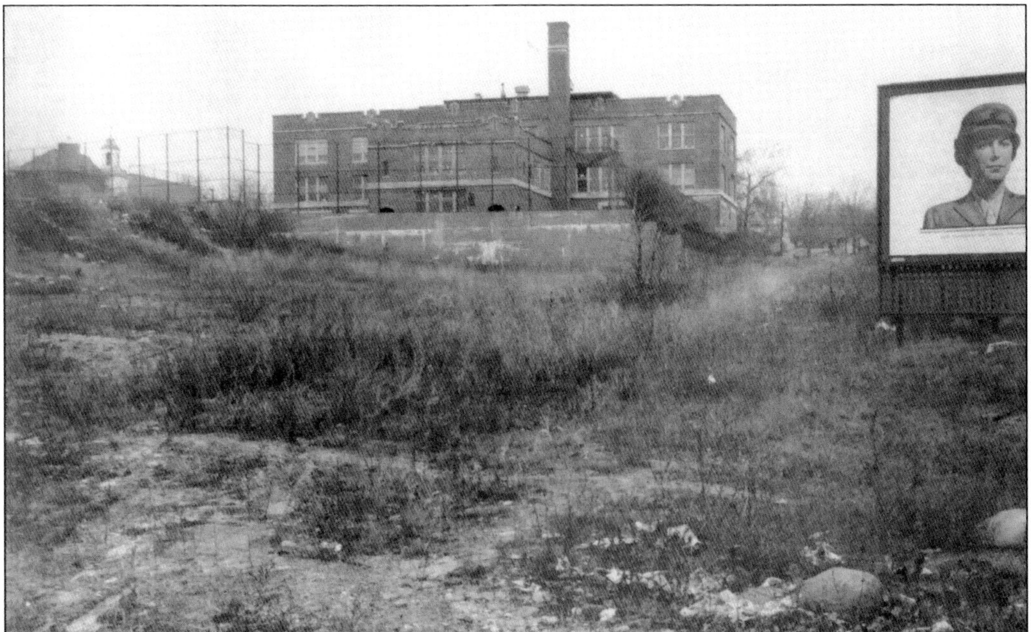

Public School 99, erected in 1923, was opened on September 11, 1924. The *Daily Star* reported on September 28, 1923: "The building will be a duplicate of the new P.S. 36 in St. Albans, and according to the plans and specification submitted by the architect, will have seventeen classrooms and accommodate 735 pupils." The architect, William H. Gompert, designed the landmarked Jamaica High School in 1927. The school is seen here from Queens Boulevard along Eighty-second Road.

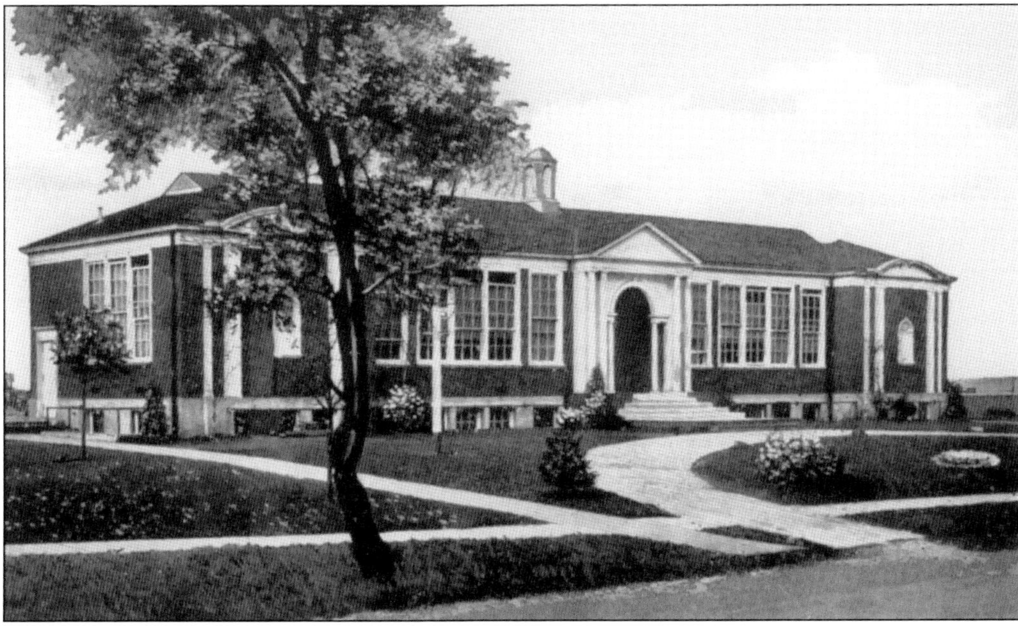

The Kew-Forest School was founded in 1918 by Louis D. Marriott and Guy Hinman Catlin. Their object was to establish a country day school with modern equipment, high standards of scholarship and discipline, and a sincere spirit of service. The school is located on Union Turnpike, west of Queens Boulevard. Notable graduates and attendees include Hank Azaria, Katharine Weber, Gideon Yago, and Donald Trump.

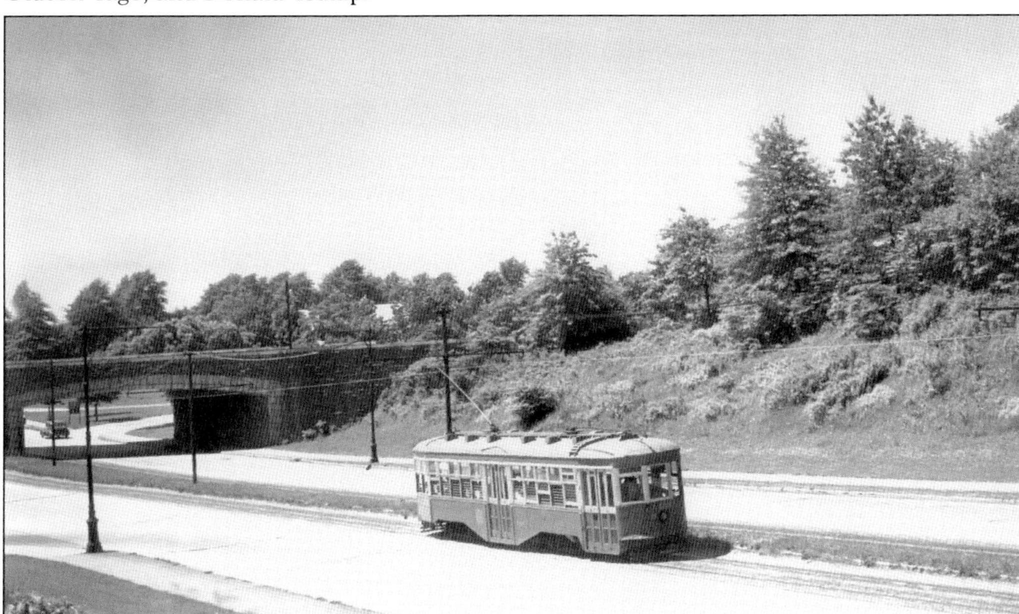

On March 30, 1909, the Queensboro Bridge was opened, connecting Queens to Manhattan. Hoffman (Queens) Boulevard was a narrow dirt road and would need to become a major artery of travel. Work started immediately, and it was soon widened and paved. On January 31, 1914, the first trolley ran on the boulevard to Jamaica. The trolley car shown here is on Metropolitan Avenue.

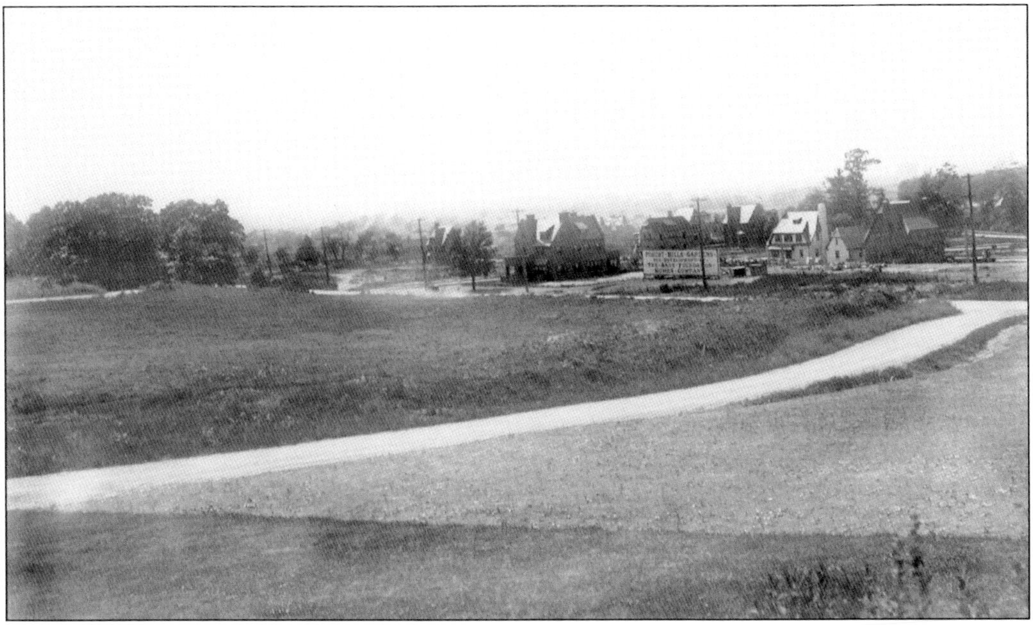

The communities of Kew Gardens and Forest Hills developed simultaneously, side by side, as seen in this photograph. An article in the *Queensborough* magazine on March 1921, stated, "A deed, filed in the Queens County Clerk's Office, covered 26 acres of land in Kew Gardens and Forest Hills. The oldest original land deed in Queens, dated March 22, 1753 by David Springsteen to his son Casparus. The consideration was 'love and affection.'" (Courtesy Ron Marzlock.)

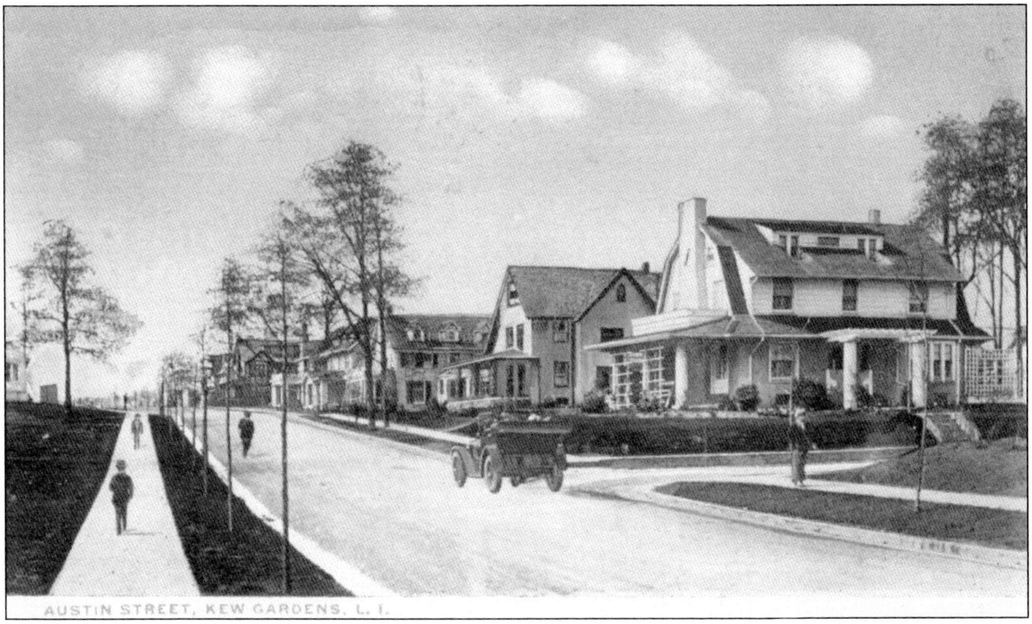

After the closing of the Richmond Hill Golf Club, Alrick Man commenced creating his new community and began cutting new streets through the old golf links. These streets and roads were given new names, and the construction of houses began. This postcard image shows Austin Street looking north to Forest Hills. The Kew Gardens station is out of view to the left. The intersection on the right marks Newbold Place (Eighty-second Road).

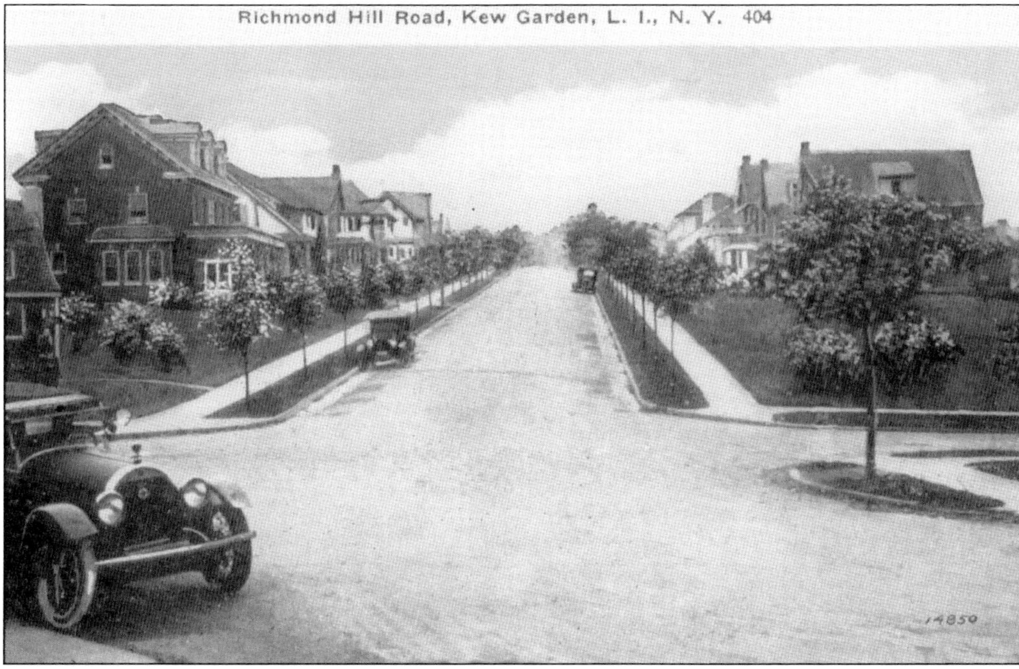

A car is parked on Lefferts Avenue (Boulevard). The viewer is looking to Richmond Hill Road (Eighty-third Avenue). The street on the right is Grenfell Street. On June 29, 1911, the *Richmond Hill Record* stated, "At this time of the year there is nothing more interesting than a walk about Kew Gardens, which is being developed by the Man Estate."

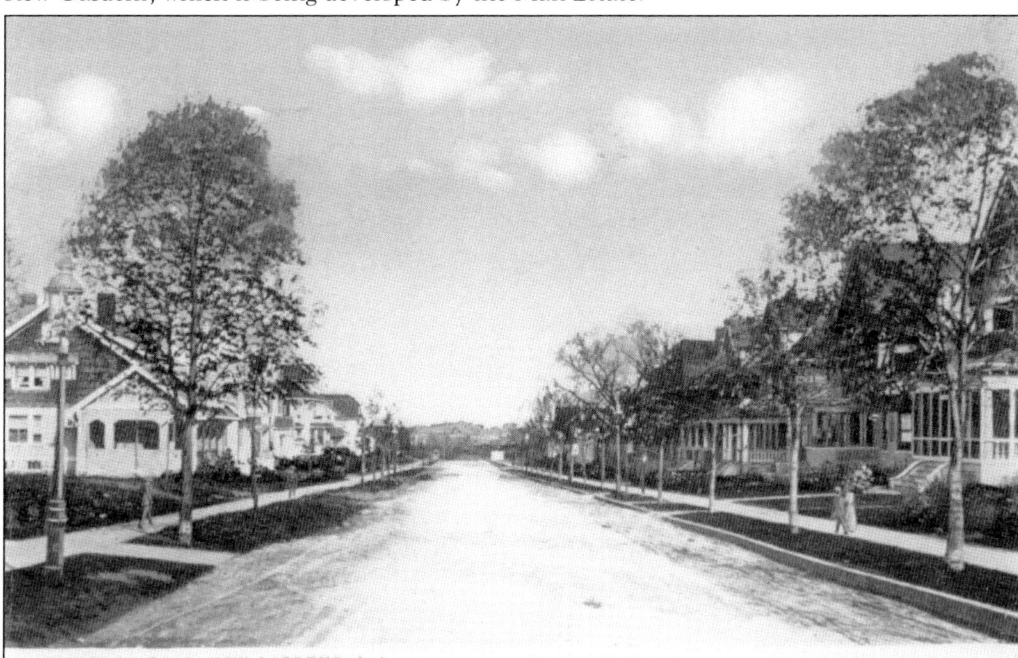

This is Abingdon Road, looking west beyond Brevoort Street. As reported in the *Richmond Hill Record* on July 12, 1912, "A comprehensive landscape gardening plan is being carried out in Kew Gardens, while at the same time the natural beauties of the place has been retained."

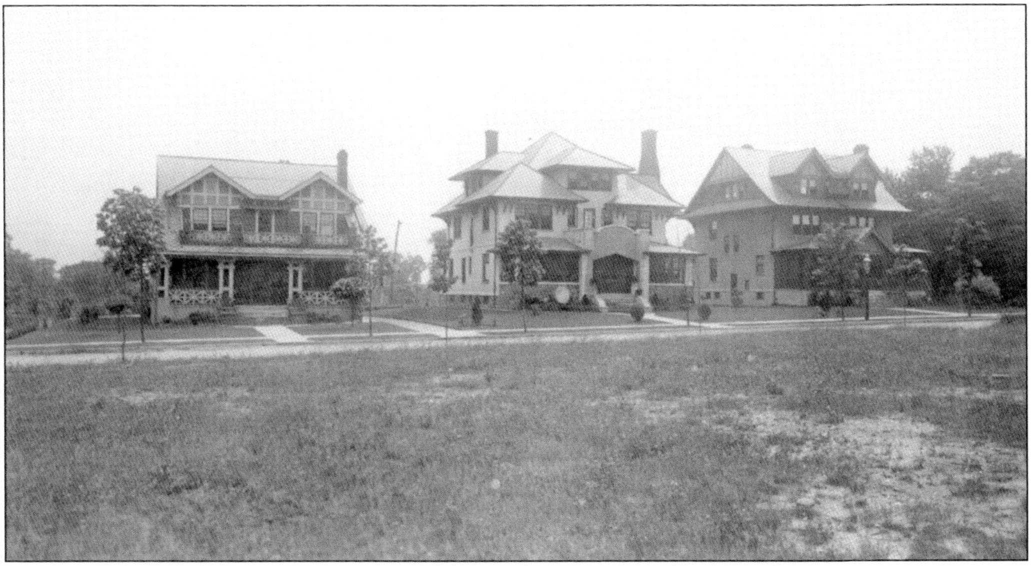

This photograph shows Abingdon Road, near Brevoort Street. The *Richmond Hill Record* of September 17, 1912, described Kew Gardens as including "the hilly part of Richmond Hill and a large portion of what is known as Kew Gardens and where there are many improvements now under way."

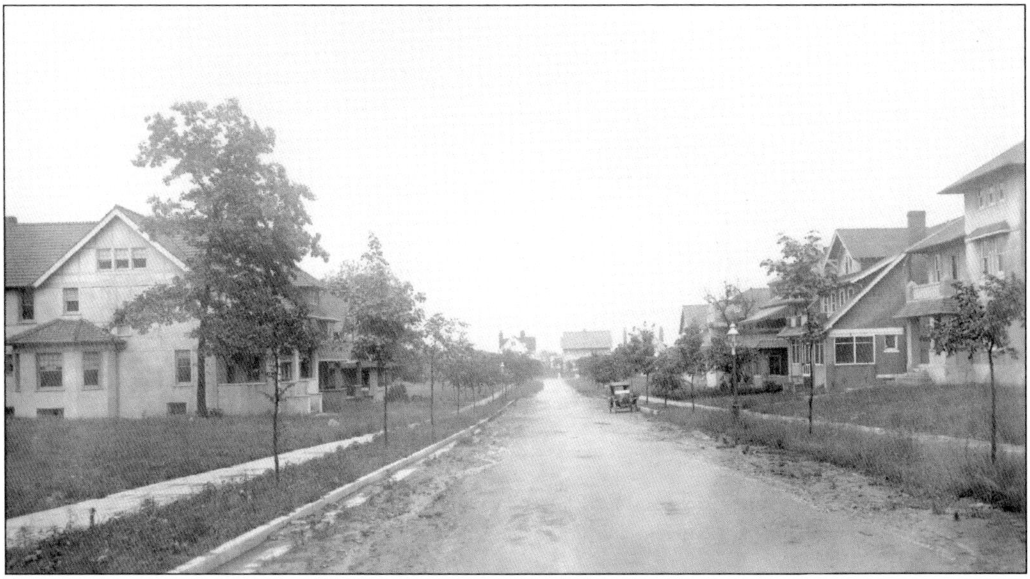

This photograph, taken from Lefferts Boulevard, looks east on Beverly Road. The *Richmond Hill Record* of September 17, 1912, reported the following: "Map of Richmond Hill and Kew Gardens. There are several wide avenues, among the number being Metropolitan Avenue, Hillside Avenue, Jamaica Avenue and Kew Gardens Road, all of which are 100 feet wide. Lefferts Avenue is laid down 60 feet in width."

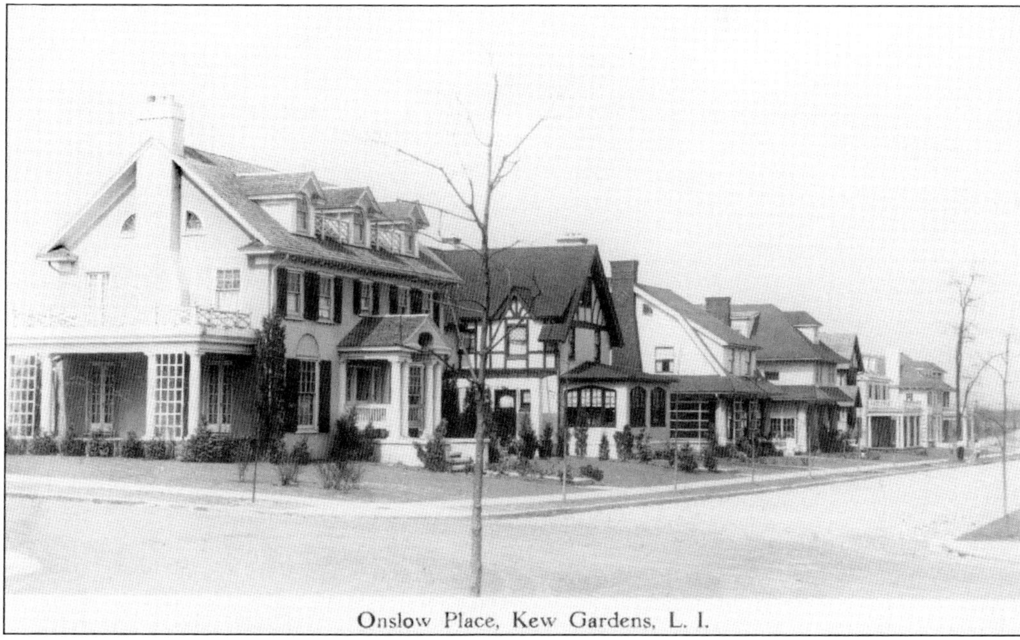

Onslow Place, Kew Gardens, L. I.

This is Onslow Place (Eighty-second Avenue), between Austin Street and Kew Gardens Road. According to the *New York Herald* of May 23, 1915, "The development of Kew Gardens, east of the railroad station, has been phenomenal. About a year and a half ago the work of opening streets was begun, not a single house having been built on this side of the station. Now there are plans for 48 new houses."

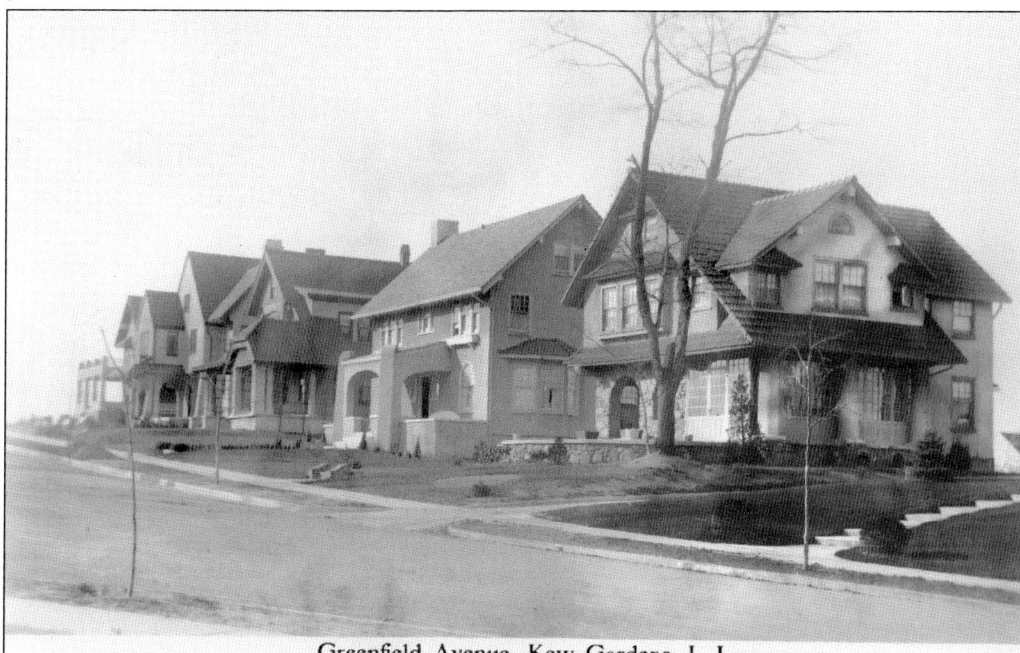

Greenfield Avenue, Kew Gardens, L. I.

Grenfell Street is seen here from Onslow Place (Eighty-second Avenue). According to the *Richmond Hill Record* of July 7, 1913, "Broad streets and avenues are macadamized, and sidewalks, curbs, gutters and sewers, water, gas, electric light, telephone service, etc., are installed by the owners."

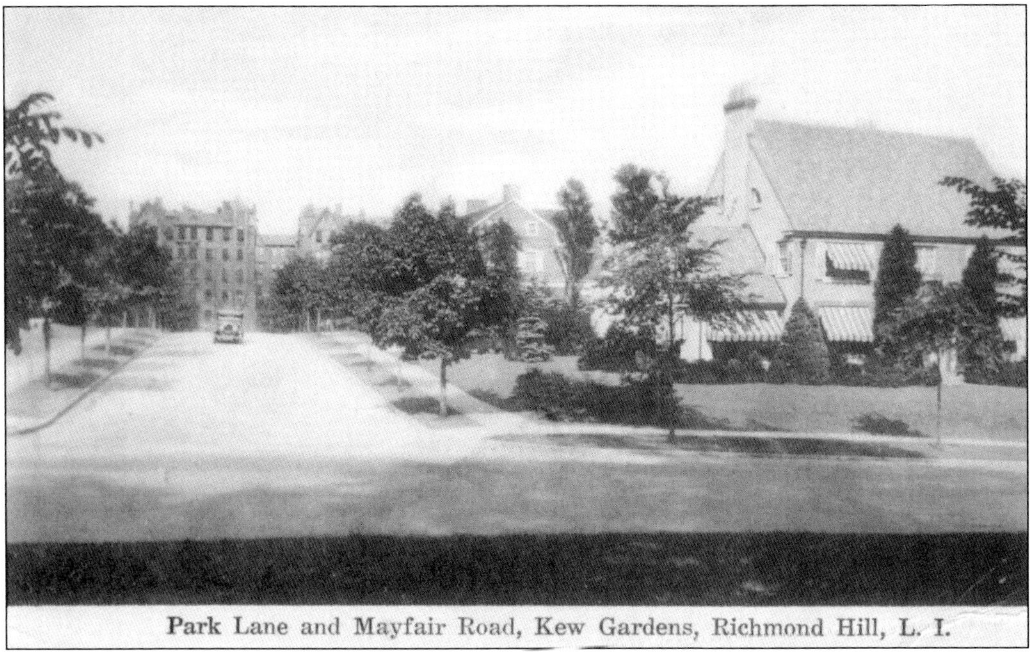

This postcard image shows Mayfair Road, looking east from Park Lane (South) to Audley Street (116th Street). According to the *Richmond Hil Record* of December 6, 1912, there was "demand for new lots. There seems to be a continual demand for building lots at Kew Gardens."

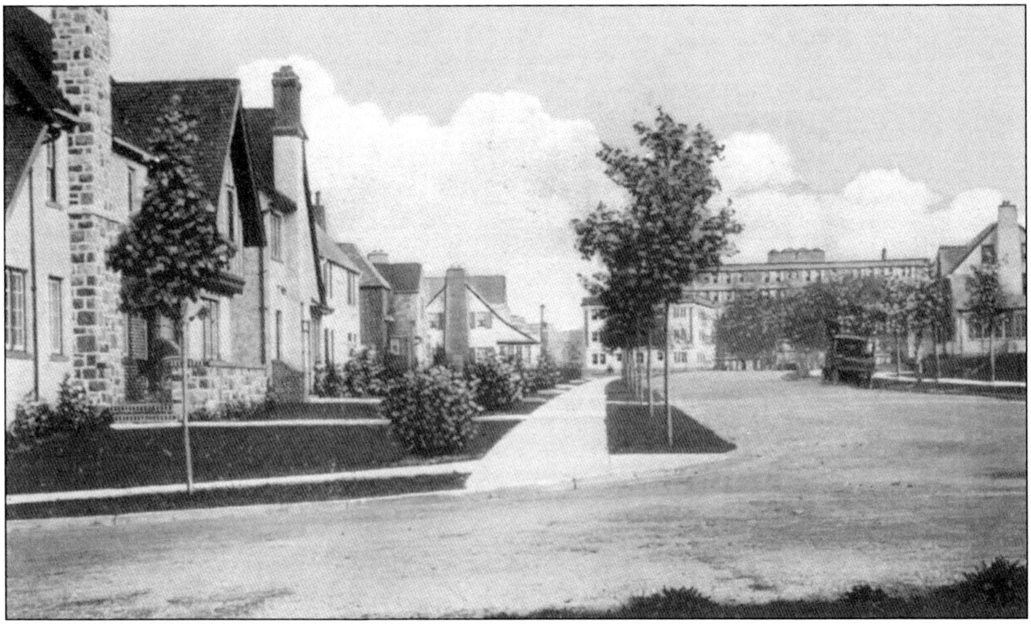

Shown here is Kew Forest Lane looking toward Union Turnpike from Seventy-seventh Avenue. The Colonial Hall apartment is in the distance. This section is part of Forest Hills above Union Turnpike. Before the Interboro Parkway separated this area, it was considered an extension of Kew Gardens.

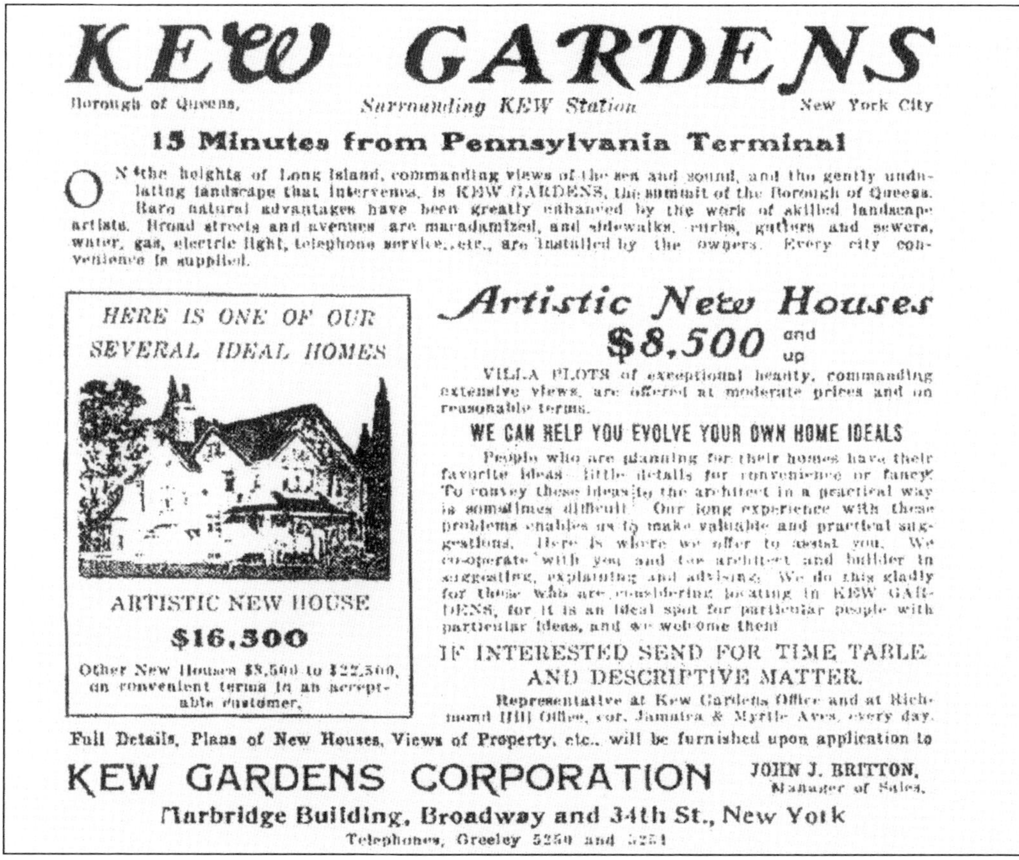

This is a 1913 Kew Gardens Corporation advertisement. In 1868, Albon Platt Man purchased a tract of land, about 400 acres, which would become the communities of Richmond Hill and Kew Gardens. He continued the development work of Richmond Hill until his death in 1891. In order to carry on this work, the Kew Gardens Corporation was formed in 1912, with the sons of Albon Man as officers and directors.

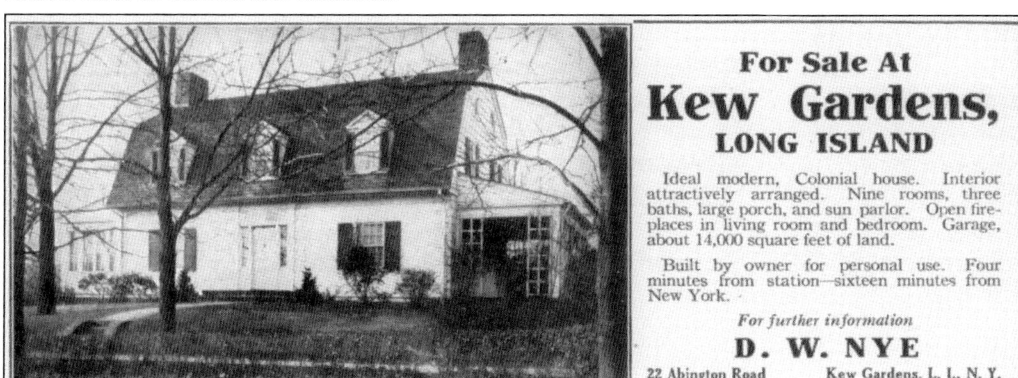

This is a 1923 advertisement for a Kew Gardens home for sale. A few years earlier, on January 27, 1919, the *Long Island Farmer* stated, "The Kew Gardens Corporation announced that for them the time for action had come, and that they are ready to build homes for those who wish to get out in suburban residential communities. The Kew Gardens Construction Co. was incorporated at Albany. It is an auxiliary of the Kew Gardens Corporation."

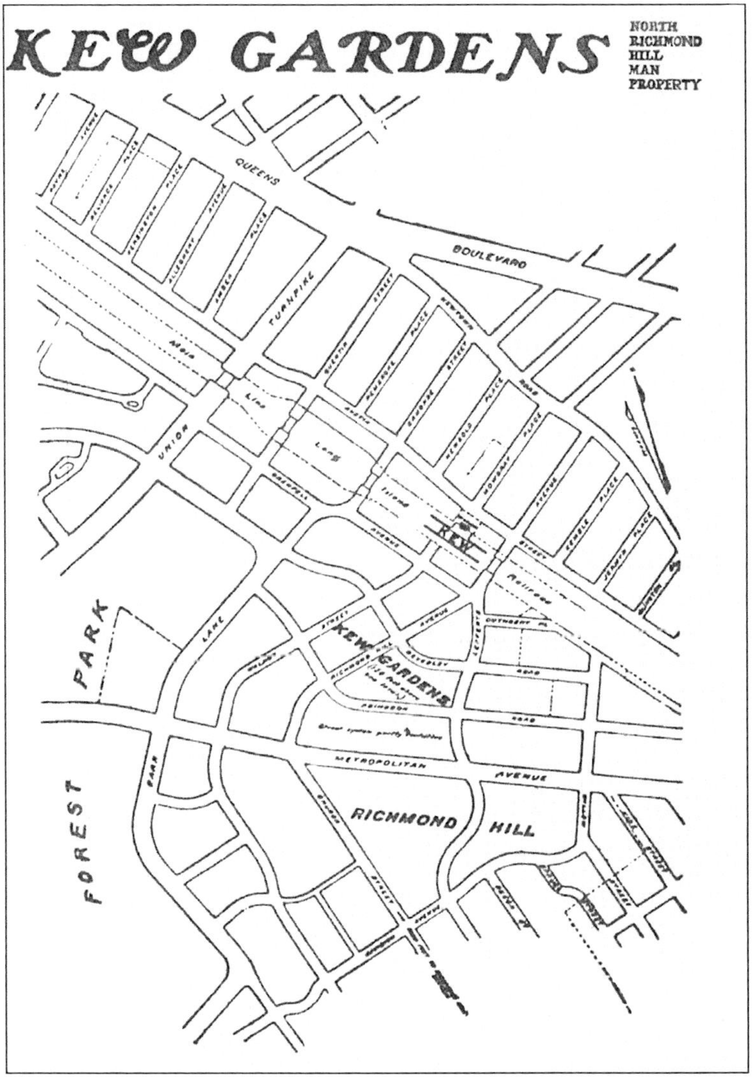

When Kew Gardens developed, new streets were created. Some have kept their name, while others have changed their names over time. Among the streets listed here, those that have changed names include the old name and, in parentheses, the new name: Quentin Street (Eightieth Road), Pembroke Place (Eighty-first Avenue), Austin Street, Onslow Place (Eighty-second Avenue), Newbold Place (Eighty-second Road), Mowbrary Place, Maple Grove Boulevard (one block long, from the Maple Grove train station to Kew Gardens Road and now part of Lefferts Boulevard), White Pot Road (Newtown Road to Kew Gardens Road), Talbot Place (Street), Grenfell Avenue (Street), Audley Street, Union Road (Union Turnpike), Park Lane (South), Beverly Road, Cuthbert Place (Street), Richmond Hill Road (Avenue to Eighty-third Avenue), Abingdon Road, Williamsburgh and Jamaica Turnpike (Metropolitan Avenue), Grosvenor Place (Road and Lane), Mayfair Road, Curzon Place (Road), Lefferts Avenue (Boulevard), Kingsley Place (Eighty-third Drive), Jemco Place (Eighty-fourth Avenue), Iris Place (Eighty-fourth Road), Hoffman Boulevard (Queens Boulevard), Richmond Hill Drive (117th Street), Willow Street (Brevoort Street), and Division (St. Ann's Avenue to Eighty-fourth Avenue). Streets between Kew Gardens Road and Queens Boulevard are Lefferts Avenue (Eighty-second Avenue), Muller Avenue (Eighty-second Road), and Augustina Avenue (Eighty-third Avenue).

Four

MAPLE GROVE CEMETERY

A COUNTRY OASIS

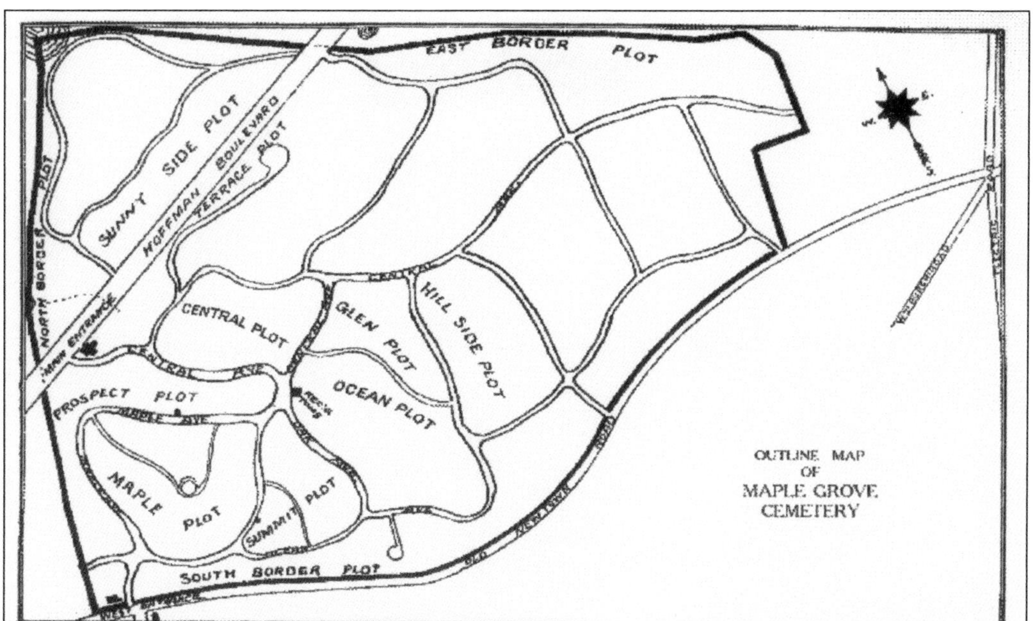

Maple Grove Cemetery, organized in 1875 with 75 acres, was purchased in an area once called Hayestown. This 1908 map includes surrounding streets; Hoffman Boulevard (Queens Boulevard), Old Newtown Road (Kew Gardens Road), and Williamsburgh Road (Metropolitan Avenue). Electric Road refers to the electrified trolley line on Jamaica Avenue. Sunny Side and North Plots were sold with the creation of the Van Wyck Expressway, reducing the cemetery to 65 acres.

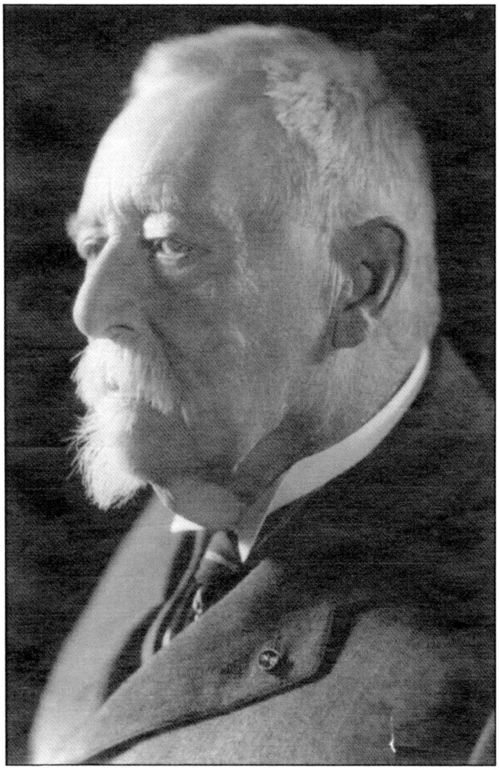

William Sterling Cogswell (1840–1935), the founding president of Maple Grove, was born in Jamaica, New York. He was commissioned in 1861 as a first lieutenant during the Civil War and fought at the battles of Antietam, Gettysburg, and others. He rose to the rank of lieutenant colonel. Cogswell studied law and practiced in Jamaica and Brooklyn. He spearheaded the formation of Maple Grove Cemetery in 1875 and served as president for 60 years.

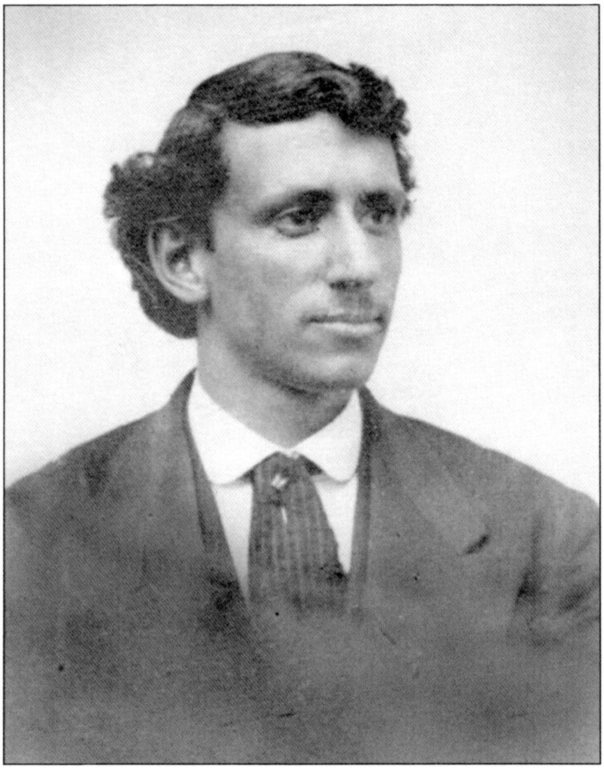

James E. Ware (1846–1918), a prolific and enigmatic New York architect, planned buildings for Maple Grove. A preeminent designer of model tenements, he was a pioneer in the American Queen Anne style. He conceived The Osborne, New York's first luxury apartment building, and the world's tallest, in 1884. Ware devised celebrated resort hotels at Mohonk and Millbrook, as well as fairy-tale-themed country estates and Madison Avenue Presbyterian Church. Ware and his family are buried at Maple Grove. (Courtesy of Bill Hurd.)

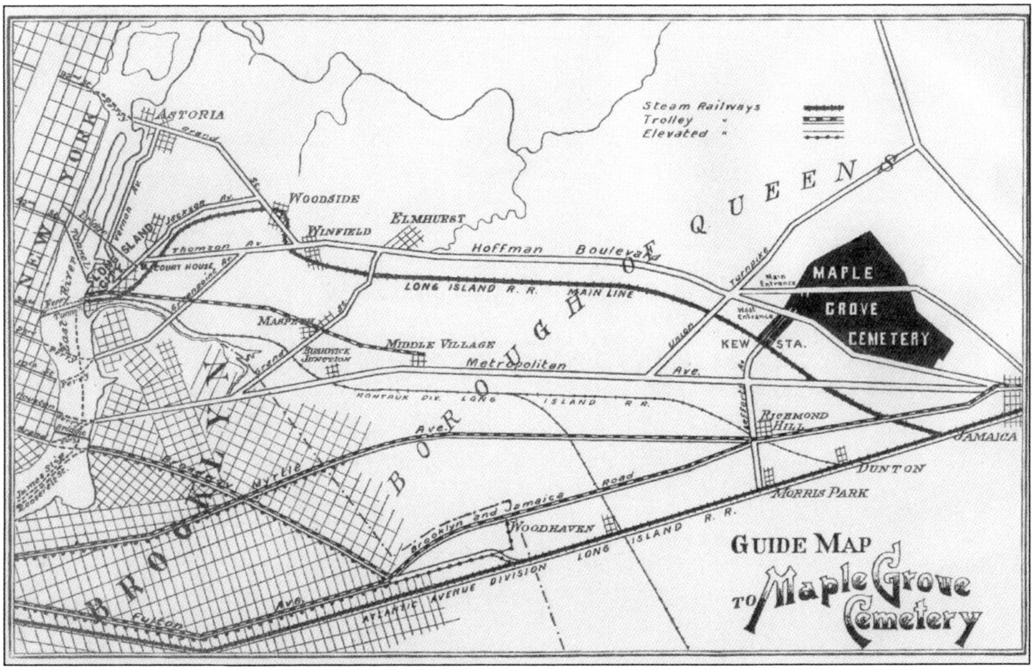

This 1908 map shows the cemetery's location in relation to Brooklyn and Manhattan. Maple Grove Station is featured, with Maple Grove Road leading from the station to the cemetery. In 1908, the curved tracks were straightened and the station moved farther south and built on what was once Crystal Lake. As seen on this map, Maple Grove Cemetery once owned the land on either side of Maple Grove Road.

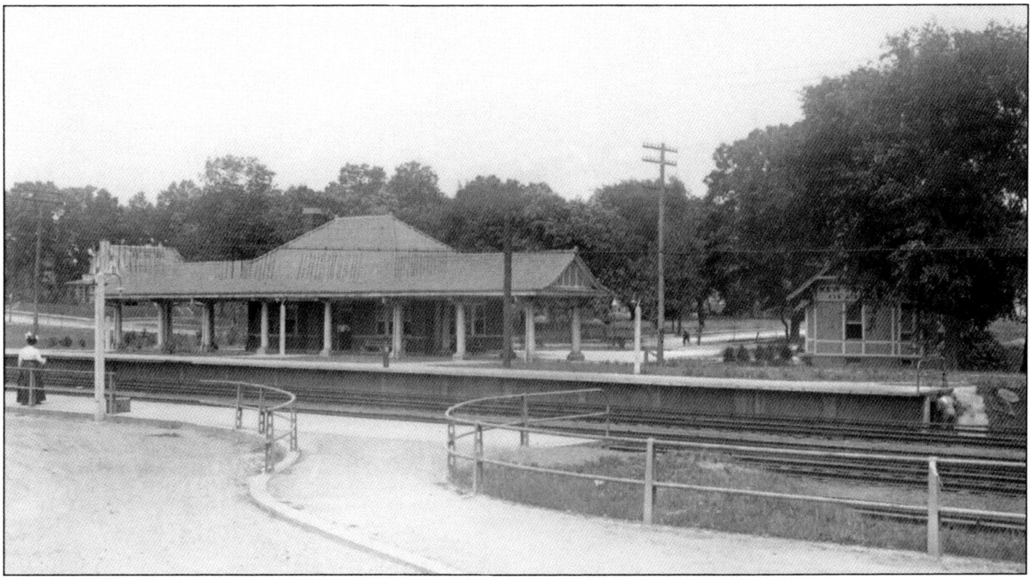

Architect James E. Ware designed Maple Grove Station in 1879. As reported in the *Newtown Register* on December 4, 1879, "Maple Grove station on the Long Island railroad at Whitepot is to have a depot master to flag trains." The old, wooden Maple Grove station (right) stands next to the new Kew Gardens station. The old station was moved south from its original position and served as the Kew Gardens office.

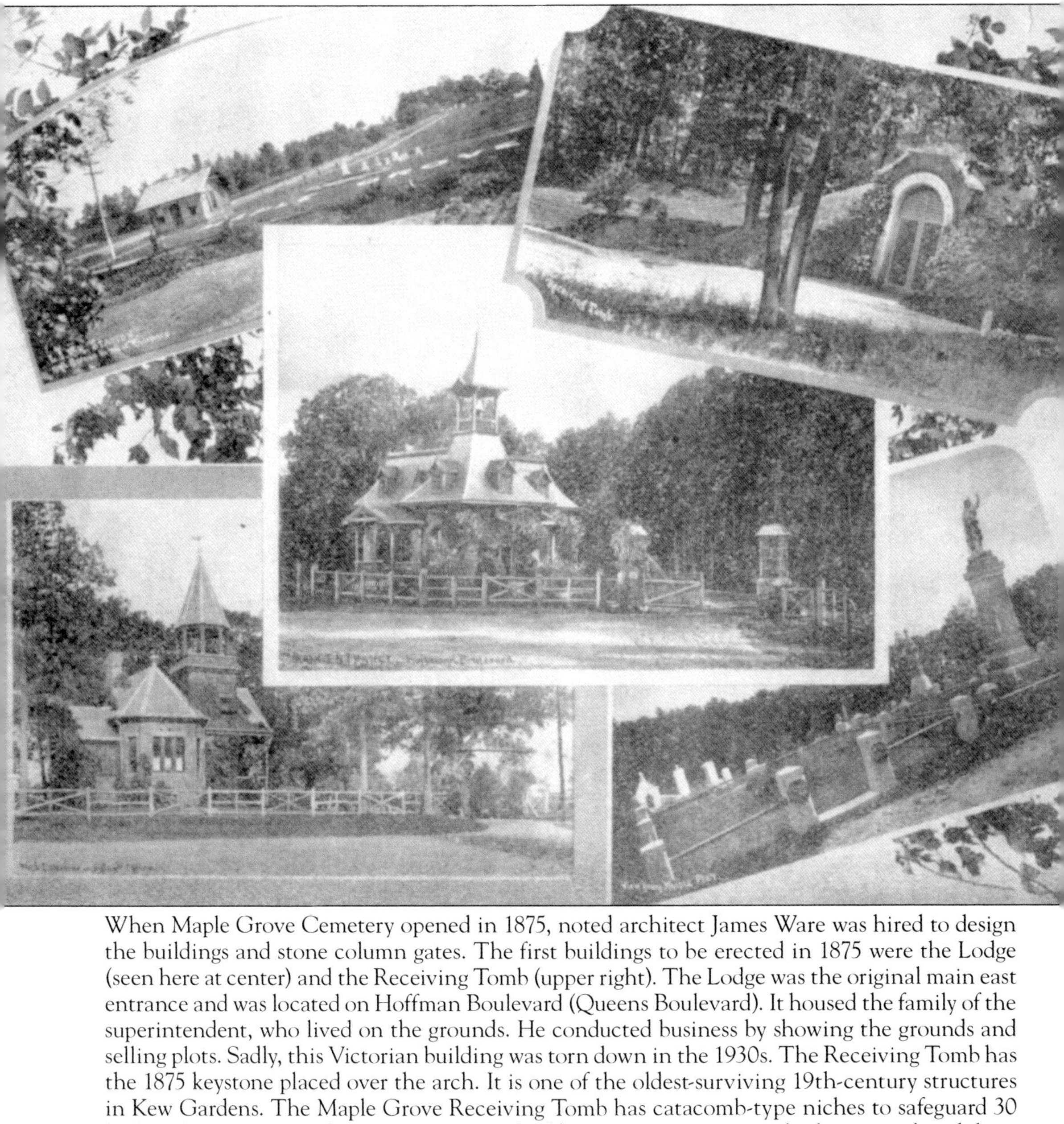

When Maple Grove Cemetery opened in 1875, noted architect James Ware was hired to design the buildings and stone column gates. The first buildings to be erected in 1875 were the Lodge (seen here at center) and the Receiving Tomb (upper right). The Lodge was the original main east entrance and was located on Hoffman Boulevard (Queens Boulevard). It housed the family of the superintendent, who lived on the grounds. He conducted business by showing the grounds and selling plots. Sadly, this Victorian building was torn down in the 1930s. The Receiving Tomb has the 1875 keystone placed over the arch. It is one of the oldest-surviving 19th-century structures in Kew Gardens. The Maple Grove Receiving Tomb has catacomb-type niches to safeguard 30 bodies. A receiving tomb was an important building in any cemetery, as bodies were placed there until the family arrived from the distant city. Also, a cemetery subject to harsh winters would store the bodies here so they could be buried in the spring, when the ground was softer. In the upper left is the Maple Grove station, and in the lower left corner is the administration building.

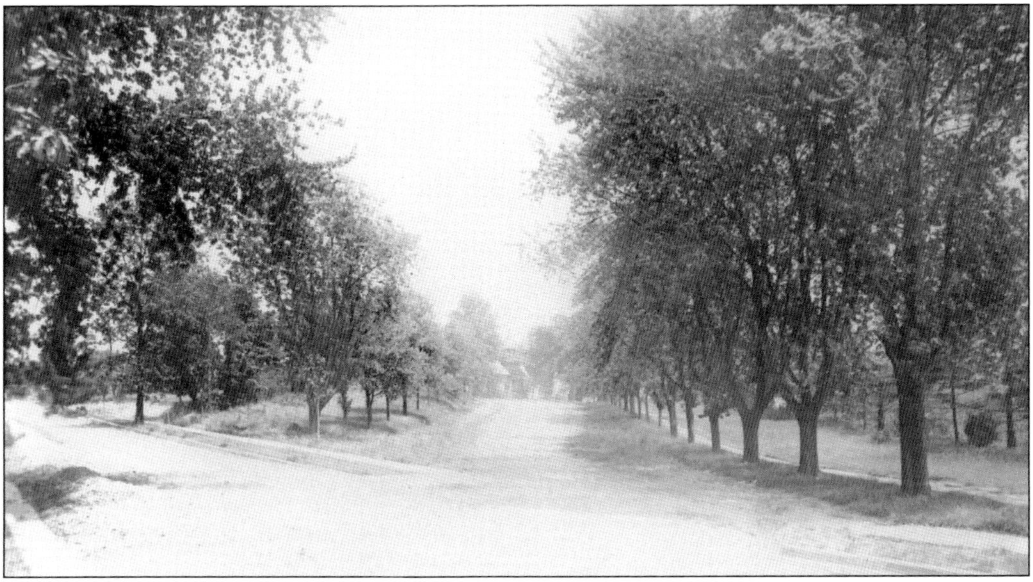

Seen here are elm trees on Lefferts Avenue (Boulevard) in the new town of Kew. The old Maple Grove Road that led from the Maple Grove train station to Kew Gardens Road is seen on the left. In 1908, a new, straighter road was cut, renamed Lefferts Avenue. The building at the end of the road is the 1880 Maple Grove Cemetery administration building on Kew Gardens Road.

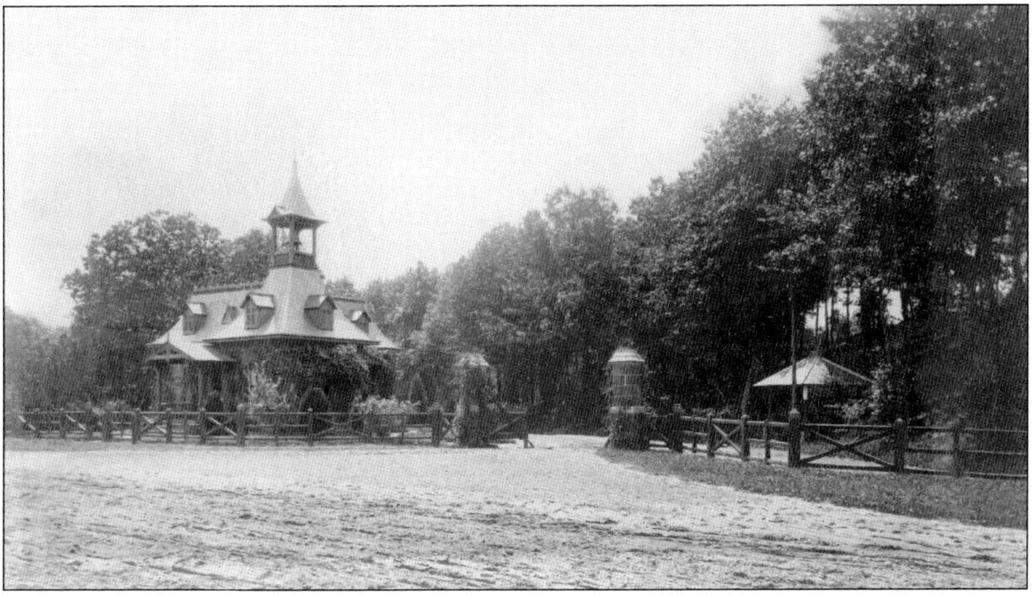

This is the 1875 lodge on Hoffman Boulevard (Queens Boulevard). This west entrance was closed and moved farther south on the boulevard. The shed to the right housed a water pump. As reported in the *Richmond Hill Record* on August 24, 1909, "Superintendent Mott of Maple Grove reports the laying of 3,000 feet of water mains and the placing of hydrants throughout the cemetery, so water may easily be secured for the purpose of watering plants, etc."

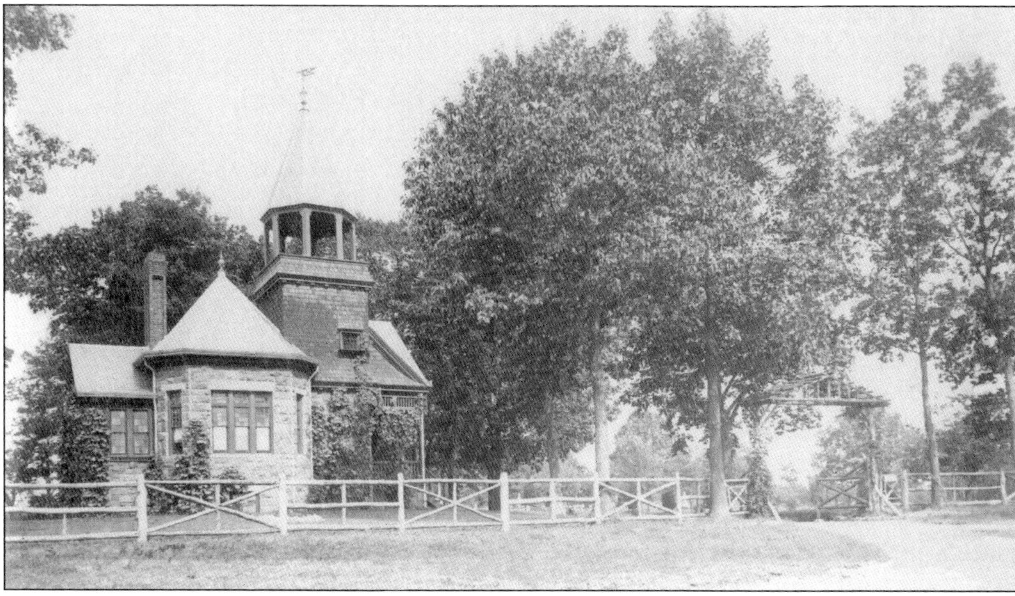

The three windows of the 1880 administration building mark the location of the chapel. The stones for the cemetery buildings came from the Maple Grove Quarry, which was located at the southern end of the cemetery. Ice Age glaciers had deposited huge amounts of rock, and this quarry helped with expenses in the early years. Stones for the foundations of many Richmond Hill homes came from the cemetery quarry.

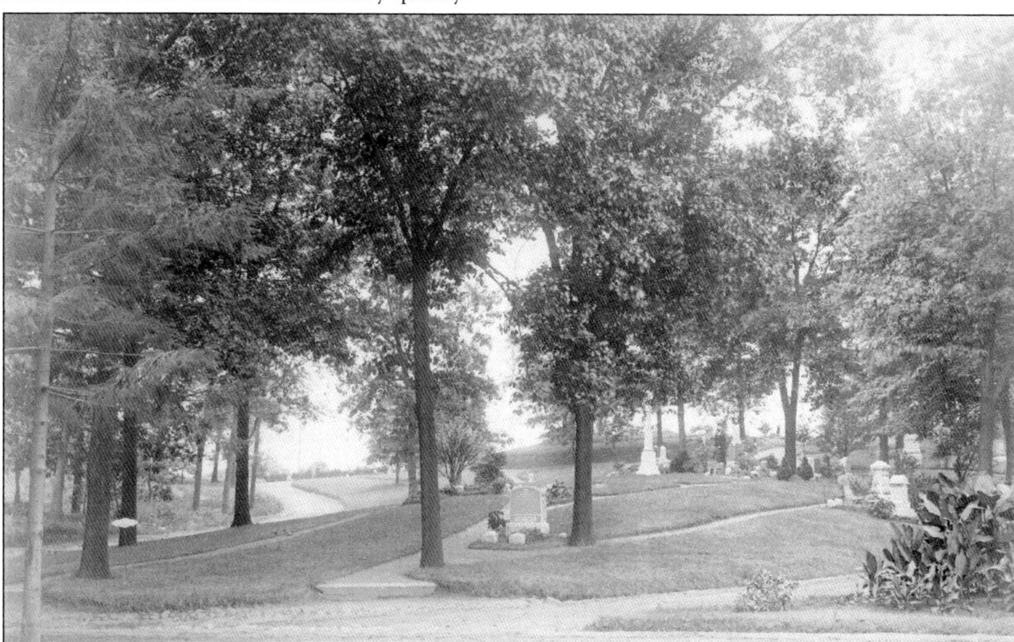

Maple Grove Cemetery was placed in the National Register of Historic Places in 2004. The cemetery is divided into two sections. The older, Victorian-era section, known as Monumental Park, makes up a third of the cemetery. The newer section, designed by George McClure in 1943, is called Memorial Park. From 1945 to 1947, massive Easter dawn services took place in this section, with scriptures read by Mayor Fiorello La Guardia.

Within Maple Grove are the resting places of those who have left their mark in the world, including Millie Tunnell, former 111-year old slave; Ann Wilkins, one of the first female missionaries to Africa; John Sutphin, Queens politician and philanthropist; jazz drummer Tony Sbarbaro; Samuel Loyd, America's puzzle king; Charles Manly, aviation pioneer; and Alfred Grebe, radio and broadcast pioneer.

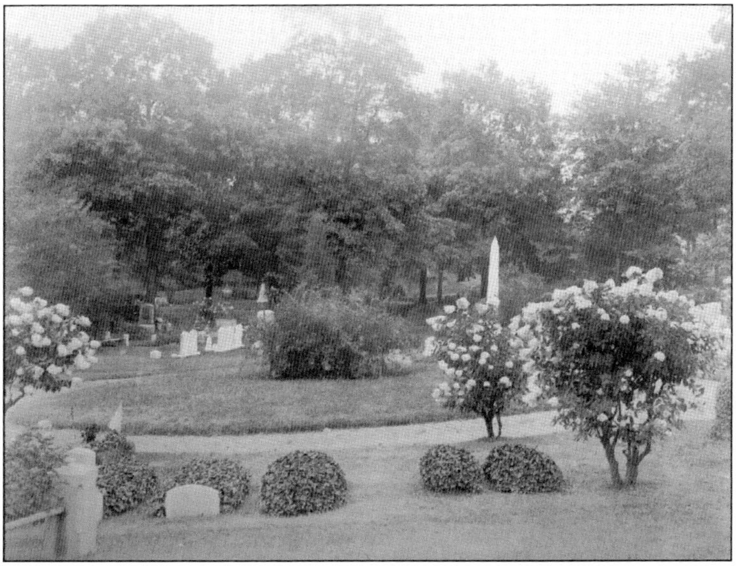

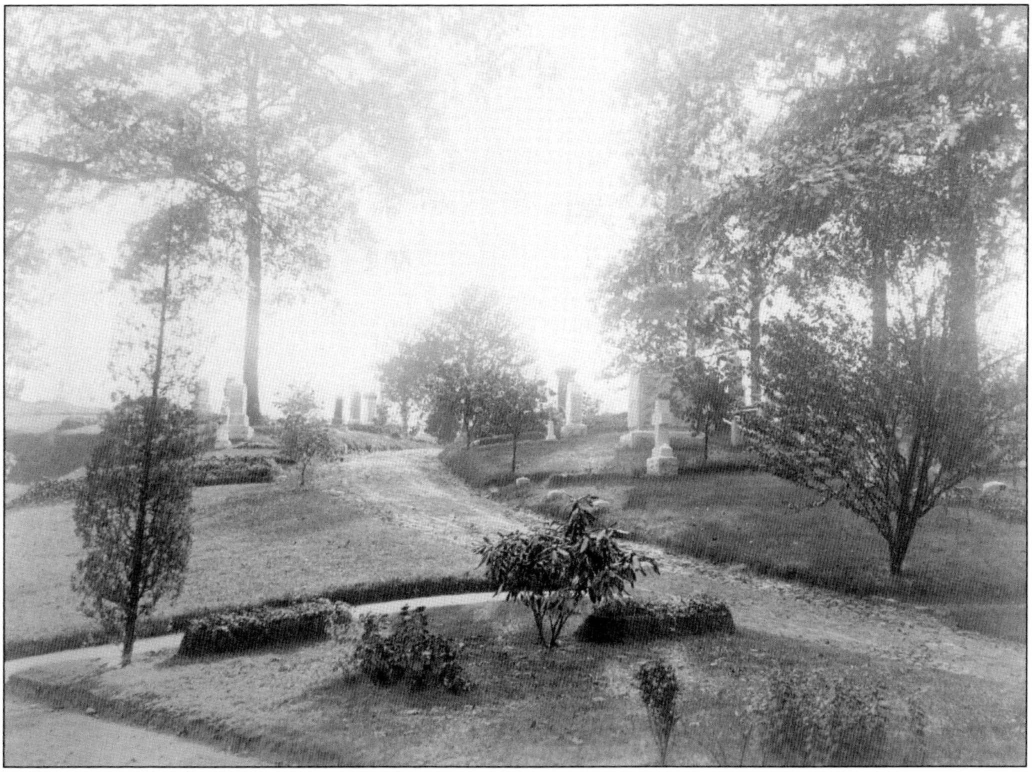

Among other noteworthy individuals interred at Maple Grove Cemetery are the following: Elisabeth Riis, wife of social reformer Jacob Riis; Russian pianists Josef and Rosina Lhevinne; Blues singer Jimmy Rushing; Rock and Roll Hall of Fame inductee LaVern Baker; recording pioneer George Washington Johnson; Winnie Winkle cartoonist Martin Branner; legendary Hollywood director Irving Rapper; Broadway singer and actress Theresa Merritt; artist Frederick Serger; playwright and poet Don Marquis; and Congressional Medal of Honor recipients George Corliss and Edward Wright.

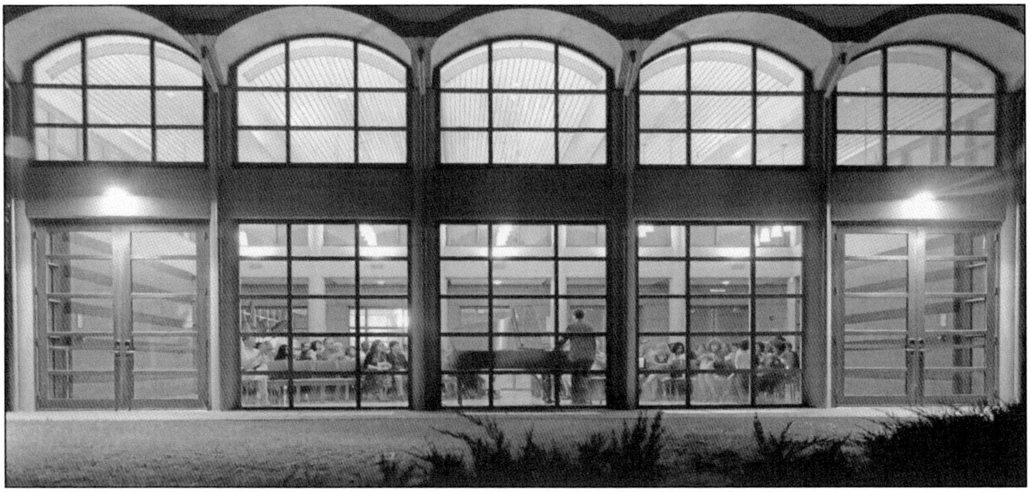

In 2009, the Center at Maple Grove opened. The 18,000-square-foot building was designed by architect Peter Gisolfi. The vision of the Center at Maple Grove was spiritual and secular, a structure to link the community and a place to engage visitors physically and culturally. It provided much-needed office space, as the administration building had become too small for the staff to support its mission to serve grieving families. In this photograph, a classical concert is held in the venue's Celebration Hall.

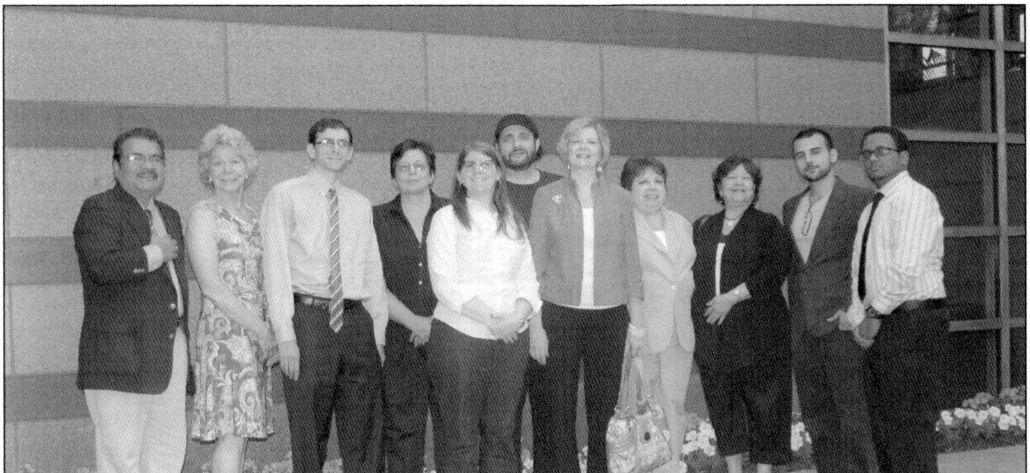

The Friends of Maple Grove Cemetery is a not-for-profit organization created for the charitable purposes of supporting and enhancing the operations of the cemetery. Members of the 2013 Friends Board are, from left to right, president Carl Ballenas; Maple Grove executive manager Bonnie Thompson Dixon; Henry Van Nunes; treasurer Lisa Erdman; vice president Andrea Crawford; vice president Andrew Koslosky; secretary Helen Day; media chair Judy Close; Carol Goldman; chair of arts and archives Gavriel Maman; and technology chair Alex Samaroo. Absent from the photograph is Cate Ludlam. (Photograph by Gavriel Maman.)

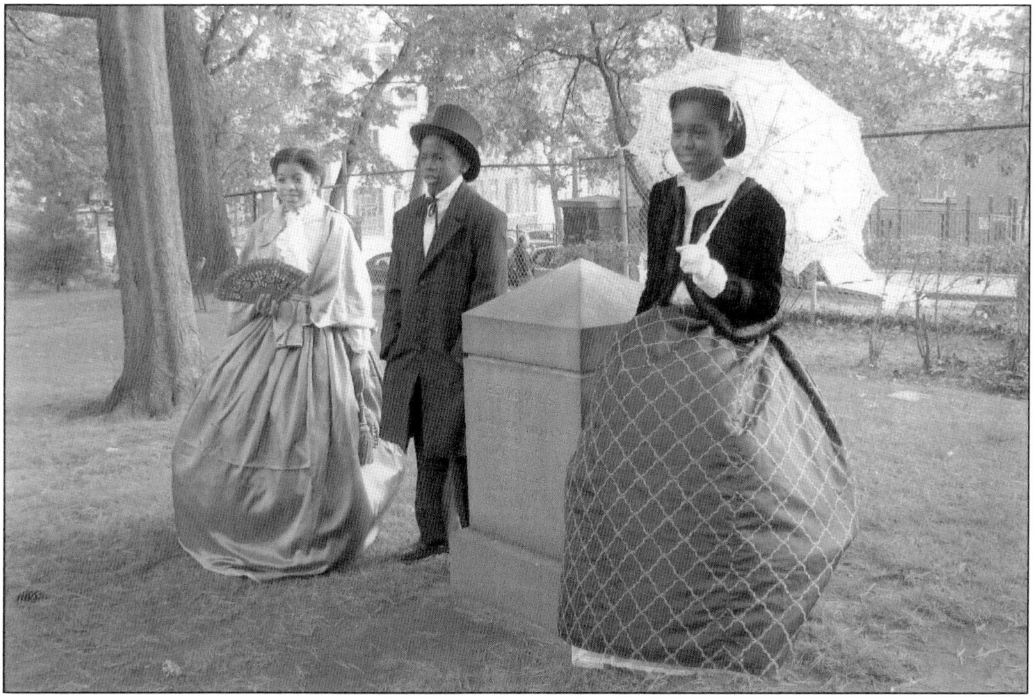

In 2004, students from the Immaculate Conception School of Jamaica paid tribute to the spirit of the people of Maple Grove by recreating the roles of noteworthy people from the past. They wore period costumes and spoke memorized speeches to reenact the lives of these people. The occasion is now an annual event called Spirits Alive. The students shown here tell the story of the recently discovered African America burial plot of the First Presbyterian Church of New York at Maple Grove.

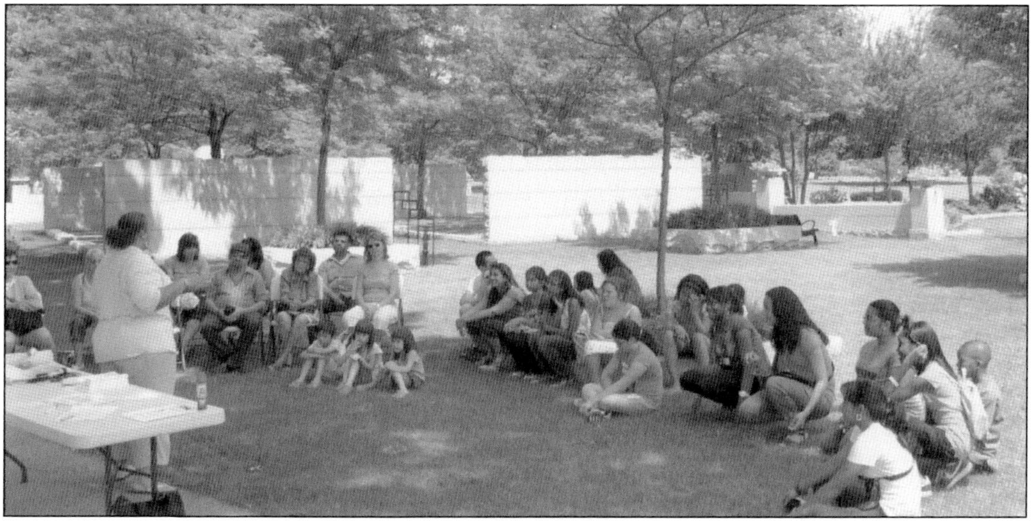

A summer series of science workshops is held in partnership with Alley Pond Environmental Center. The outreach program takes place at Maple Grove. All events and programs sponsored by the Friends of Maple Grove Cemetery have a connection to the history of the cemetery. This science program honored all the great scientific minds at Maple Grove, such as Koleman and Julius Czito, assistants to Nicola Tesla.

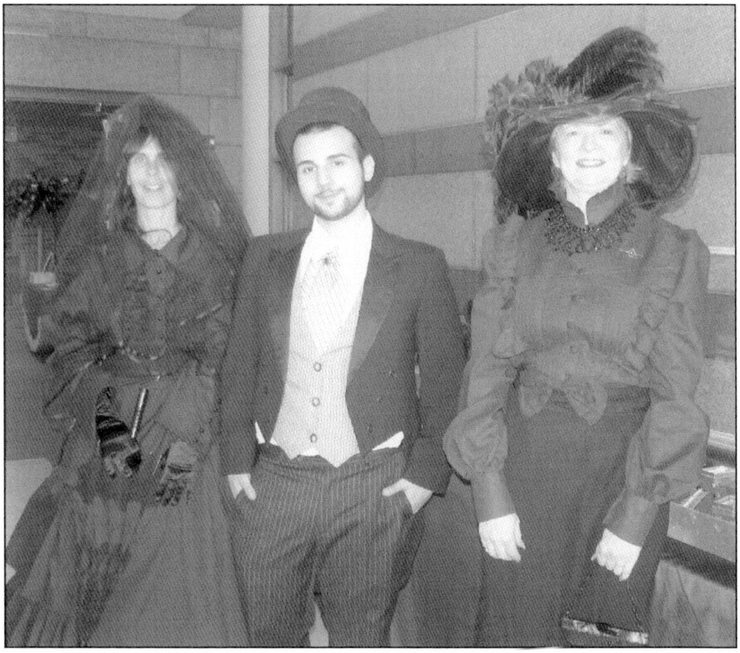

The Friends of Maple Grove Victoriana Day explored the Victorian Era and its social practices, superstitions, mourning attire, jewelry, and rituals. It included a walking tour through Monumental Park and a Victorian funeral tea with music of the period. The volunteers shown here are dressed in full Victorian attire. Other activities sponsored by the Friends include walking tours, lectures, jazz concerts, magic shows, and filmmaking workshops.

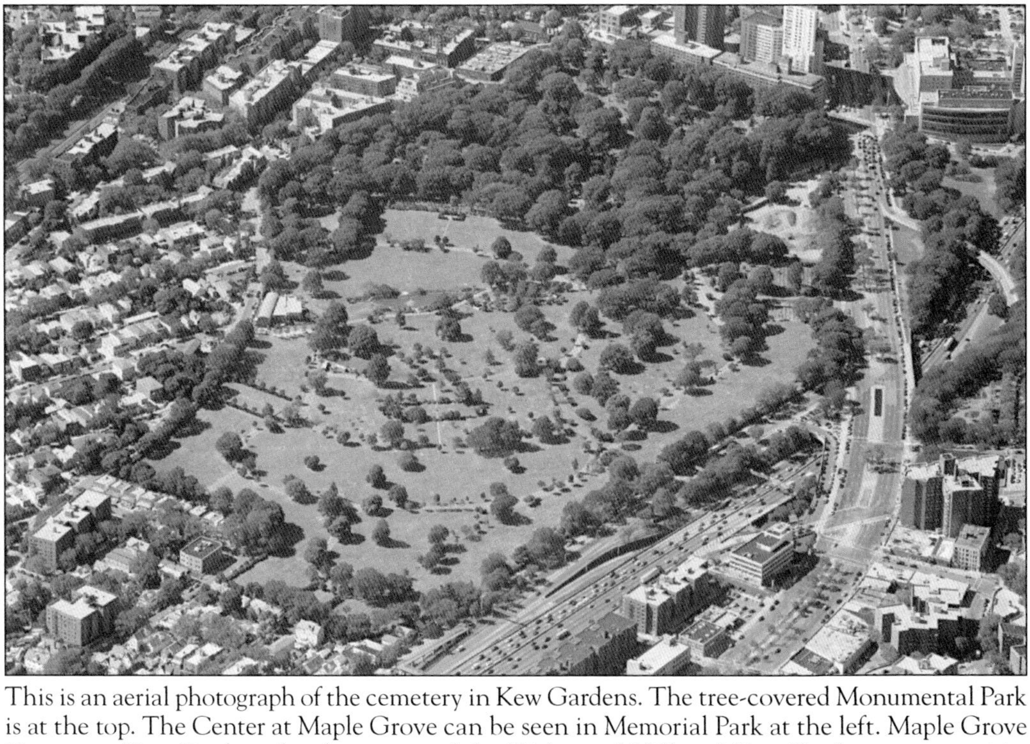

This is an aerial photograph of the cemetery in Kew Gardens. The tree-covered Monumental Park is at the top. The Center at Maple Grove can be seen in Memorial Park at the left. Maple Grove Cemetery, Kew Gardens, has been part of the Richmond Hill and Kew Gardens communities since 1875. The innovative events and programs held at the Center at Maple Grove make the cemetery a unique cultural haven for the community.

Five

Home Life

Private Homes and Apartment Buildings

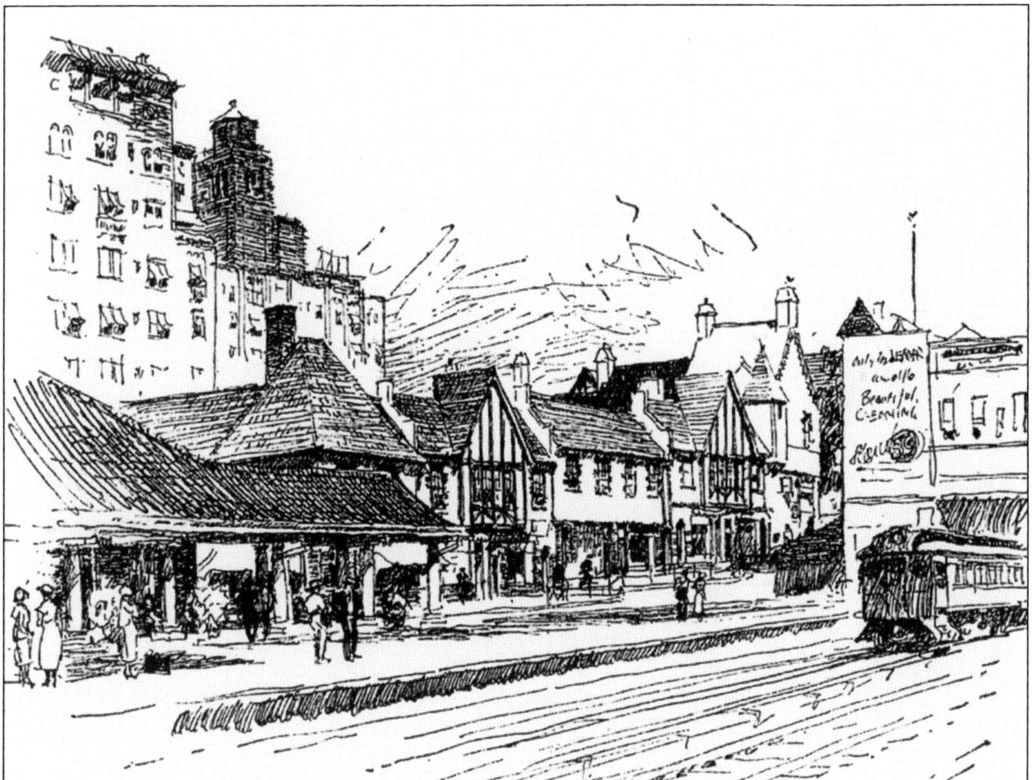

The *Brooklyn Daily Eagle* of May 20, 1927, reported the following: "Residents of the country and Europe wishing to live in New York, yet not desiring the congestion of the city streets and depressing influence of city blocks visiting here are charmed with the views of greenery, well kept lawns, trees and shrubbery and a cultivated population, evident by the architecturally beautiful homes. The growth of Kew Gardens is only limited by its lack of room for further development."

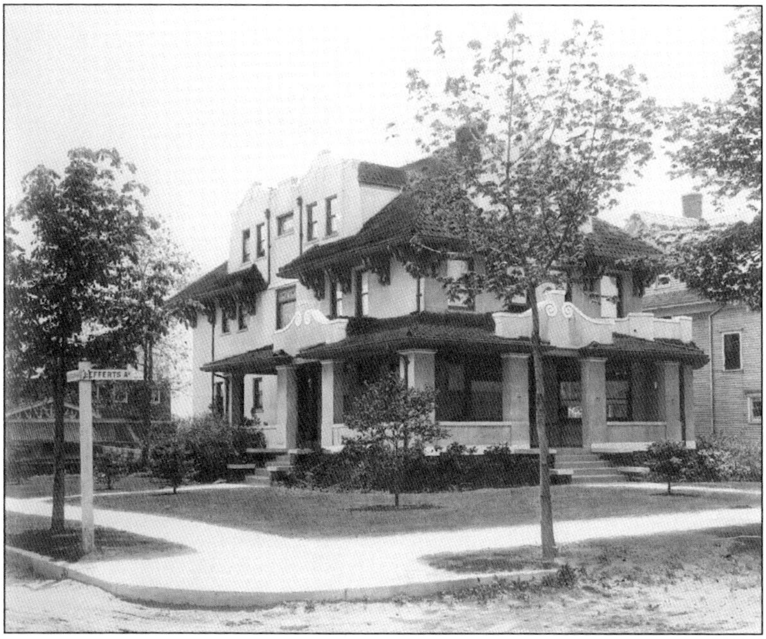

This home on the corner of Lefferts Avenue and Abingdon Road became the Dupont Funeral Home and is now the site of the Shaare Tova Synagogue. A c. 1930 report from the files of Alrick H. Man states, "Millions of yards of rocks and soil were moved in grading out the construction of a practicable street system through and across Kew Gardens' rough hills and deep hollows."

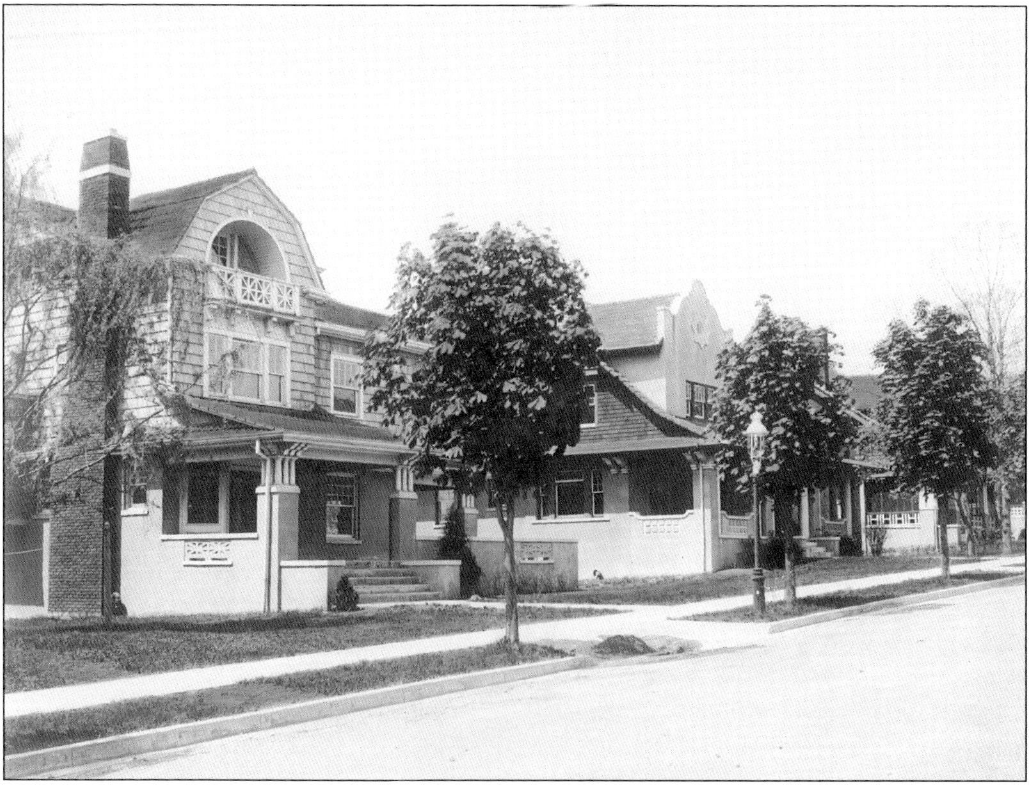

Shown here is Abingdon Road, off Lefferts Avenue (Boulevard). The *New York Herald* reported in 1918, "In the Spring of 1912 Kew Gardens was but a name, with practically nothing but the railroad station to mark the spot. Now it is one of the most highly developed communities on Long Island, with an individuality all its own."

This view is of Eighty-second Avenue, looking toward Kew Gardens Road. As reported in the *Richmond Hill Record* on June 29, 1911, "The development is of the highest order and yet houses and lots are not prohibitive in price to those who want fine homes."

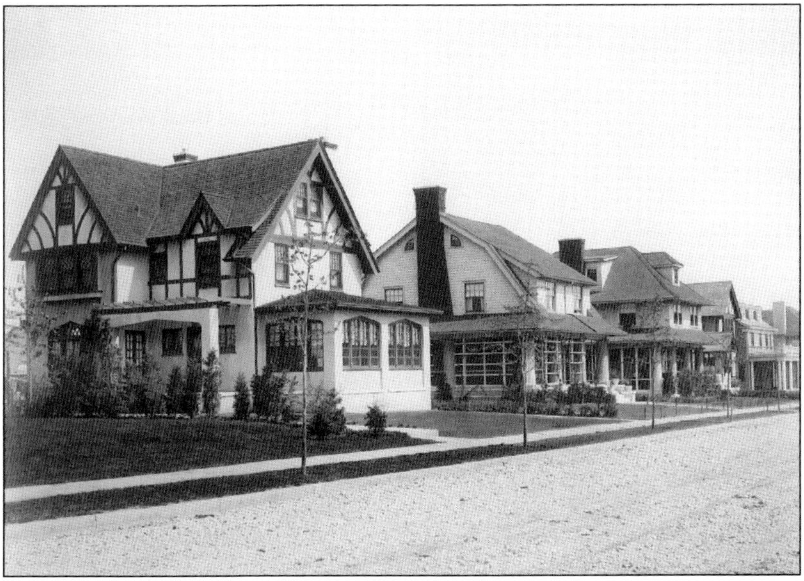

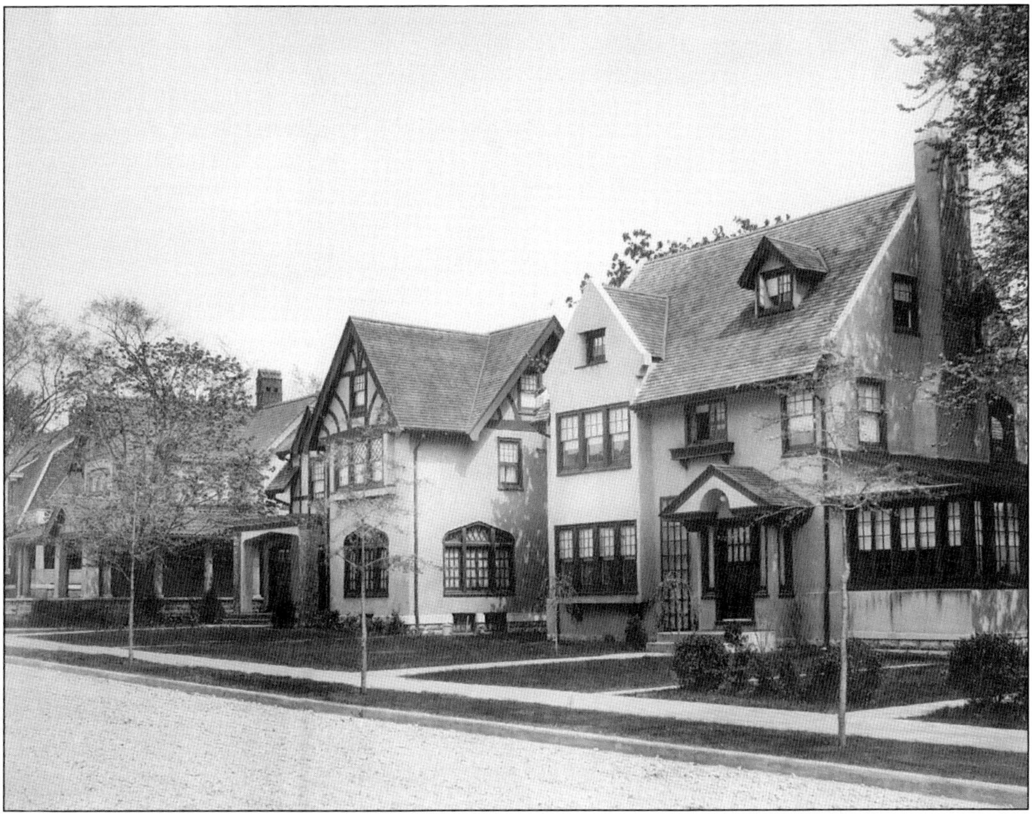

This view is of Eighty-second Road looking toward Kew Gardens Road. The house at the right belonged to the brother of the artist George Overbury "Pop" Hart, best known as a watercolor painter. His work can be found in major museums throughout the United States and around the world. George Hart spent many summers here and used Kew Gardens scenes for some of his works.

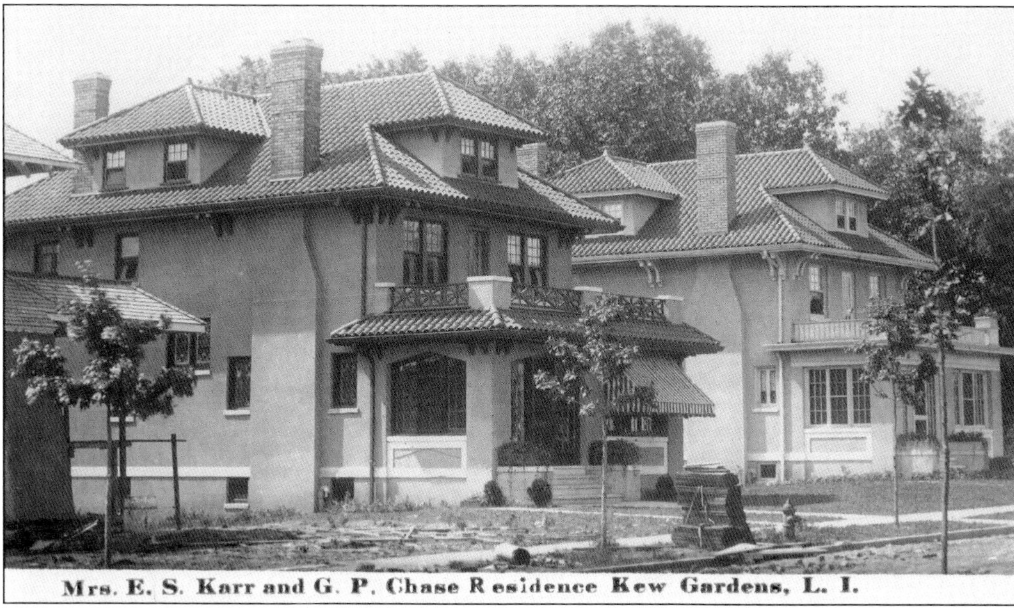

These are the residences of E.S. Karr and G.P. Chase on Onslow Place (Eighty-second Avenue) between Austin Street and Kew Gardens Road. Anaïs Nin and her family stayed at the Chase home, which belonged to her maternal uncle. As reported in the *Richmond Hill Record* of January 17, 1913, "Builders are active in the Kew field, where the demand for houses and lots has been greater than in any other section of Queens."

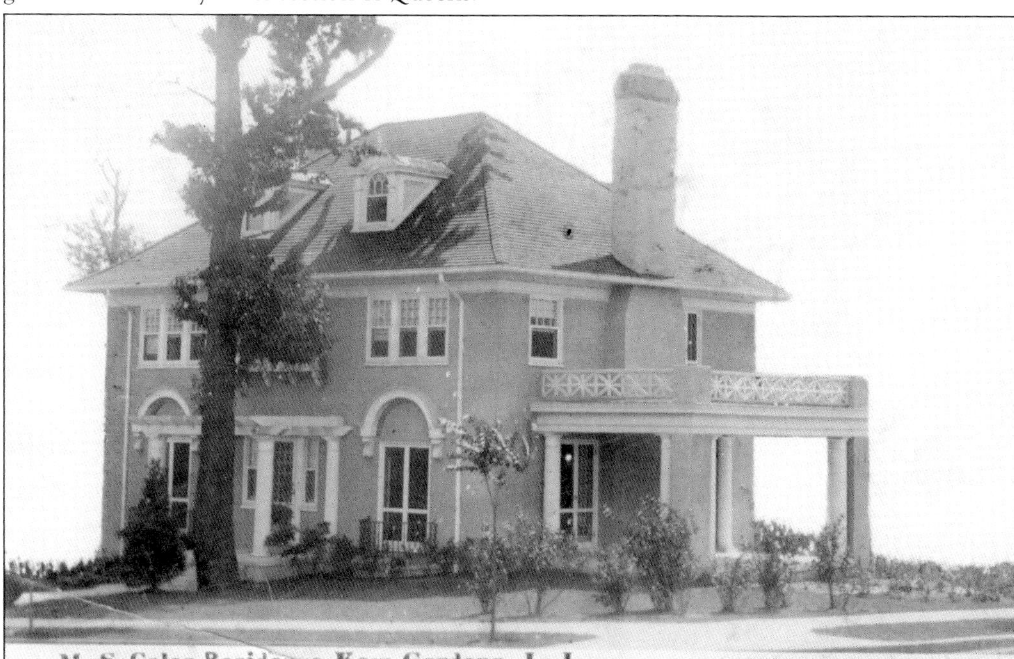

This residence stands on Pembroke Place (Eighty-first Avenue). The *Richmond Hill Record* of August 26, 1911, described Kew Gardens houses as "of high standard of architecture and construction and built of fireproof blocks, roofs of tile, and some made of roofs of hand-made shingles, with 8 to 12 rooms; 1 to 2 baths; $13,000 to $20,000; lots 25 x 100."

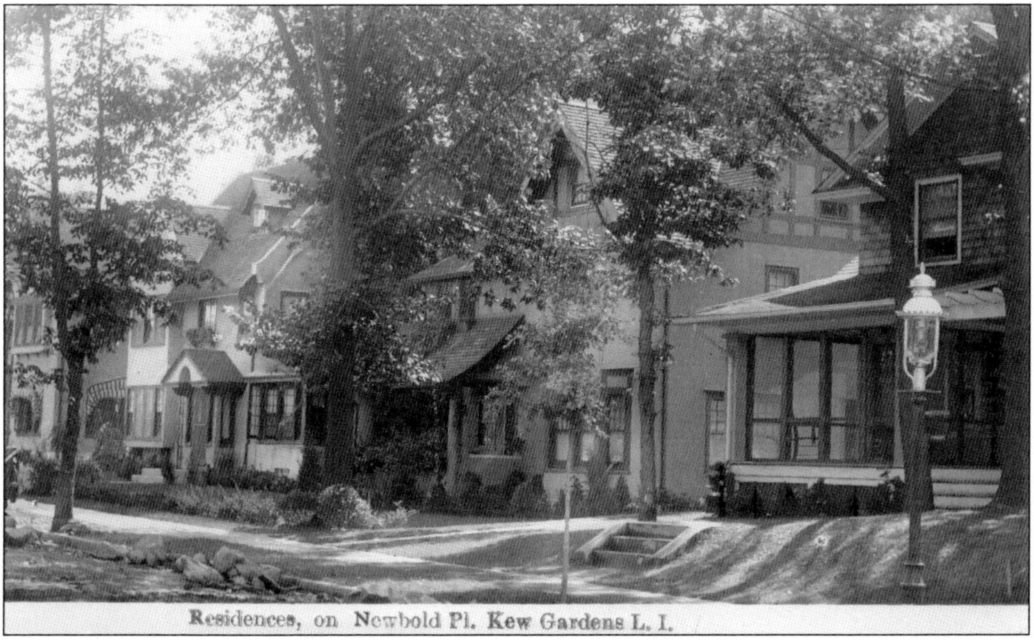

These are homes on Newbold Place (Eighty-second Road) between Austin Street and Kew Gardens Road. According to the *Brooklyn Daily Eagle* of September 8, 1916, "The magnificent facilities offered by Kew Station and the Pennsylvania Tunnels bring this area nearer, in point of time to the center of activities in New York. Thus residents of Kew Gardens may reach the Manhattan Opera House or the Waldorf-Astoria in twenty minutes."

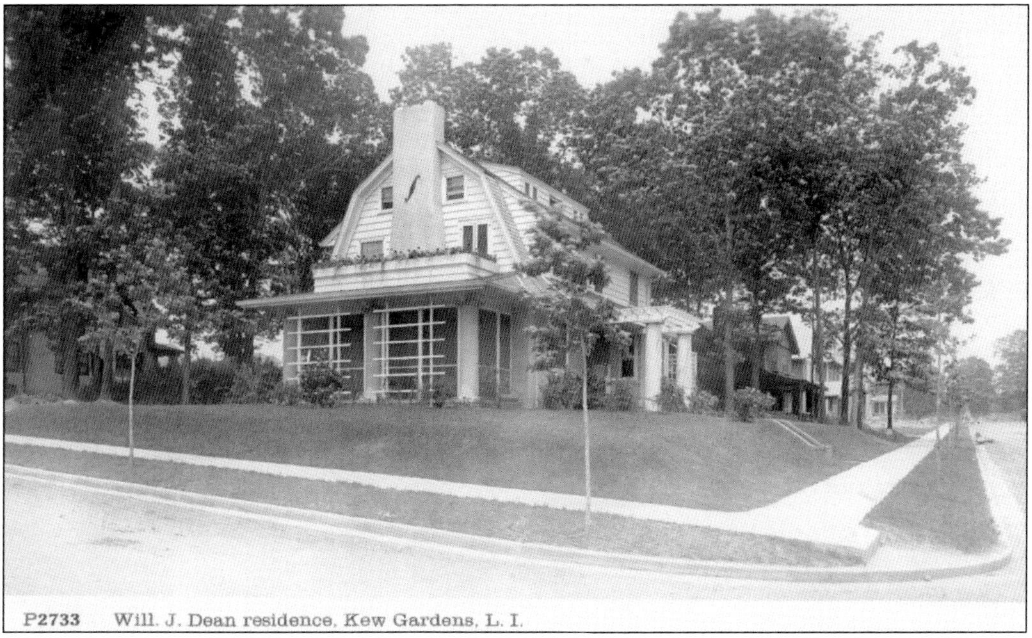

Shown here is Newbold Place (Eighty-second Road) from the corner of Austin Street. The *New York Herald* reported on May 23, 1915, "Nowhere in the residence section of New York or its nearby suburbs is there greater substantial building activity than at Kew Gardens, in the borough of Queens."

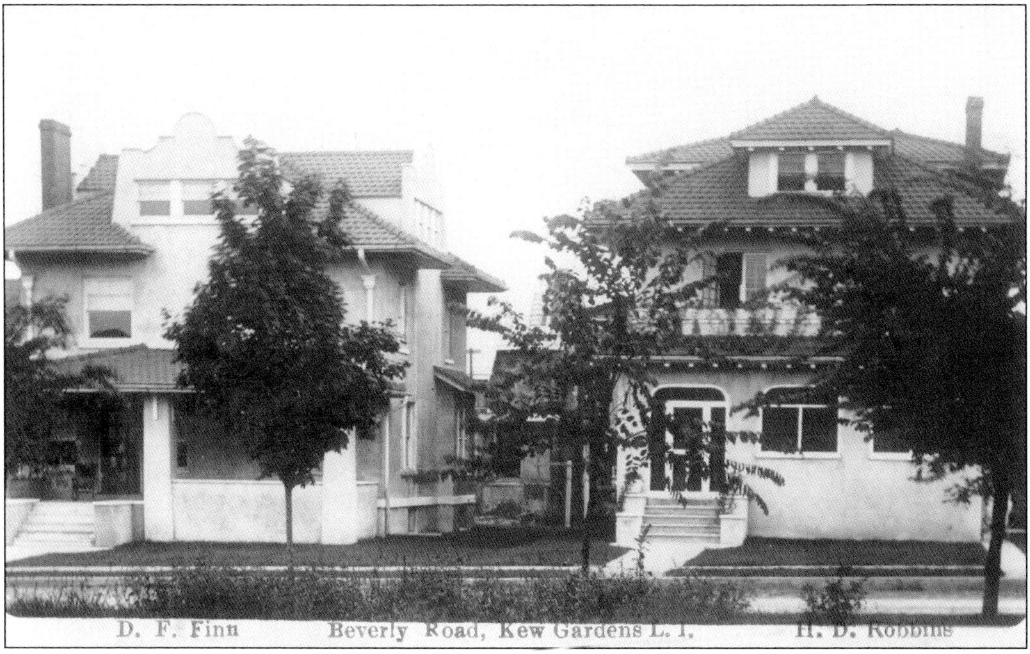

These residences are on Beverly Road. The house on the left once belonged to the actress Margorie Gateson. As reported in the *Richmond Hill Record* on October 24, 1913, "Plans have been completed for the erection of 30 additional new houses during the fall and winter season, and it is prophesied that next spring will even see greater building activities at Kew Gardens."

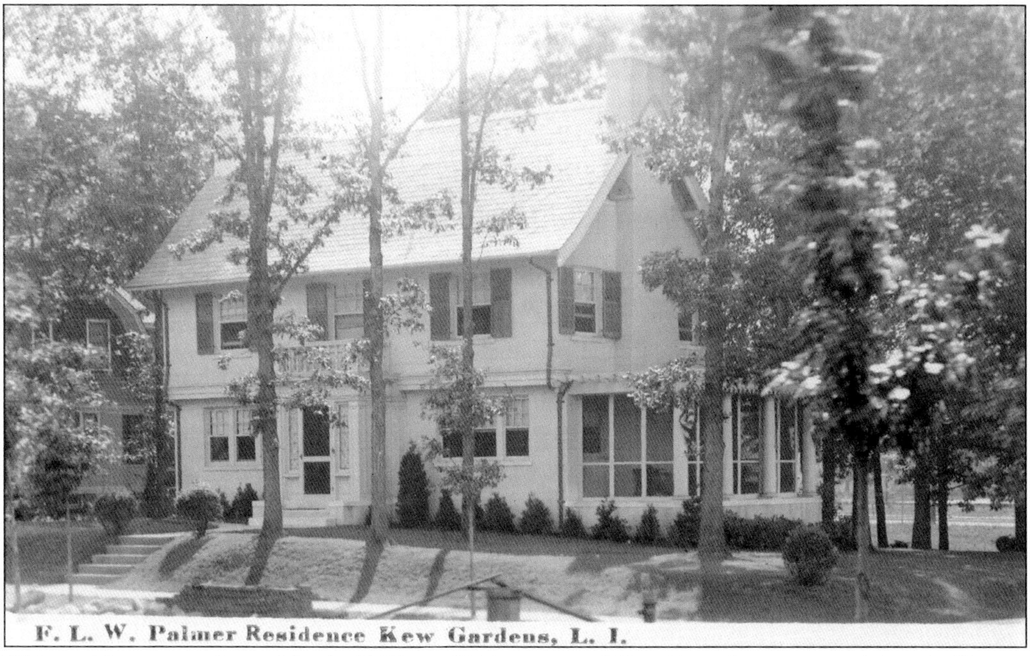

This residence stands on Newbold Place (Eighty-second Road) at the corner of Austin Street. According to the *Richmond Hill Record* of July 12, 1912, "Several new homes of an attractive type have recently been started at Kew. Pleasant drives have been laid out, and sewers, water, gas and electricity installed."

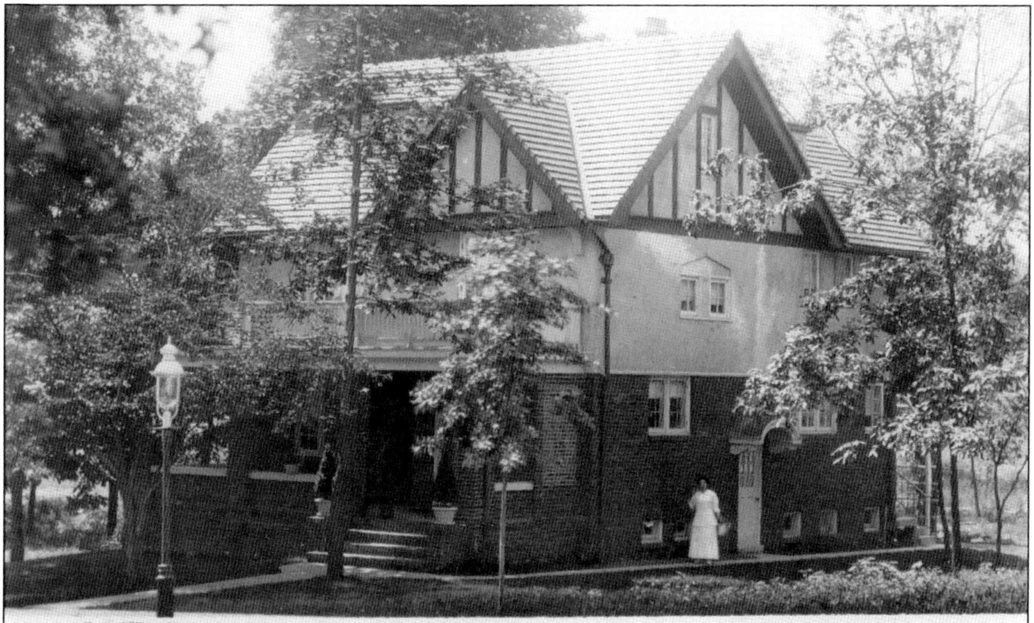

C. W. Baronburg's Residence, Kew Gardens L. I.

This residence is at Grenfell Street between Lefferts Boulevard and Eighty-second Avenue. A c. 1930 description found in the files of Alrick H. Man reads as follows: "The policy of the Kew Gardens Corporation was to render Kew Gardens unique, and by the preservation of its natural beauty, the imposition of salutary restrictions, the supervision of all proposed plans of building and the maintenance of high standards of landscape architecture to render it the most attractive residential section of the City."

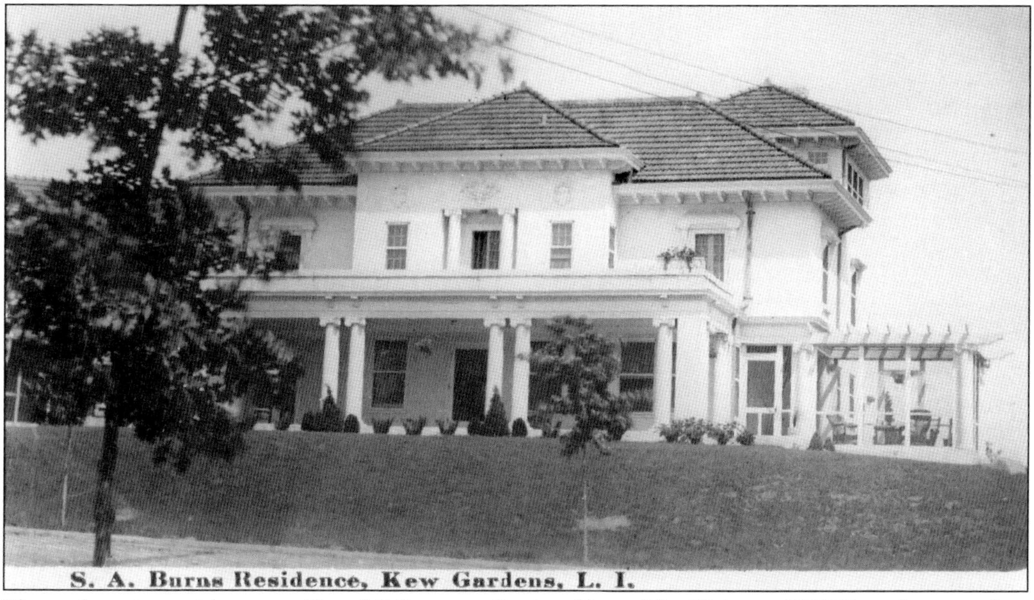

S. A. Burns Residence, Kew Gardens, L. I.

Shown here is a residence on Grenfell Street at Onslow Place. The *Richmond Hill Record* reported on January 14, 1911: "Plots in Kew Gardens are sold only to those who propose prompt and substantial improvement. The opportunity is afforded to persons already identified with Richmond Hill to make selections at present prices before the completion of development."

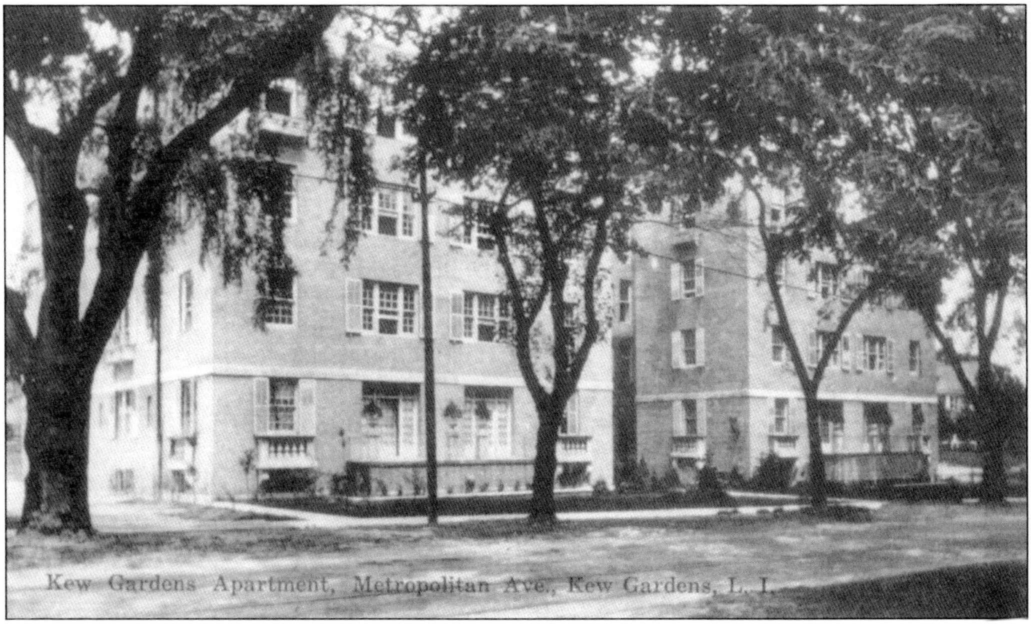

The Kew Gardens Apartment, built by the Kew Gardens Corporation, was the first apartment building in Kew Gardens. Designed by Andrew Thomas, it opened in 1918. This 16-family, four-story building was an experiment and claims a world's first. According to the *Richmond Hill Record* on July 7, 1919, "Kew Gardens is notable in the building world, as the place where the first four-story elevator apartment was erected." It is located on Metropolitan Avenue and was renamed Le France.

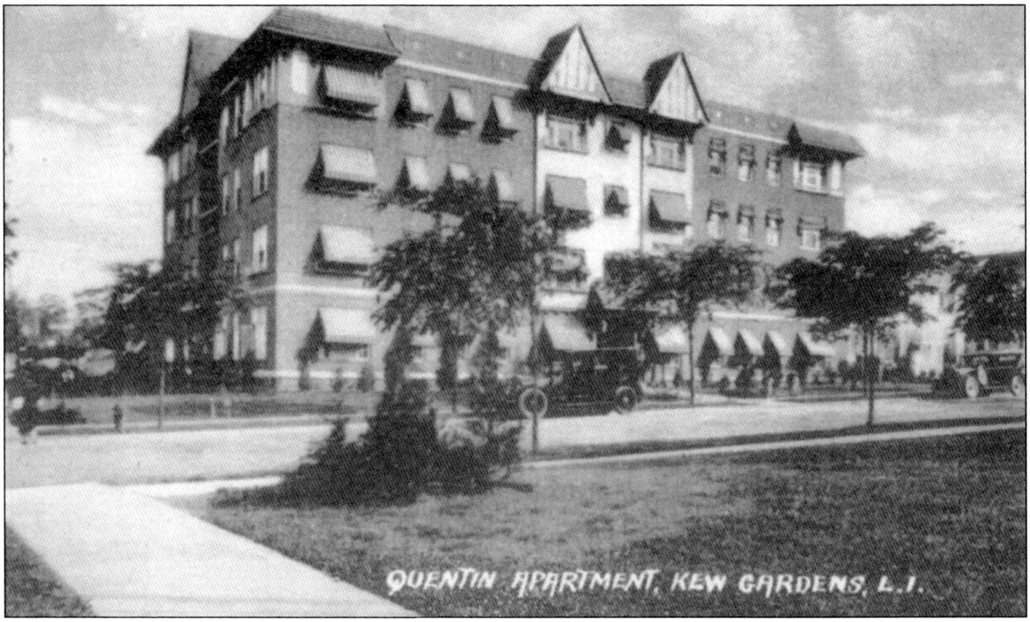

As reported in the *Long Island Daily Press* on September 21, 1921, "At the corner of Kew Gardens Road and Quentin Street, just opposite the Kew Gardens Inn, the Garden Road Construction Co. has erected a modern apartment—Quentin Apartments. Although the interior is not yet finished, about one-half of the apartments are leased."

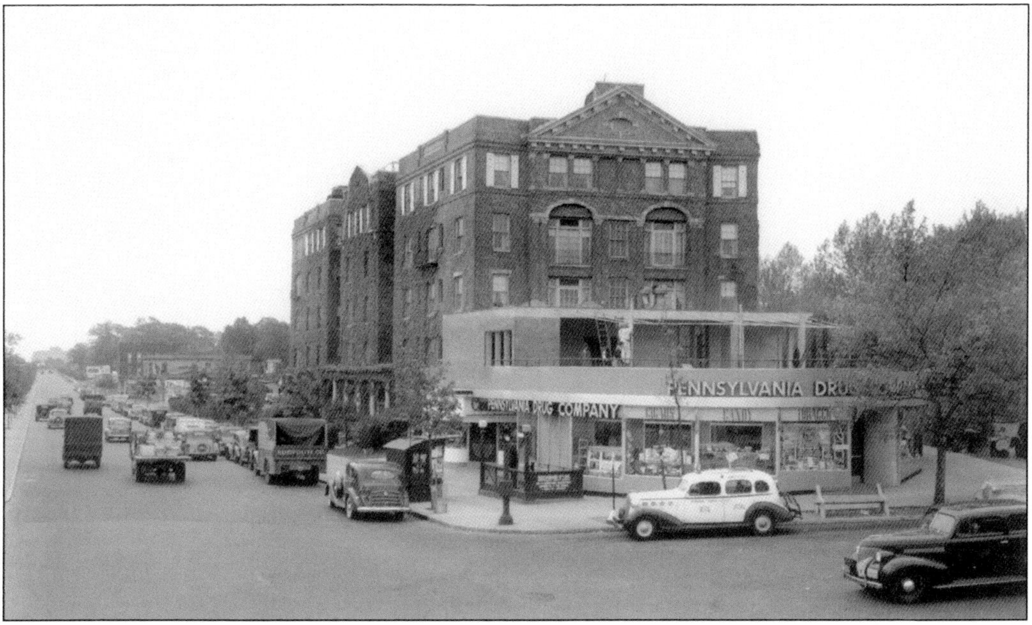

The *Long Island Press* reported the following on January 4, 1936: "Sarah Bolmer, daughter of Daniel Foulk, was president of the Bolmer Construction Company, organized in 1923, which built the Kew Bolmer Apartments on land which once was part of her father's farm purchased in 1851. The building was completed in 1924." The building was erected on a triangular lot between Queens Boulevard (left) and Kew Gardens Road. (Courtesy Ron Marzlock.)

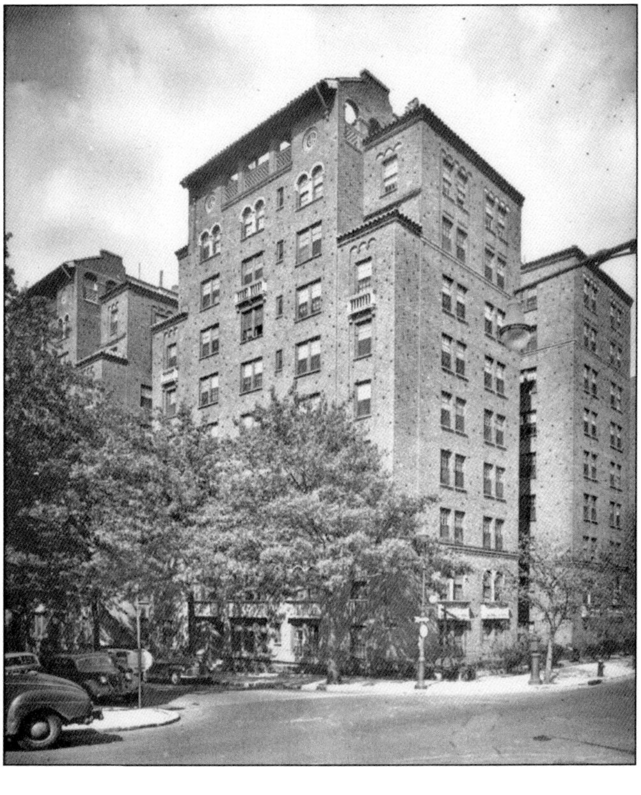

The Mowbray Apartment was built on the corner of Lefferts Boulevard and Austin Street. The *Brooklyn Daily Eagle* of May 22, 1927, mentioned the new building: "Kew Gardens, this exclusive and highly restricted suburban section as planned by Alrick H. Man, is being invaded today by an influx of the ubiquitous multi-family house ranging from the original 16-family apartment that was built in 1918 to the palatial nine-story Mowbray Apartment, with every modern convenience for 142 families, built at a cost of $1,500,00."

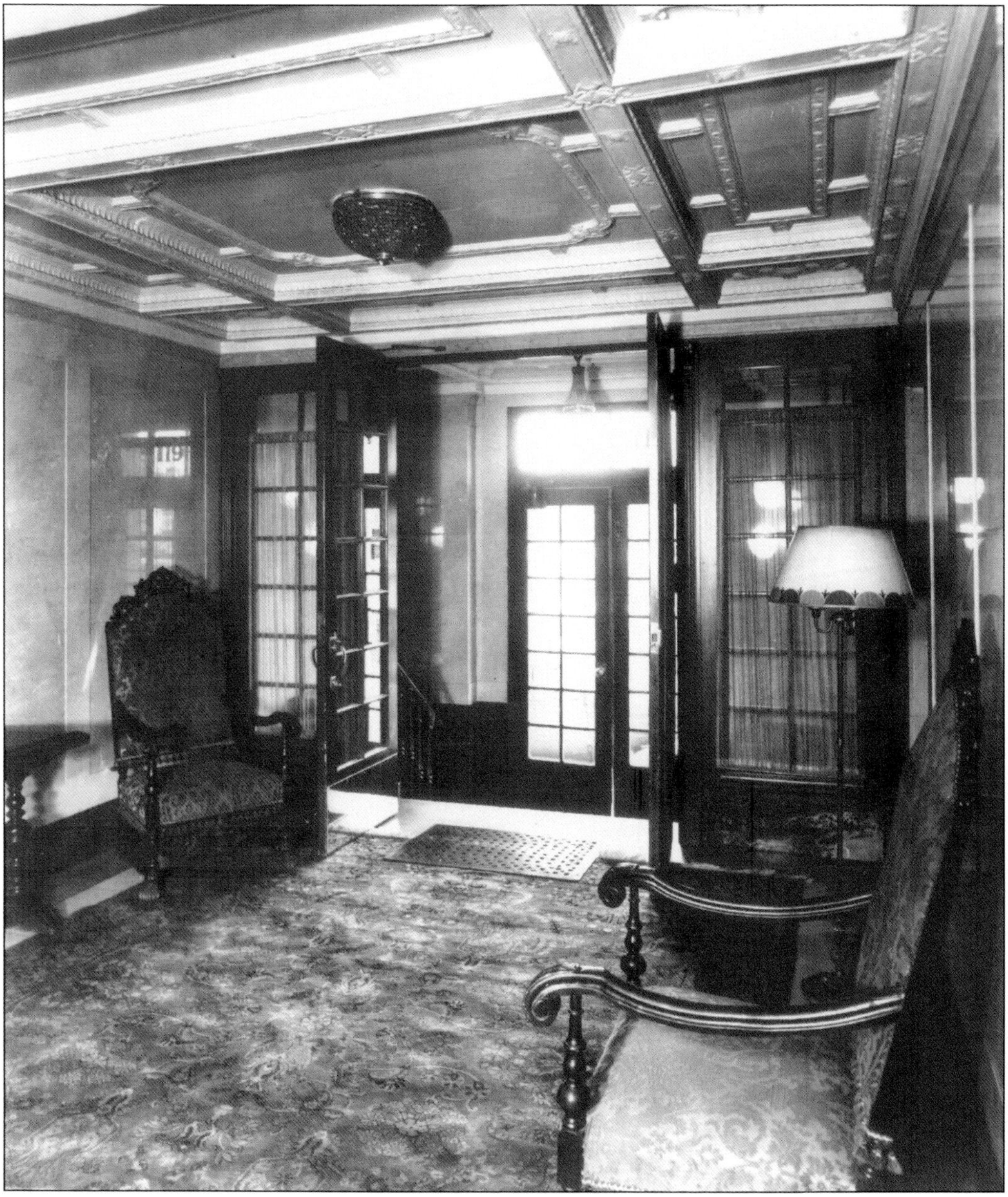

According to the *Long Island Daily Press* of August 17, 1929, "Housing of high class character in Central Queens was augmented recently by the completion of the Colonial Hall apartments at Kew Gardens." This photograph shows the Colonial Hall lobby. The *Brooklyn Daily Eagle* reported the following on May 22, 1927: "There have been built in Kew Gardens in the last two or three years a score of big apartments that will rank well with the most up-to-date multi-family houses of Manhattan in service and equipment. The average rentals in the Kew Gardens apartments run from $25 to $32.50 per room." These apartment buildings were mentioned in the article as being recently built or approaching completion: The Kew Terrace, Kew Kensington Court, Arlington Court, Colonial Apartments, The Forest Park Apartments, Kew Arms, Kew-Lefferts, Kew Beverly, Kew Bolmer, Quentin Apartments, Kew Towers, and the Kew Brevoort. (Courtesy Ron Marzlock.)

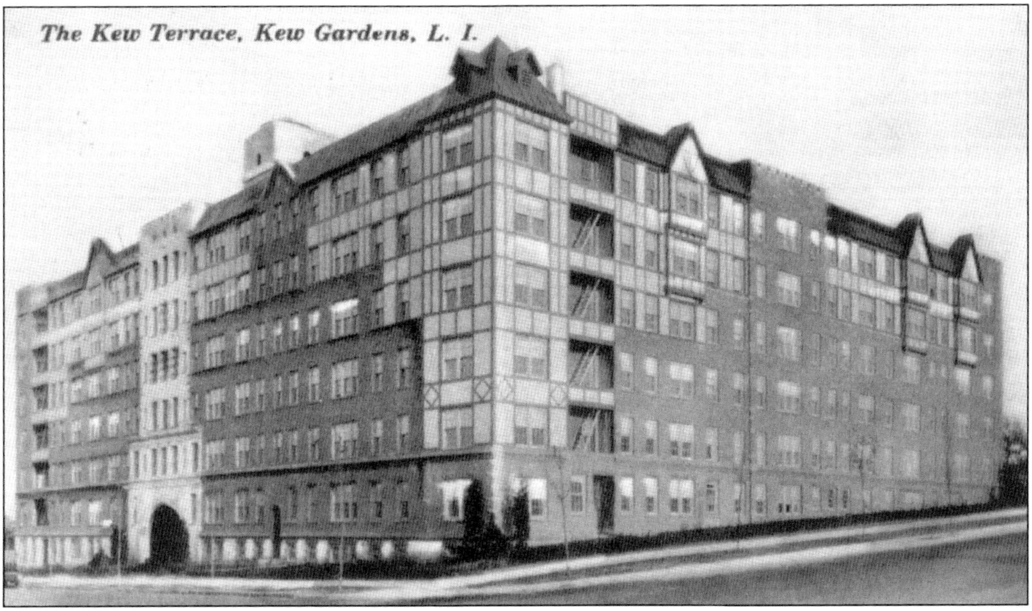

Shown here is the Kew Terrace on Union Turnpike and Park Lane South. A nearby apartment building included a new feature, as described in the *Daily Star* on August 19, 1930: "Visible only to sunshine and aviator, women tenants of the recently completed apartment on Union Turnpike, acquire fashionable tans in a solarium which the builders have thoughtfully provided on the roof, believed to be the first of its kind installed on an apartment in Queens."

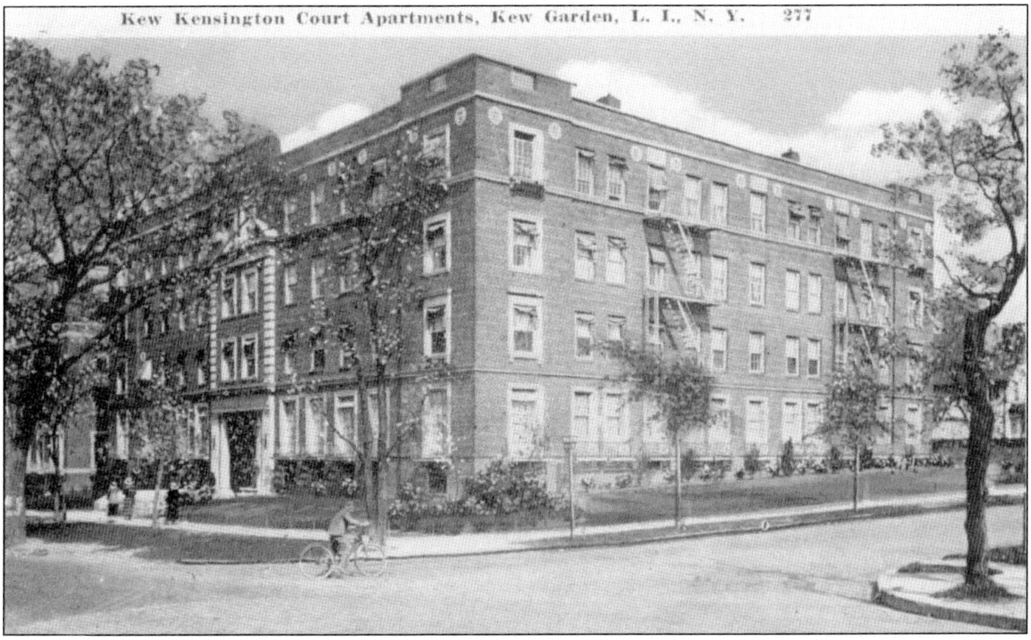

This is Kew Kensington on Union Turnpike. An advertisement in the *New York Times* on January 14, 1923, stated the following: "New Apartments at Kew Gardens, Kew-Arlington, Kew-Kensington. Delightfully situated within three minutes of the Kew Gardens Station. Now available—A limited number of these handsomely appointed apartments of 3 and 4 rooms $1,800 upward. Open for inspection today."

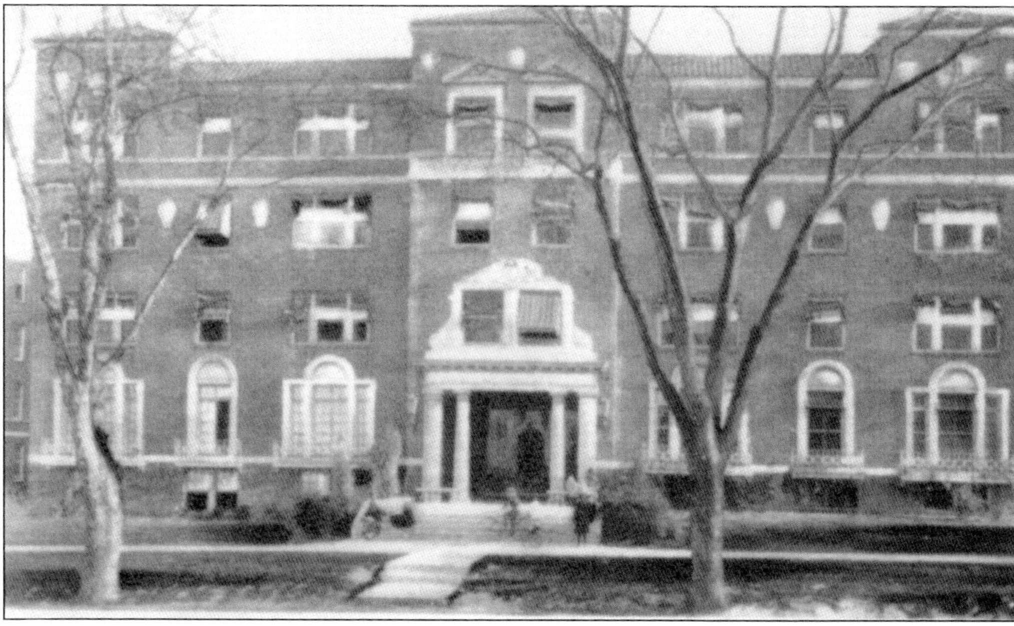

This is Kew Arlington on Union Turnpike. According to the *Long Island Daily Press* on May 10, 1923, "Mrs. Daniel Hiltz of Kew Arlington appointed Queens County chairman of the NYS Division Women's Organization for National Prohibition Reform. Queens County has an overwhelming majority of citizens who favor repealing the 18th Amendment and the substitution of a system of state liquor control as a means of promoting real temperance and curbing lawlessness."

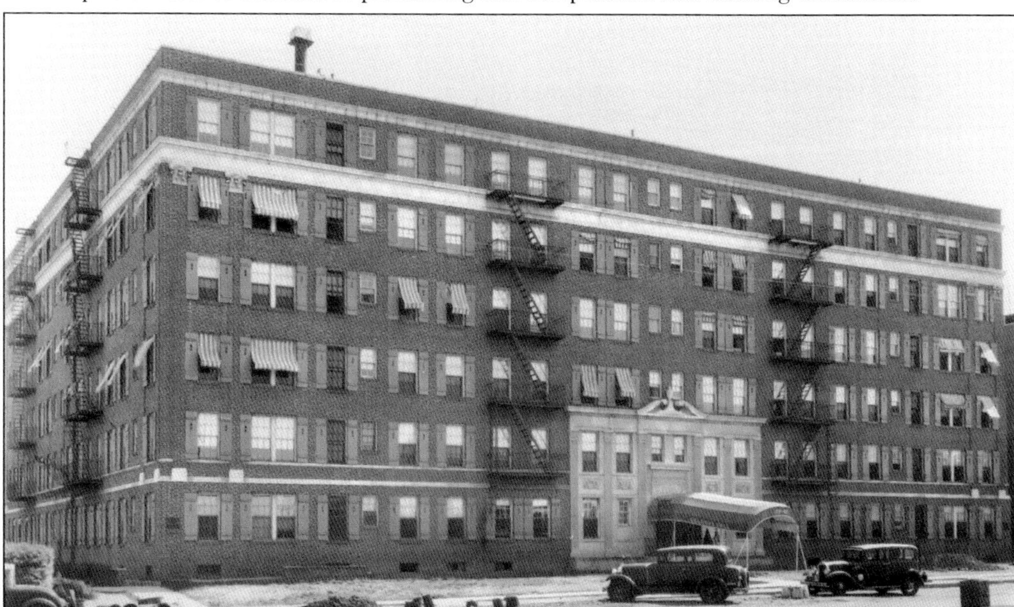

The Colonial Apartment stands on Union Turnpike. Kew Gardens was intended to be a safe haven from the congestion and noise of urban city life. The Kew Kensington, Kew Arlington, and Colonial had grand entrances with canopies, lush green front lawns, trees, and other greenery. When the Interborough Parkway was built, these garden apartments along Union Turnpike lost their natural front settings, and tenants faced a scene of cars and concrete.

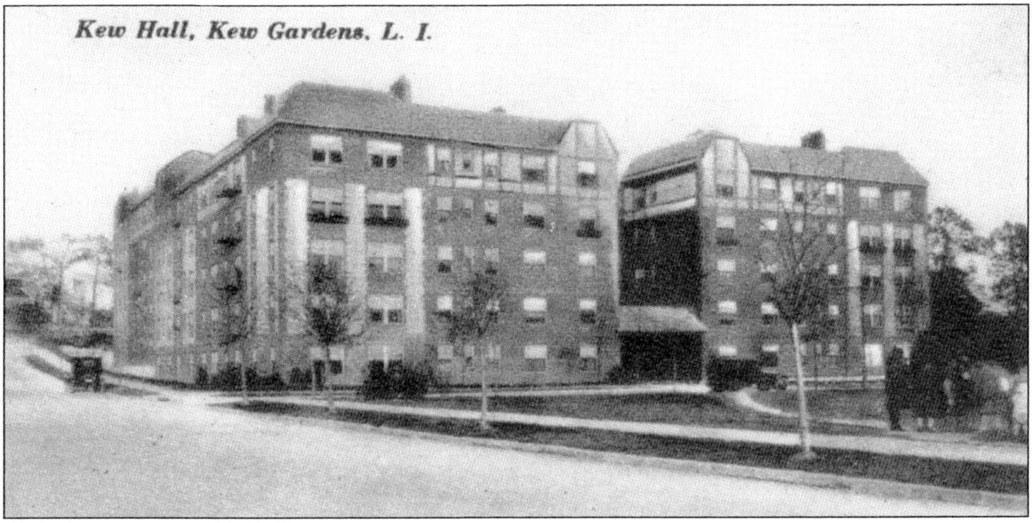

This is Kew Hall, at the corner of Lefferts Boulevard and Talbot Street. The *Brooklyn Daily Eagle* described the building on August 24, 1924: "Located in the heart of beautiful Kew Gardens, a short block from the station and separated from it only by the Kew Gardens Country Club, there has been erected Kew Hall, of charming English architecture, the last word in modern apartment house design. 100% cooperative, and constructed of fire-proof material."

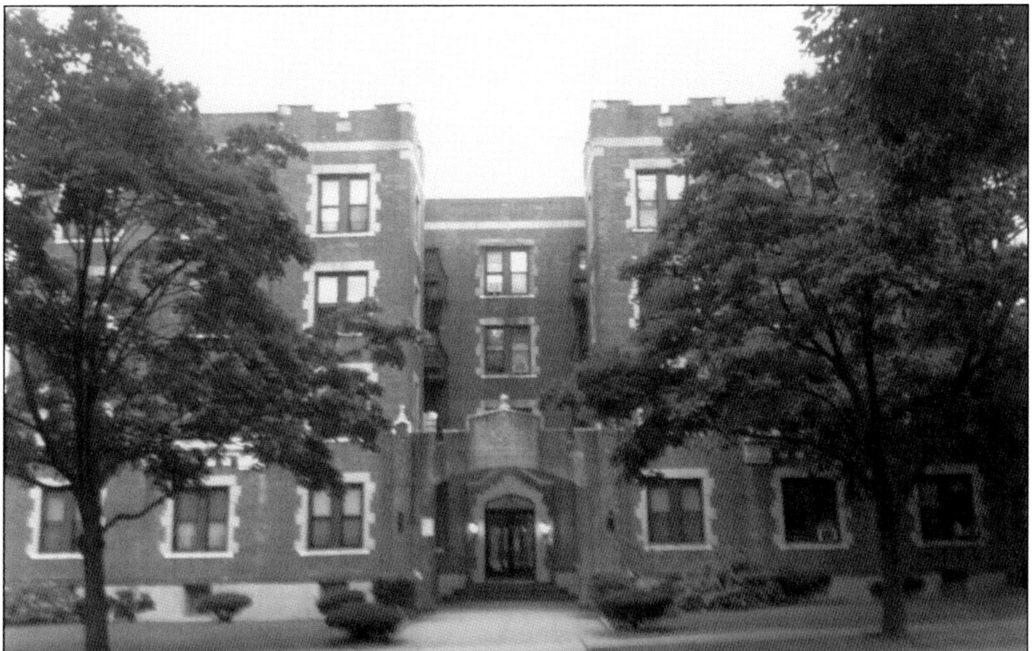

This garden apartment stands at the corner of Metropolitan Avenue and Park Lane South, overlooking Wallenberg Square and Forest Park. It is a four-story walk-up with two entrances. This parcel of land belonged to the estate of Albon Platt Man. A deed was filed on November 11, 1911. Hank Gallo, former *New York Daily News* entertainment reporter and, later, television producer (*Politically Incorrect*, *The Daily Show*), was a former occupant. (Courtesy Malini Singh McDonald.)

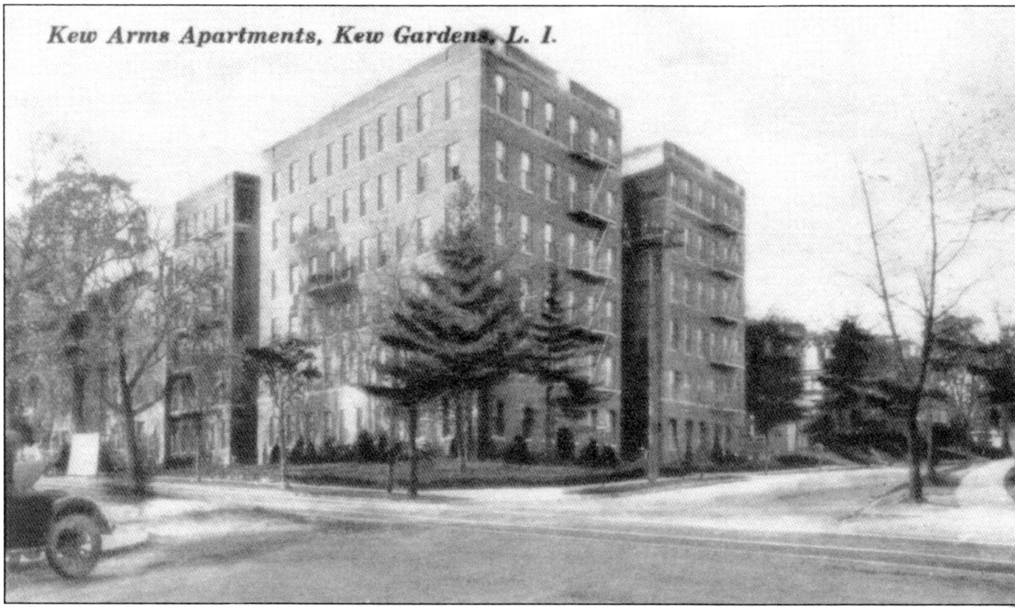

Kew Arms stands at the corner of Lefferts Boulevard and Metropolitan Avenue. As reported in the *Richmond Hill Record* on December 26, 1924, "Special Meeting of the Kew Gardens Civic Association. The objective was the consideration by members of a proposed agreement which the officers of the Civic Association considered advisable to make with the Kew Gardens Corporation. Under this agreement, it would become impossible for apartment houses to be erected in certain areas."

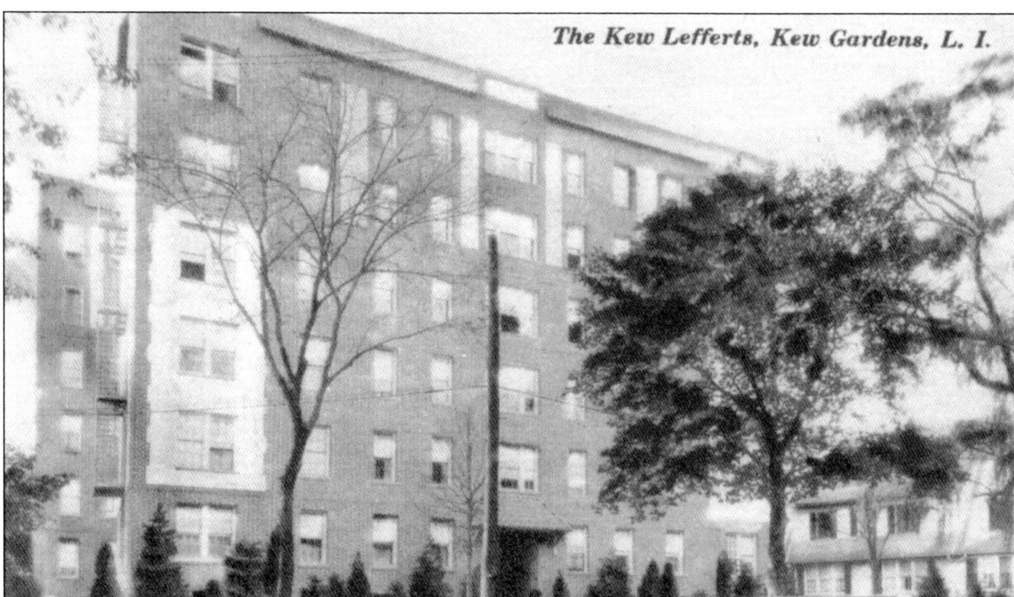

The Kew-Lefferts building stands on Lefferts Boulevard, south of Metropolitan Avenue. According to the *Brooklyn Standard Union* of August 10, 1924, "Kew Gardens has seen the erection of several multi-family houses in the last few months. The latest apartment is the Kew-Lefferts at Lefferts Avenue. It is a six-story elevator building of red brick, attractively trimmed with white stucco and green Spanish tile. The owner expects it ready for occupancy in early September."

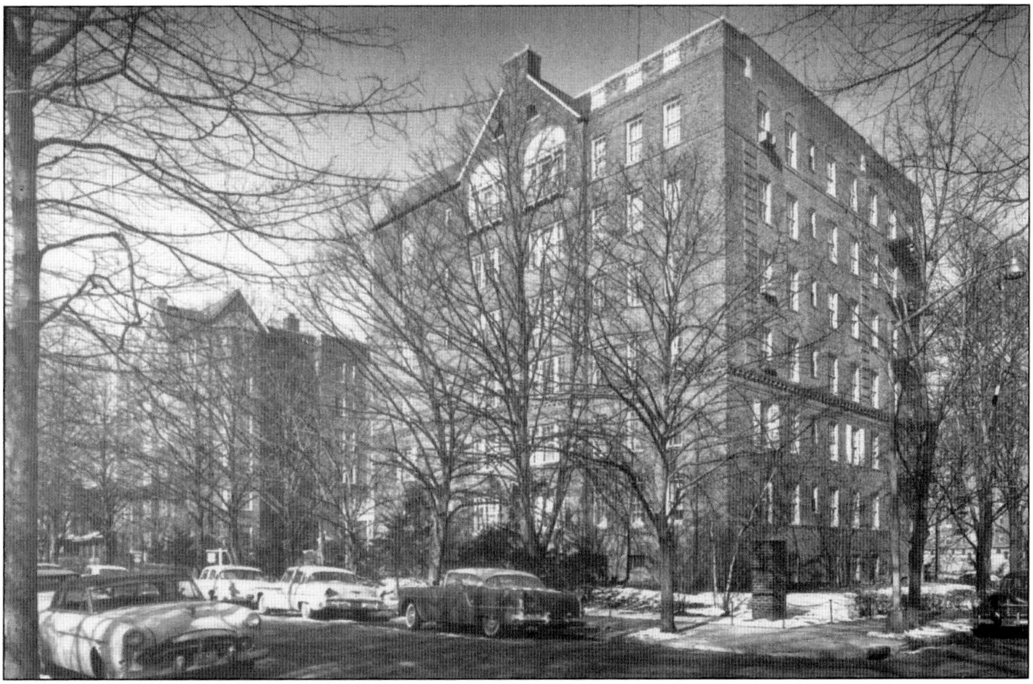

The Beverly House stands on the former site of the mansion of Joseph Fleischman, a millionaire florist who died in 1938. According to the *Brooklyn Daily Eagle* of October 29, 1939, "Notable Addition to Attractive Area. The Beverly House on Beverly Street built for the Beverly Gardens Corporation by Sam Ageloff."

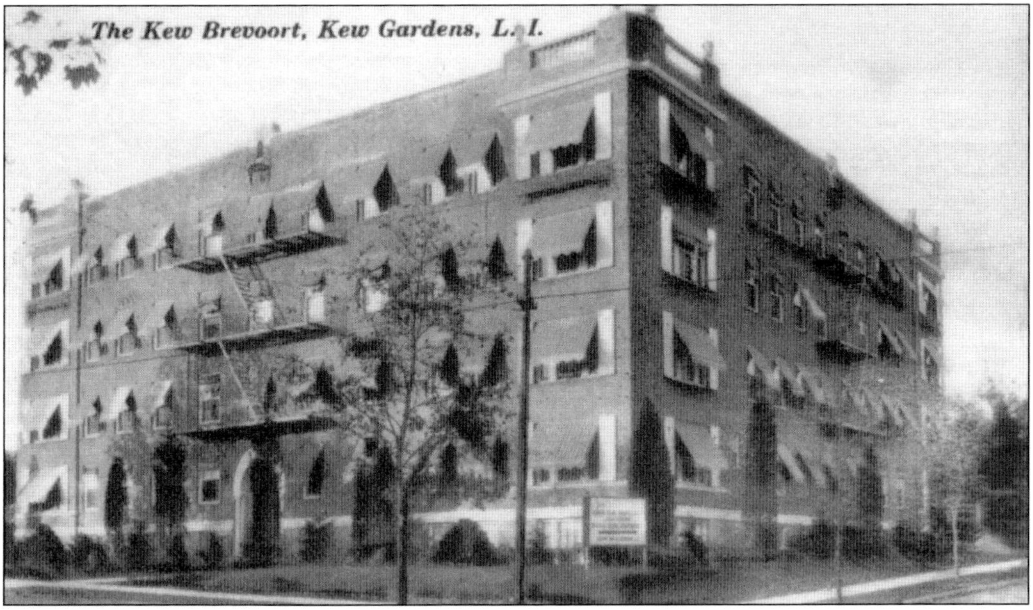

The *Brooklyn Daily Eagle* of November 9, 1924, reported, "An auspicious beginning has been made at Kew Gardens where several big apartments have been built, planned to form a circle outside the colony of high-class private dwellings, costing from $200,000 to $750,000 each. The Brevoort [seen above], a 60-family structure, located at Metropolitan Avenue costs $350,000."

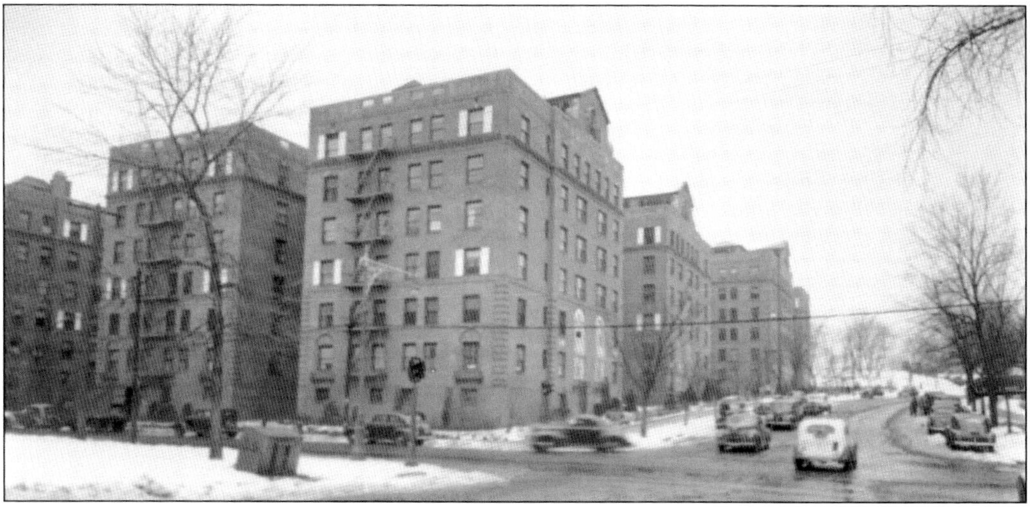

Kent Manor/Hampton Court is located at the corner of Metropolitan Avenue and Park Lane South. As reported in the *Brooklyn Daily Eagle* on August 29, 1937, "The third and fourth units of Kent Manor, one of Kew Gardens' largest apartment house developments, will be ready for occupancy on October 1. The apartment, which consists of four buildings and will house 316 families, is surrounded by Forest Park on three sides."

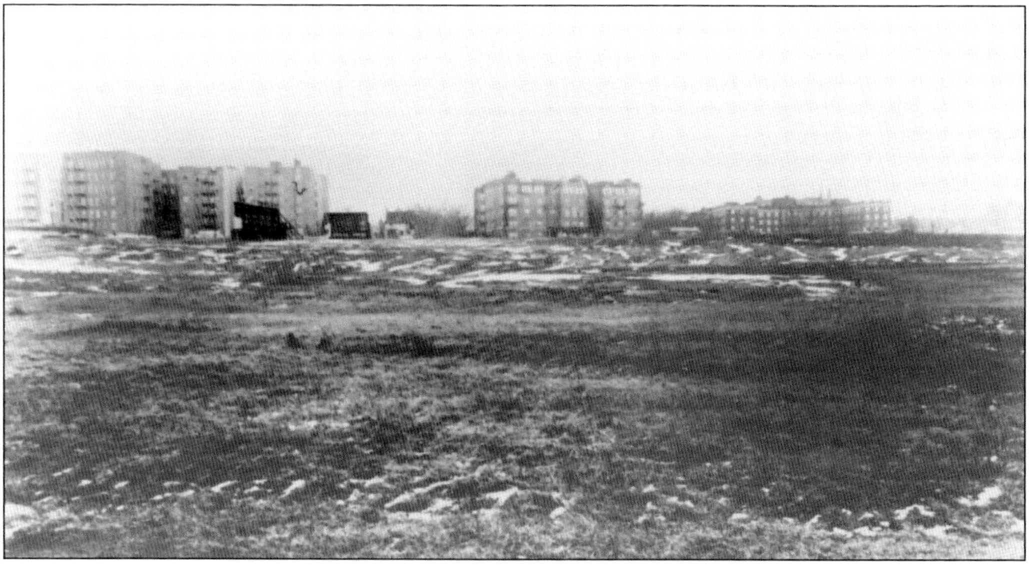

Shown here is the future site of Queens Borough Hall. At center are the Kew Bolmer and Kew Gardens Inn on Queens Boulevard. Recounts Barry Lewis, "Kew Gardens apartment houses are a varied lot: low-rise or high-rise, walk-up or elevator, central courtyard, central common, or pin-wheel in layout, massive tower or charming 'townhouses.' All are coddled with verdant trees and threaded with gardens. These are apartment houses we can learn from. These are city dwellings, but done in a unique American fashion."

Six

People, Places, and Events

Making Kew Gardens Unique

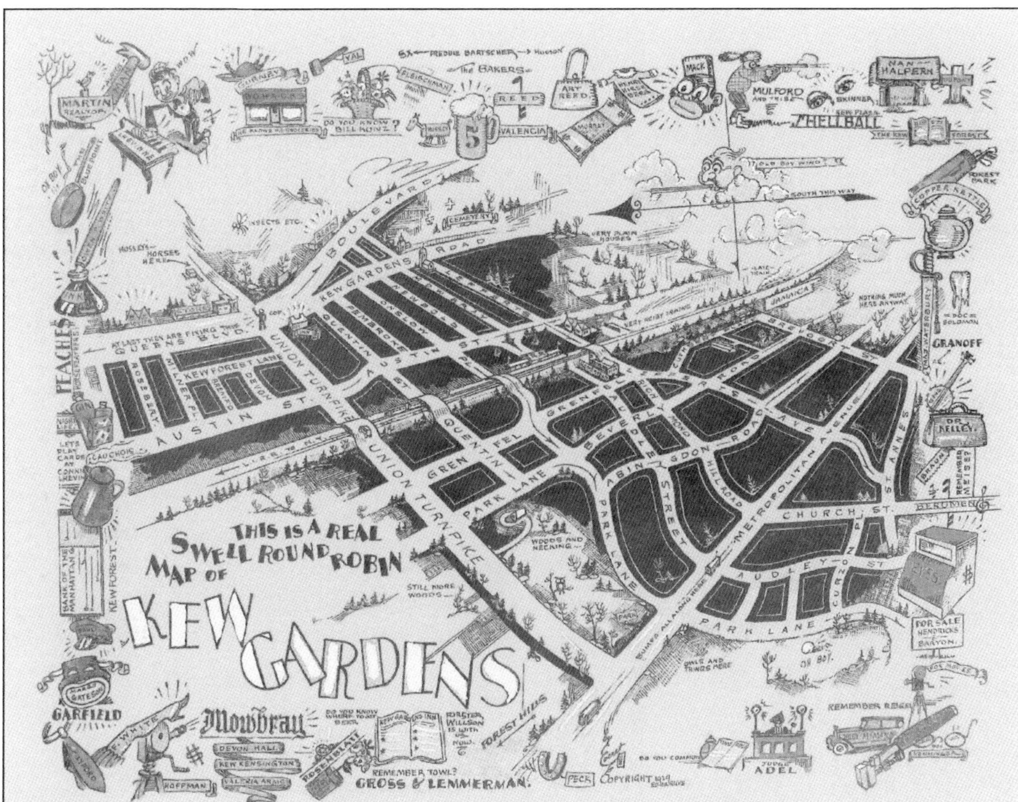

This 1929 Kew Gardens "Round Robin" map lists many local landmarks and people, including the following: Kew Gardens Movie Theater; Kew Gardens Inn; the swamps (where Queens Borough Hall stands today; its mosquitoes were a plague to Richmond Hill and Kew Gardens); Maple Grove Cemetery; First Church of Kew Gardens; Kew Gardens Country Club; Homestead Hotel; and Overlook. People mentioned include Alrick Man, the Lhevinnes, Henry Bohack, Joseph Fleischman, Nan Halpren, Judge Abel, and many more. (Courtesy Roger Sabo.)

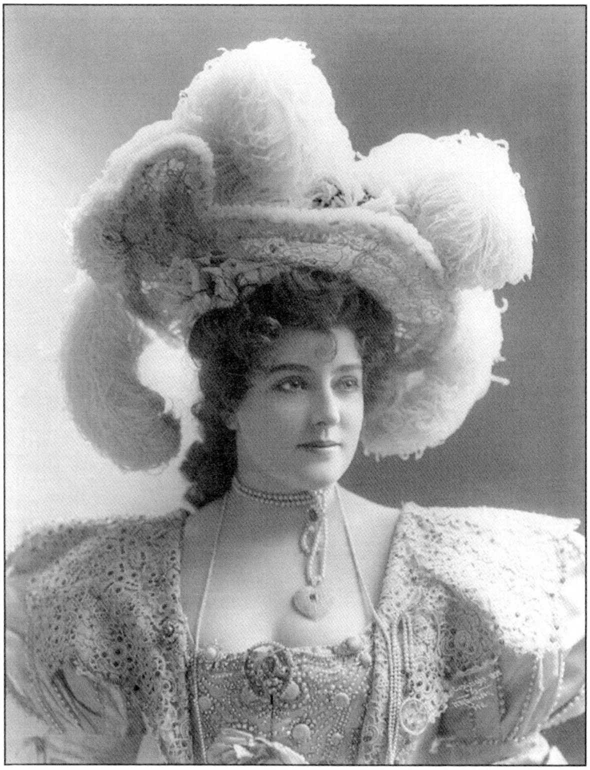

Lillian Russell (1860–1922), the famous actress and singer of the late 19th and early 20th centuries, was known for her beauty, style, and stage presence. Her daughter Dorothy Russell Calvit resided in Kew Gardens and was cut off from her mother's will. Dorothy fought her stepfather for her mother's possessions. "All I want is my mother's personal jewelry and her paintings," said Dorothy Calvit in the *Daily Star* on October 27, 1930.

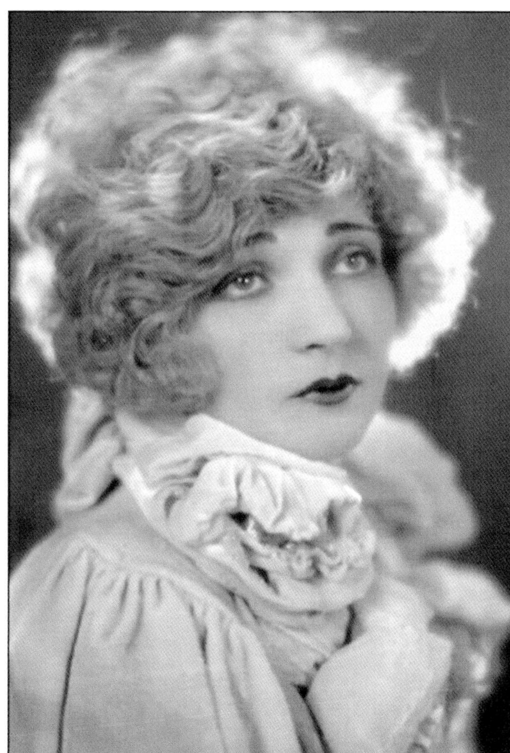

Belle Bennett (1891–1932) was a stage and screen actress who started her professional career in vaudeville. Samuel Goldwyn selected her for the leading role in *Stella Dallas* (1925). The film has been ranked as one of the finest movies of all time. In 1932, she resided at the Kew Gardens Inn, just a few months before her death at age 41.

Pedro de Cordoba (1881–1950) was a classically trained actor who did extensive Broadway work. His first silent film was Cecil B. DeMille's version of *Carmen* (1915), and he became a popular leading man in Hollywood, appearing in such classics as *Captain Blood*, *Saboteur*, *The Song of Bernadette*, and *Samson and Delilah*. Cordoba was born in New York City, and he resided in Kew Gardens during the 1930s.

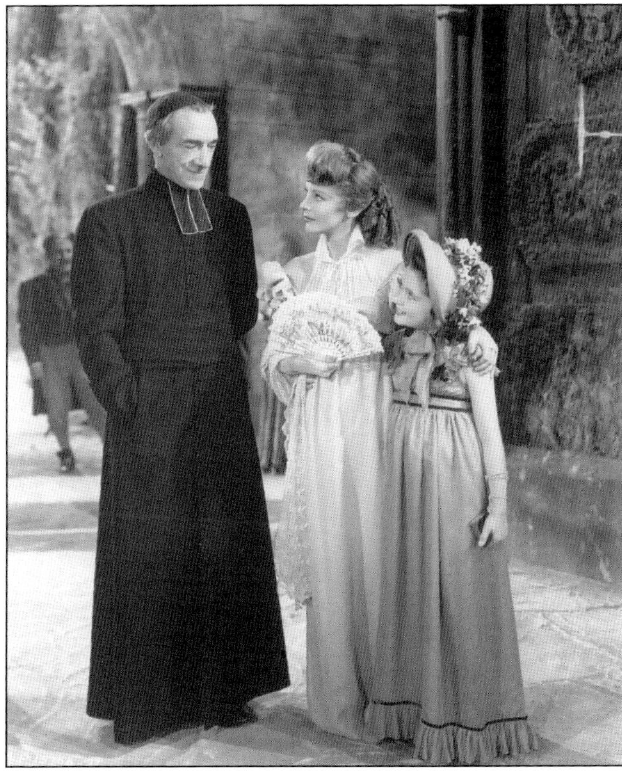

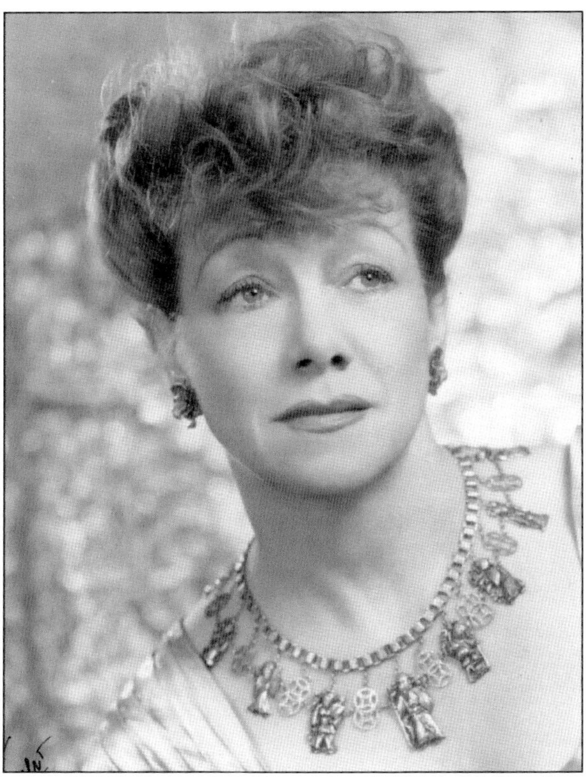

Marjorie Gateson (1891–1977) played opposite Mae West in *Goin' to Town* and with Harold Lloyd in *The Milky Way*. She enjoyed television success as matriarch Grace Tyrell on the daytime soap opera *The Secret Storm*. As reported in *Kew-Forest Life* on November 23, 1929, "Marjorie lives at 68 Beverly Road. 'We chose Kew Gardens chiefly on my account. One gets so much more relaxation away from the city and its noises, and Kew Gardens is so conveniently near New York.'"

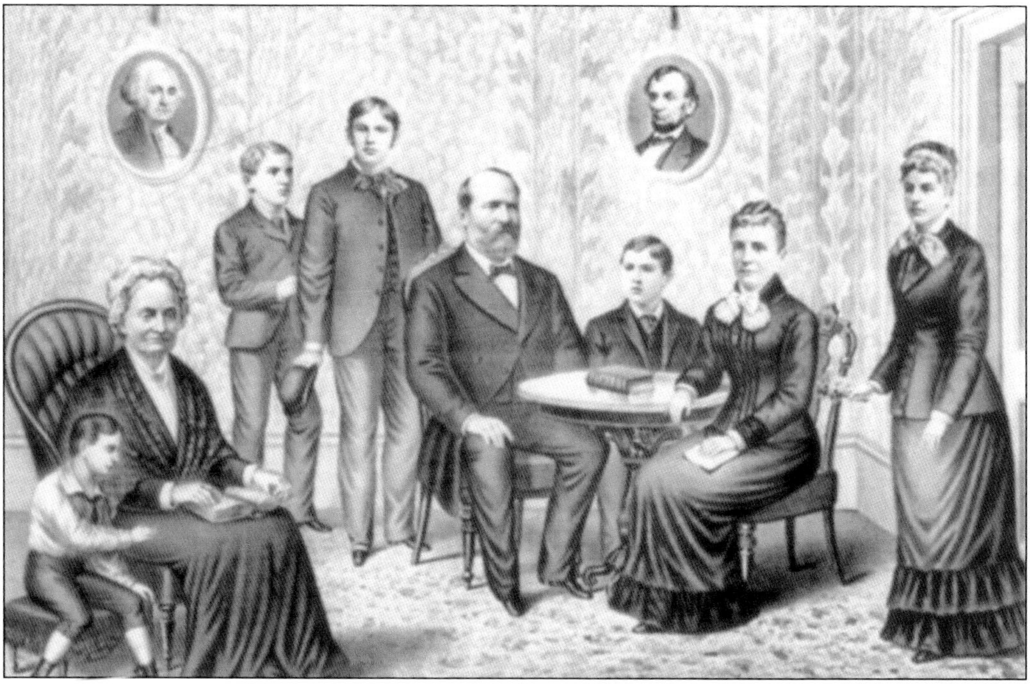

Mary "Mollie" Garfield Stanley-Brown (1867–1947) was the daughter of assassinated president James Garfield. Shown at the right in this engraving, she moved to the White House at age 14. She married Joseph Stanley-Brown, her father's secretary. The *Kew-Forest Life* reported the following on January 18, 1930: "The Stanley-Browns have lived in Kew Gardens since 1914. They have a very attractive and artistic home on Quentin Street, planned and designed by Mr. Stanley-Brown and his son."

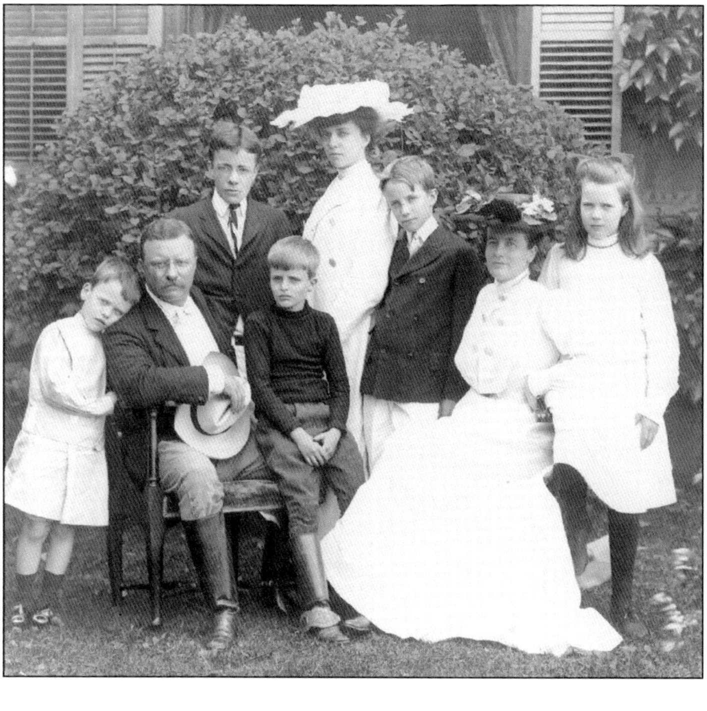

Edith Roosevelt (sitting at right), the wife of Pres. Theodore Roosevelt, and Eleanor Roosevelt (not pictured), wife of Pres. Franklin Roosevelt, attended meetings at the Kew Gardens Country Club. Eleanor Roosevelt spoke to a 1928 woman's meeting, saying that women should play a larger part in the selection of members of their own sex for public office. In 1932, Edith Roosevelt, Long Island director of the Needlework Guild, congratulated the branch on collecting and distributing clothing to needy persons.

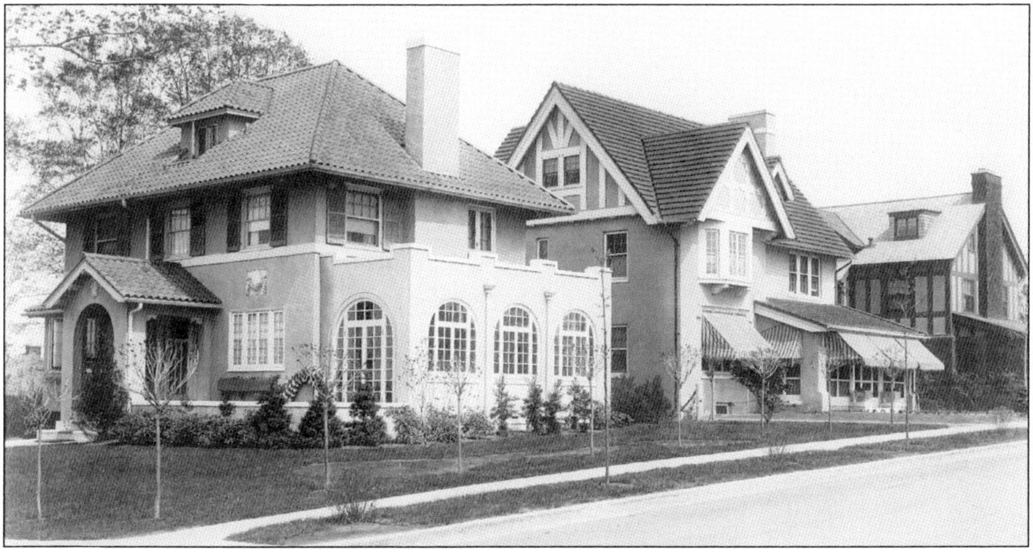

An electronic industry hero of the 1950s and 1960s was Saul B. Marantz (1911–1997), who lived at the corner Austin Street and Eighty-first Avenue (far right). Working at home, he pioneered the use of the laser in the development of compact, high-quality, well-designed music amplification equipment. Marantz went on to develop a series of vacuum-tube components that became yardsticks for the hi-fi industry, and he gained worldwide acclaim in the process.

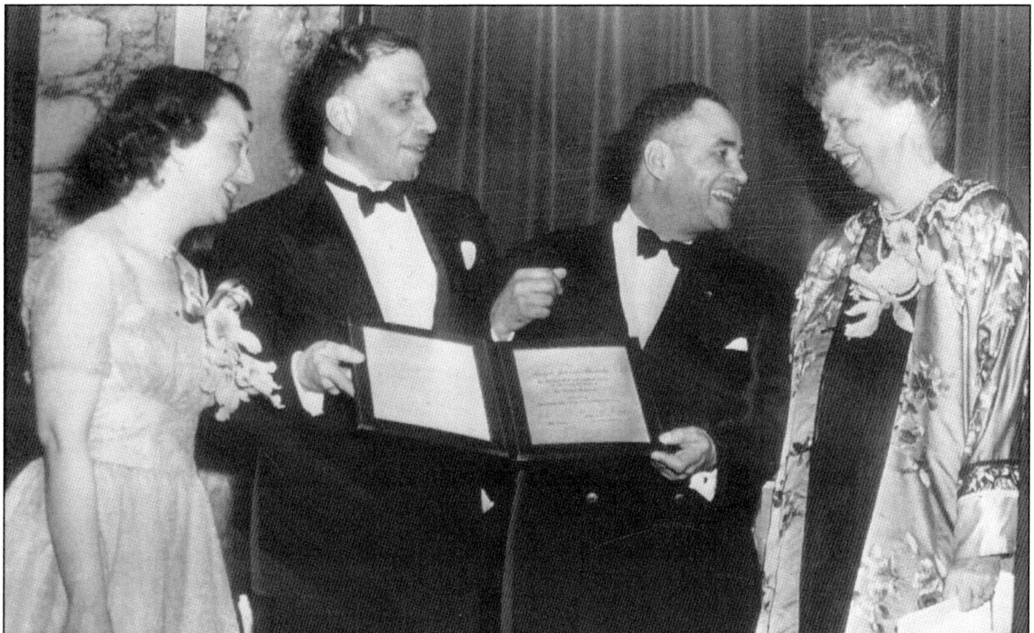

Ralph Bunche (second from right) talks to Eleanor Roosevelt at a 1949 tribute. At left is Mrs. Bunche and Oscar De Lima, an award committee member. Dr. Bunche (1903–1971), a political scientist, academic, and diplomat, received the 1950 Nobel Peace Prize for his mediation in Palestine. He was the first African American to be so honored. Involved in the formation of the United Nations, he was awarded the Medal of Freedom by President Kennedy. He lived on Grosvenor Road, Kew Gardens.

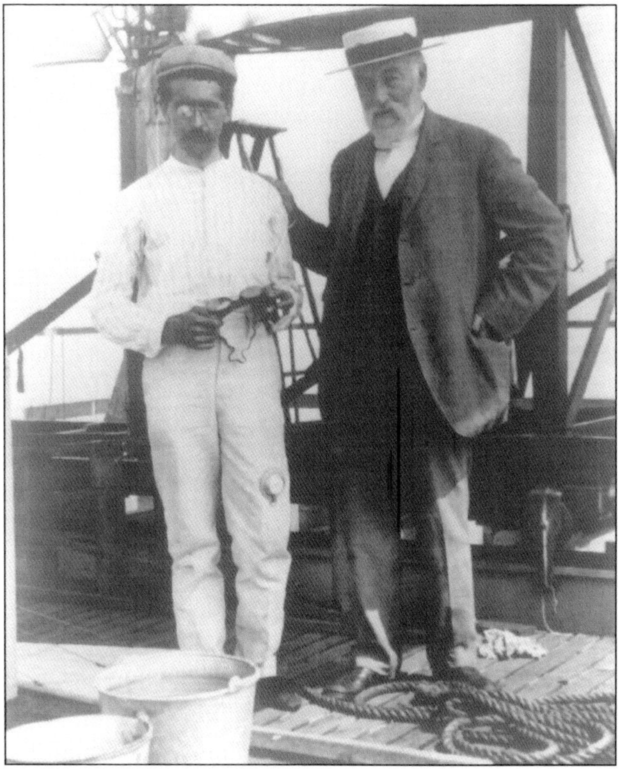

Charles Manly (1876–1927), at left in this photograph, an engineer and Smithsonian Institution secretary, and Samuel Langley (pictured on the right) built the Great Aerodrome, a flying machine. On December 8, 1903, Manly attempted to fly the plane, but a strong winter wind ripped off the tail and the plane crashed, severely injuring Manly. Nine days later, the Wright Brothers flew into aviation history. In June 1914, Glenn Curtiss successfully flew the original Langley/Manly craft.

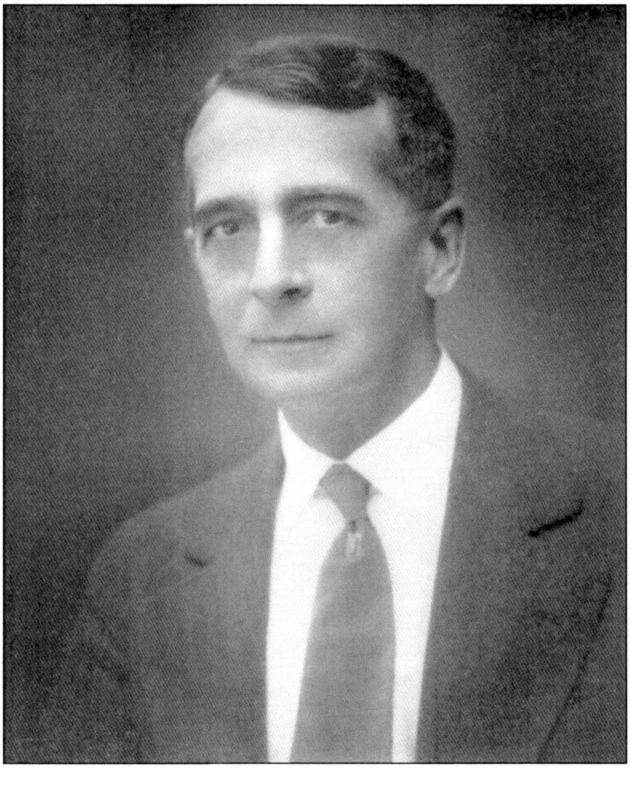

The Wright Brothers were first in flight, but Charles Manly (seen here) and Samuel Langley were the first to experiment with flight, making aviation possible. As reported in the *Corning Evening Leader* on December 27, 1929, "The late Charles Manly and Com. Richard E. Byrd are placed by Smithsonian Institute in its 'Aviation Hall of Fame' with Wilbur and Orville Wright, Glenn Curtiss, and Charles Lindbergh." Manly lived at the Kew Arms Apartment and is buried at Maple Grove Cemetery.

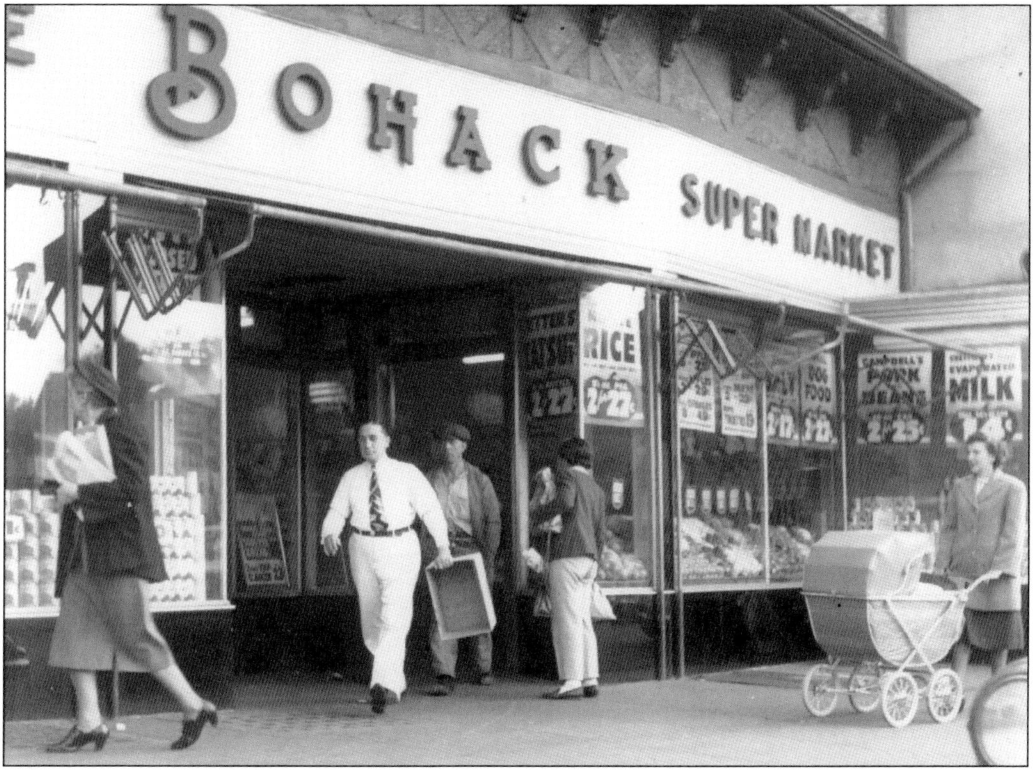

Shown here is the Bohack store on Lefferts Boulevard. Henry Bohack's first job at a grocery store earned him $7 a month. By 1889, he opened his first independent store. By the age of 35, he owned five stores. In 1903, the H.C. Bohack Company was organized, and by 1931, the company had 735 branch stores in Queens, Brooklyn, and Long Island. Bohack (1865–1931) lived in Kew Gardens on Beverly Road.

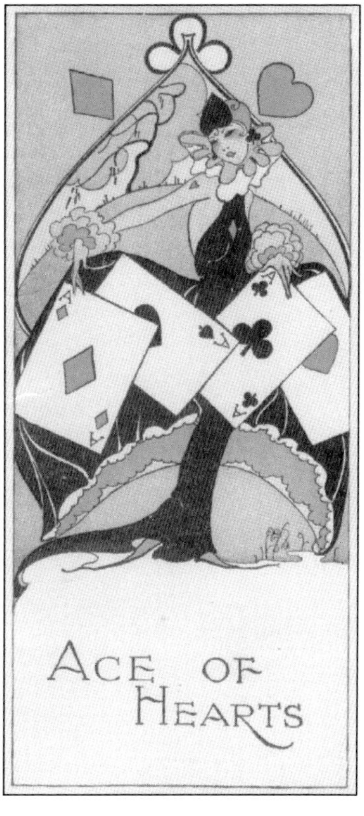

Charles S. Clark (1875–1932) established a successful greeting card company. The *Bookseller and Stationer* of May 15, 1992, quoted his business philosophy: "This is a business not of production, but one that requires quality, good taste and above all, limited to the manufacturing of merchandise that is absolutely useful." He lived on Newbold Place (Eighty-second Road) and took an active role in the community. Displayed here is a Clark Company card from 1920.

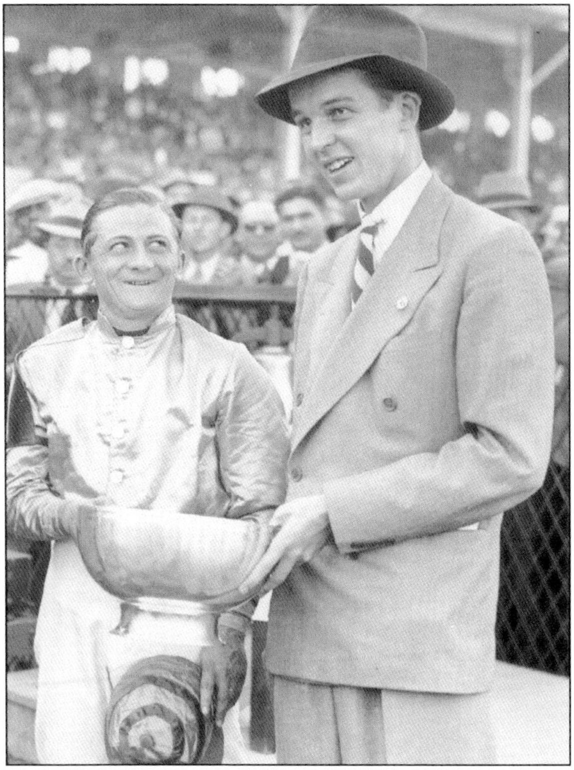

Don Meade (1913–1996) was a noted jockey who won the 1933 Kentucky Derby riding Brokers Tip in a fight to the finish line. In 1939, the president of the Maryland Jockey Club, Alfred Vanderbilt (right) presents Meade with the Dixie Cup. Meade lived with his family on 118th Street in Kew Gardens.

Shown here is the 1933 Kentucky Derby's famous "Fighting Finish," with jockey Don Meade riding Brokers Tip (right) and Herb Fisher on Horse Play. They used their riding crops on their mounts and on each other as they raced head-to-head down the stretch. Brokers Tip beat Horse Play by a nose and was declared the winner.

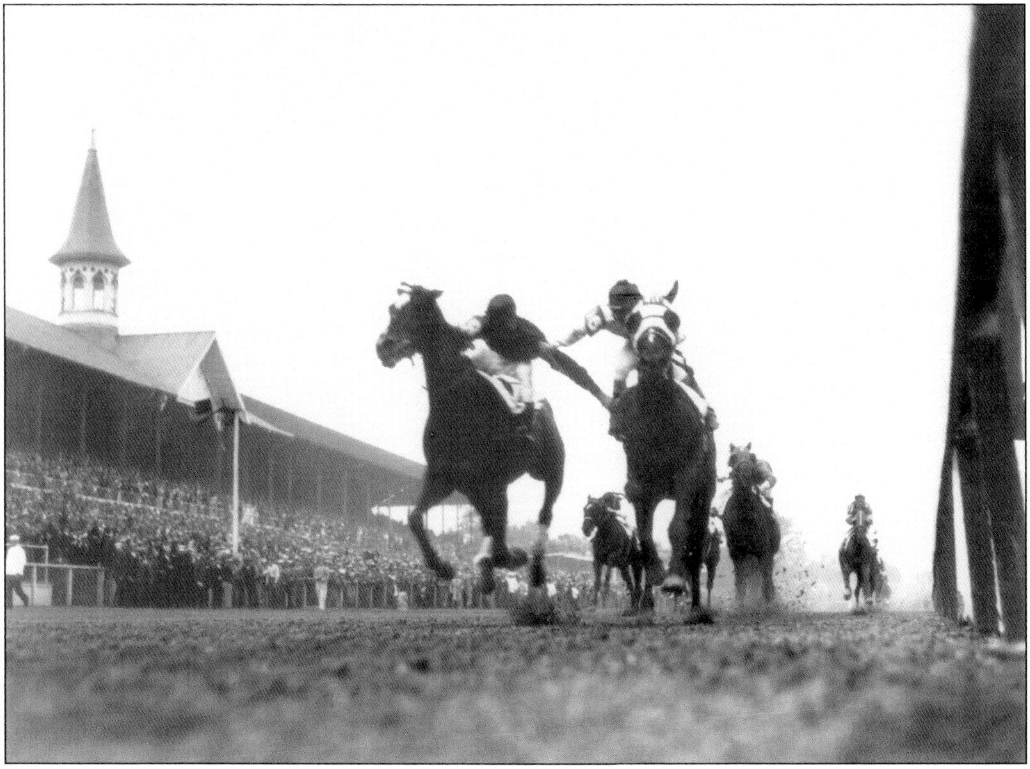

Earl Sande (1898–1968), a resident of the Kew Hall Apartments, was one of the most popular jockeys of the 1920s and 1930s. He rode many great horses to victory, such as Man o' War, Sir Barton, Zev, and Gallant Fox. In 1923, he won 39 stakes, including the Kentucky Derby and Belmont Stakes. Sande's most famous wins came aboard Gallant Fox in 1930, when he won the Triple Crown.

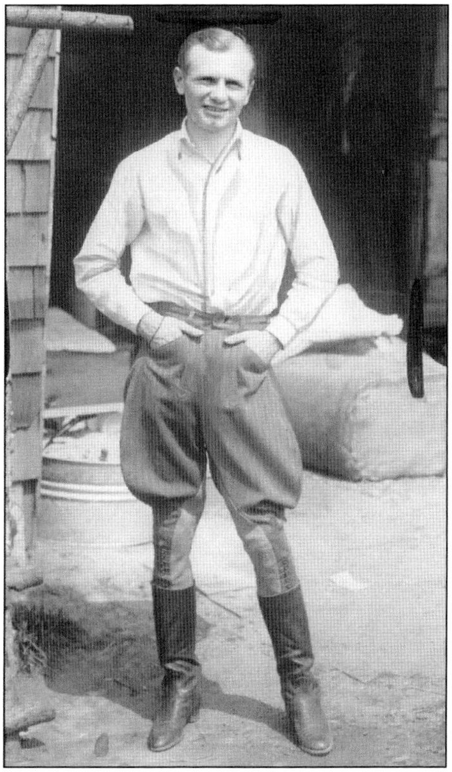

Earl Sande is shown here on Man o' War. In 1955, he was inducted into the National Museum of Racing and Hall of Fame. Featured in an article in *Kew-Forest Life* on April 6, 1932, he said, "There is a thrill of some sort in every race but perhaps the biggest thrill of all was when I rode Gallant Fox to victory against Questioneer by a nose in the Lawrence Realization."

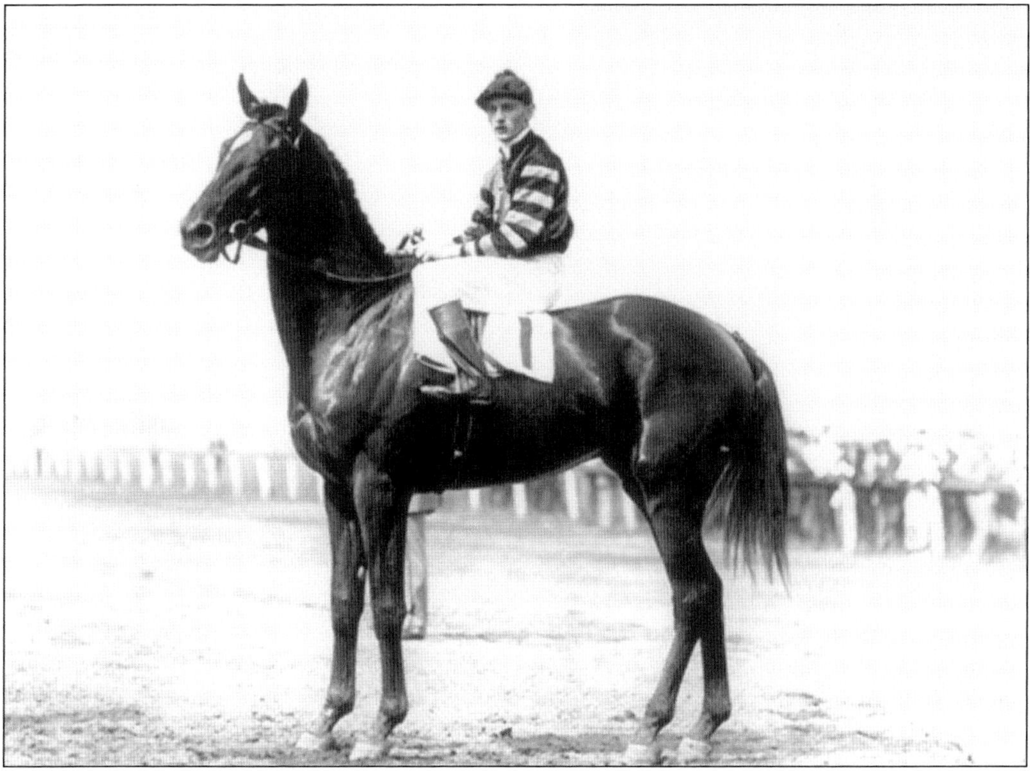

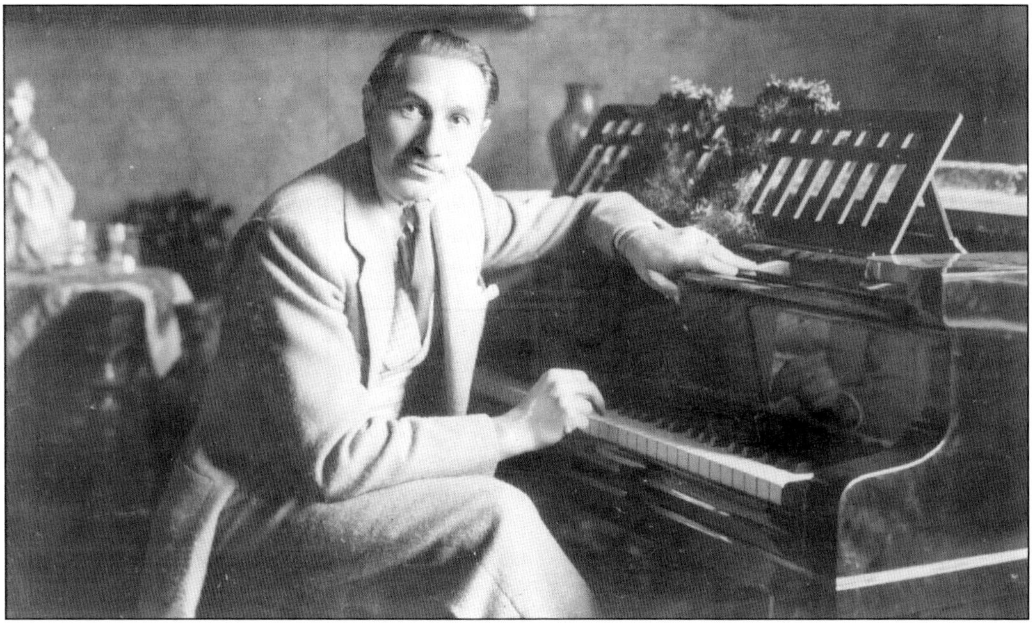

Rudolph Friml (1879–1972) was a composer of operettas, musicals, songs, and piano pieces. His best-known works are *Rose-Marie* and *The Vagabond King*, which enjoyed success on Broadway and were adapted into films. "Indian Love Call," a song from *Rose-Marie*, achieved great popularity and remains Friml's best-remembered work. The *Daily Star* reported on December 26, 1929, "Friml has a beautiful suite in the Kew Gardens Inn, with a piano and every convenience for composing."

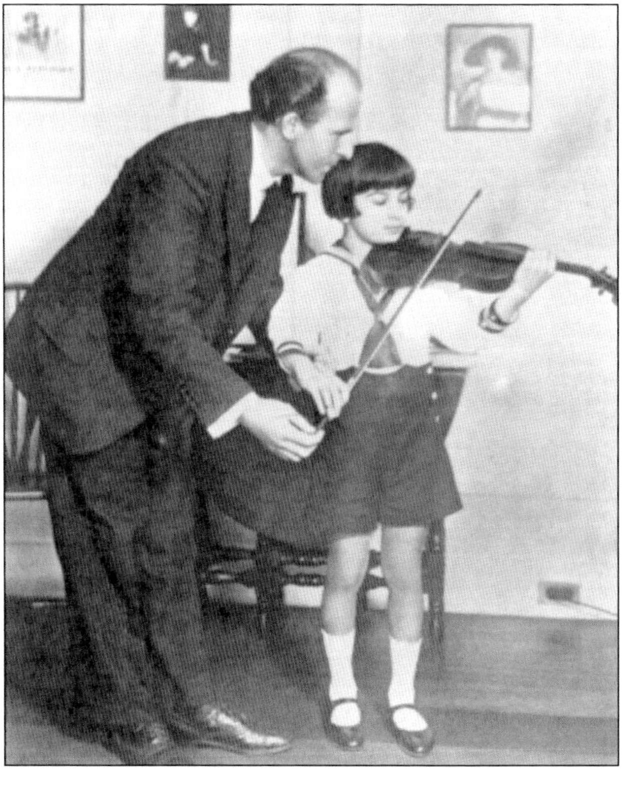

Violinist and pianist Louis Persinger (1887–1966) trained at the Leipzig Conservatory. He was a concertmaster of the Berlin Philharmonic and the Royal Opera Orchestra. Persinger embarked on a solo career as a preeminent violinist. In the 1920s, he became a violin teacher and taught at Juilliard. He is best known as the teacher of such great violinists as Yehudi Menuhin, Ruggiero Ricci, Isaac Stern, Camilla Wicks, Almita Vamos, and many others. He lived on Union Turnpike in Kew Gardens.

Josef and Rosina Lhevinne were famed classical pianists. Both won the coveted gold medal from the Moscow Imperial Conservatory. Leaving Russia, they immigrated to America, joining the faculty of the Institute of Musical Art, which became The Juilliard School. Josef embarked on a series of concert tours across the country and around the world. He was regarded as one of the supreme pianists of his day by virtually all of his famous contemporaries.

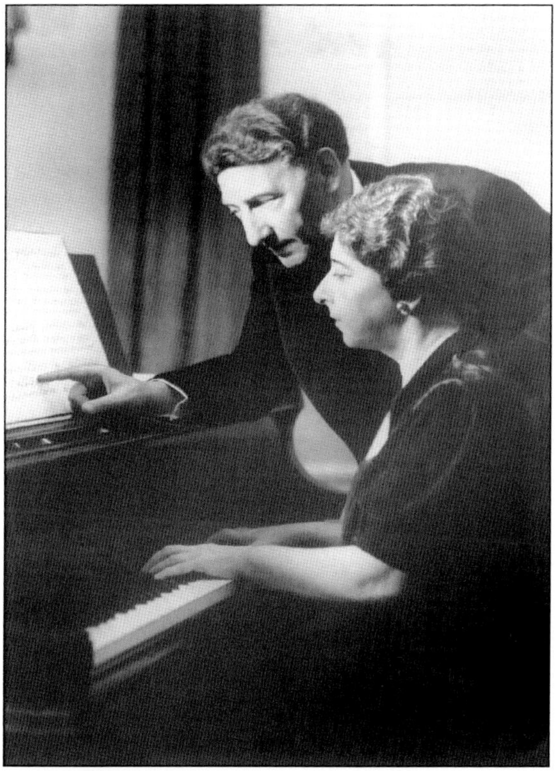

In 1919, the Lhevinnes built this spacious home in Kew Gardens on Eighty-third Avenue. Remembering the Russian winters, Rosina had a fireplace built in almost every room. Among Rosina's students were many of the best young pianists of the 1940s, 1950s, and 1960s, including Van Cliburn. At the height of the Cold War, in 1958, Van Cliburn was awarded first prize at the inaugural Tchaikovsky Competition in Moscow.

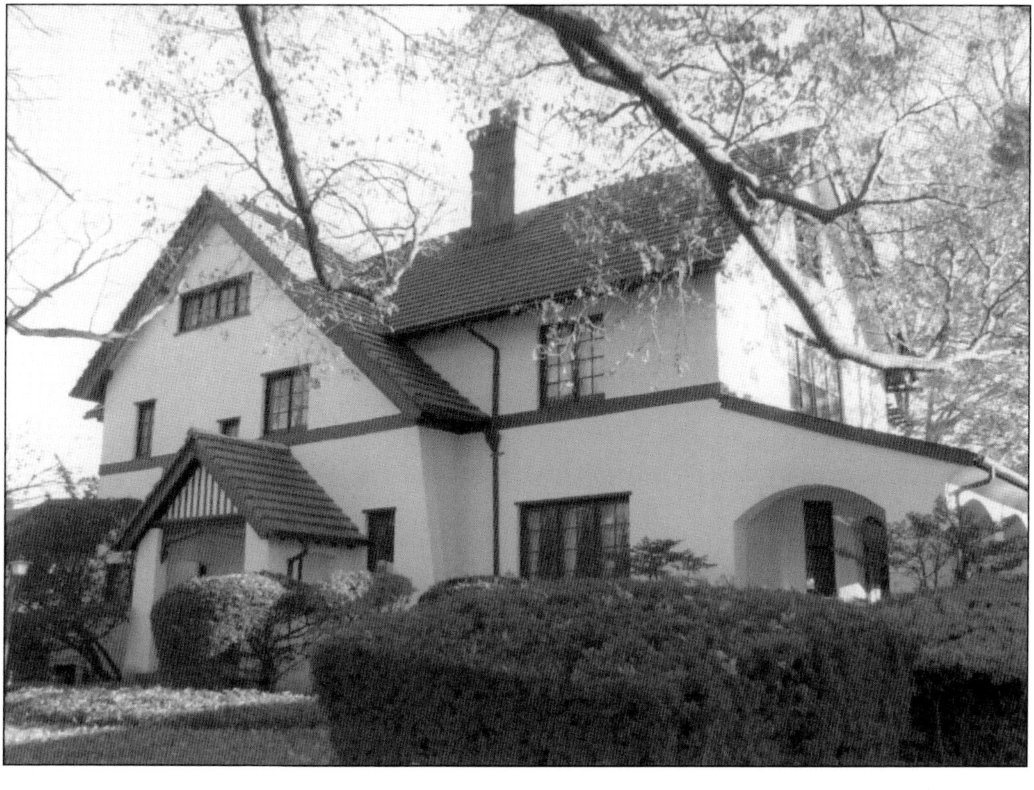

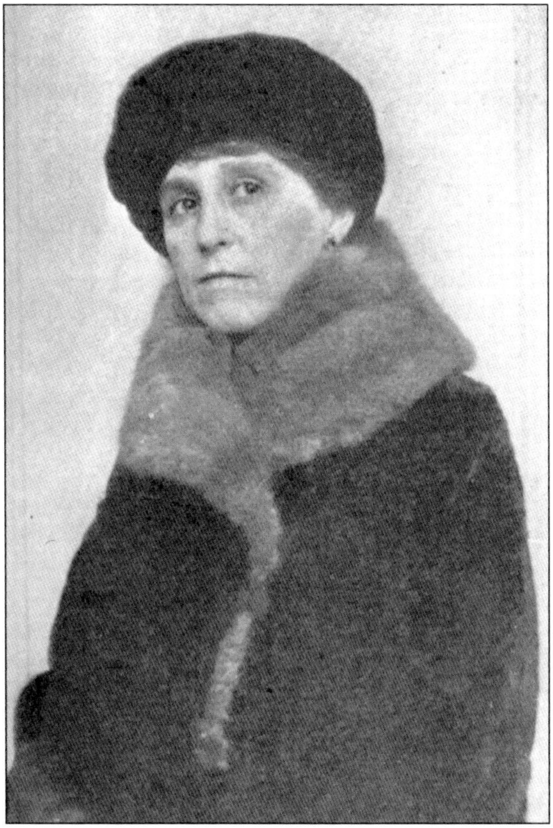

The artist Ethel Paxson (1885–1982) attended the Pennsylvania Academy of Fine Arts and studied under William M. Chase and Cecilia Beaux. *Kew-Forest Life* mentioned her on February 15, 1930: "Mrs. Paxson has lived in Kew Gardens for seventeen years. She devotes her afternoons to painting in a studio. Portraits, flower arrangements and landscapes, charming in color and composition, line the walls of her studio." (Courtesy QBPL Archives, Periodical Collection.)

Henry Clive (1882–1960) was an artist in Hollywood who acted in silent films. He began painting Ziegfeld Follies girls, which led to work painting screen stars. He was the art director for Paramount Pictures, and his work appeared on many movie posters, including that for the Rudolph Valentino film *The Sheik*. Charlie Chaplin used Clive as his art director. His artwork appeared on many movie magazine covers. He and his family resided at the Kew Gardens Inn.

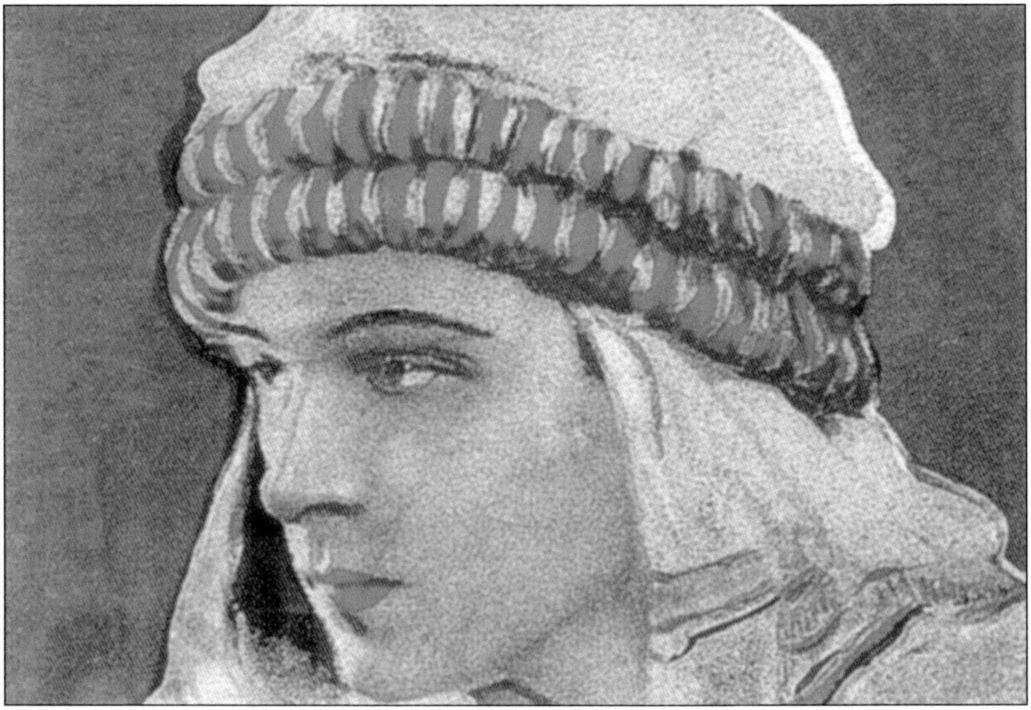

The writer Adele Whitely Fletcher (1897–1979) lived at the Kew Hall. She started as a secretary and, by the 1920s, was editing *Motion Picture* magazine and *Movie Weekly*, writing 300 articles and reviews for *Motion Picture*, covering everyone from Gloria Swanson to Burt Reynolds. She became editor for *Photoplay* as well as feature editor for the *American Weekly*. She gave showgirl Lucille LeSeur her movie-star name: Joan Crawford. (Courtesy QBPL Archives, Periodical Collection.)

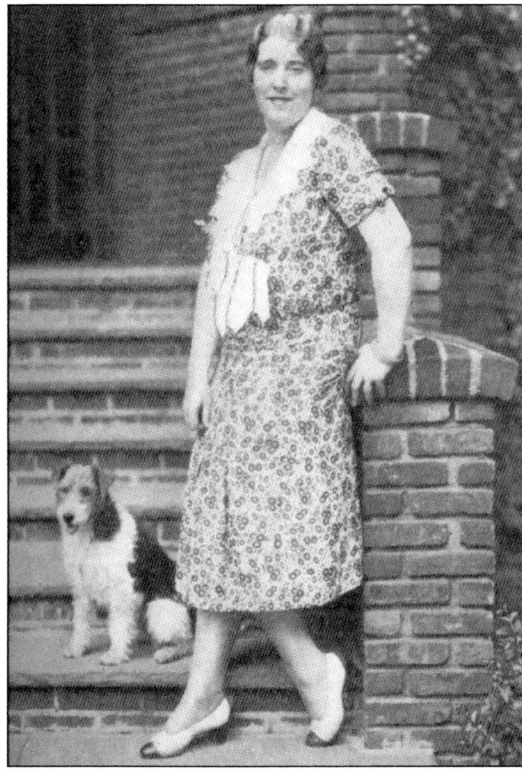

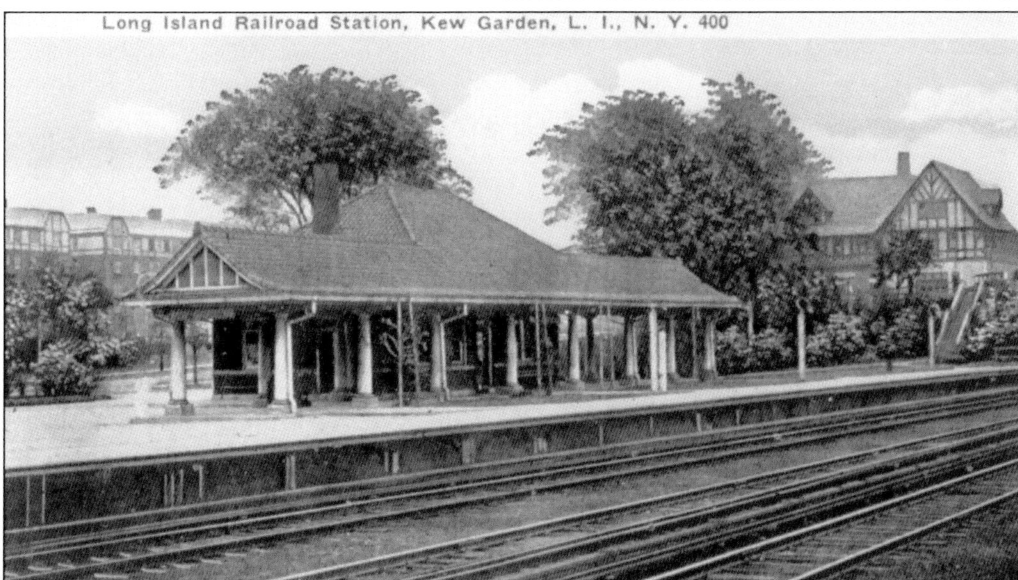

The writer Thyra Samtar Winslow (1885–1961) lived at the Kew Hall Apartment. She wrote stories between 1915 and 1955 for American magazines, including *Century*, the *New Yorker*, *American Mercury*, *Cosmopolitan*, and *Redbook*. In 1935, Doubleday published *My Own, My Native Land*, with stories that had appeared in the *New Yorker*. Winslow wrote the film screenplay for *She Married Her Boss*, starring Claudette Colbert and Ronald Colman. In this postcard image, the Kew Hall can be seen on the left.

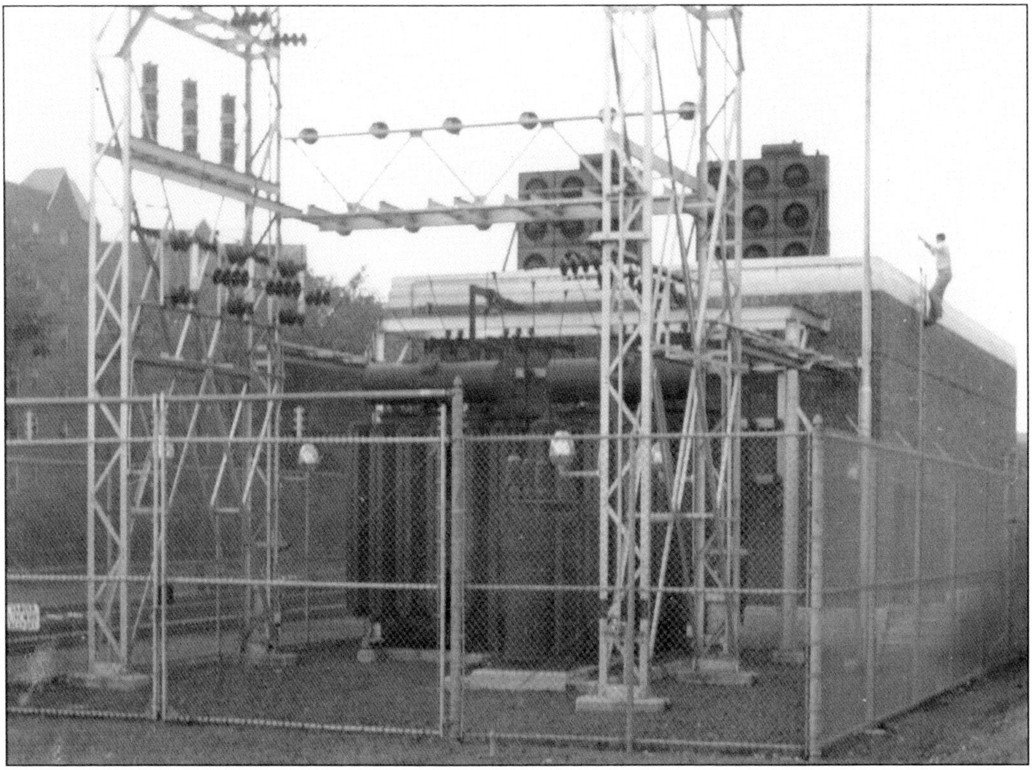

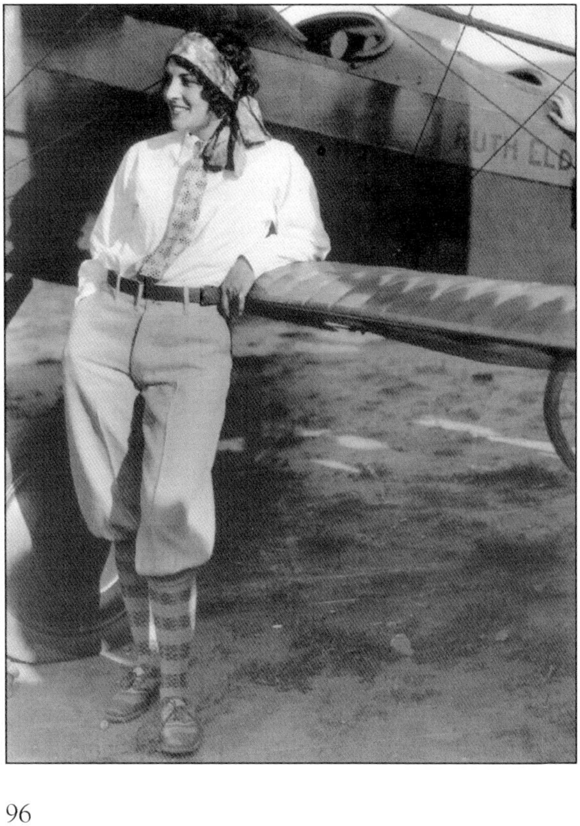

Shown here is the Kew Gardens Electrical Power Plant. Lloyd Espenschied (1889–1986), a coinventor of the coaxial cable, which made today's television possible, lived at the corner Eighty-second and Kew Gardens Roads. An alumnus of the AT&T staff of brilliant engineers headquartered on West Street, he became part of the creative Bell Labs team. Espenschied, a graduate of Pratt Institute, developed over 100 patents in various fields of the communications industry.

Ruth Elder (1902–1977) wanted to be the first woman to fly across the Atlantic, and she was the first woman to attempt this flight. In October 1927, Elder and companion George Haldeman departed from Roosevelt Field. After nine hours at the controls, foul weather forced them to ditch into the ocean, but they were rescued. They stayed at the Kew Gardens Inn while preparing for this flight.

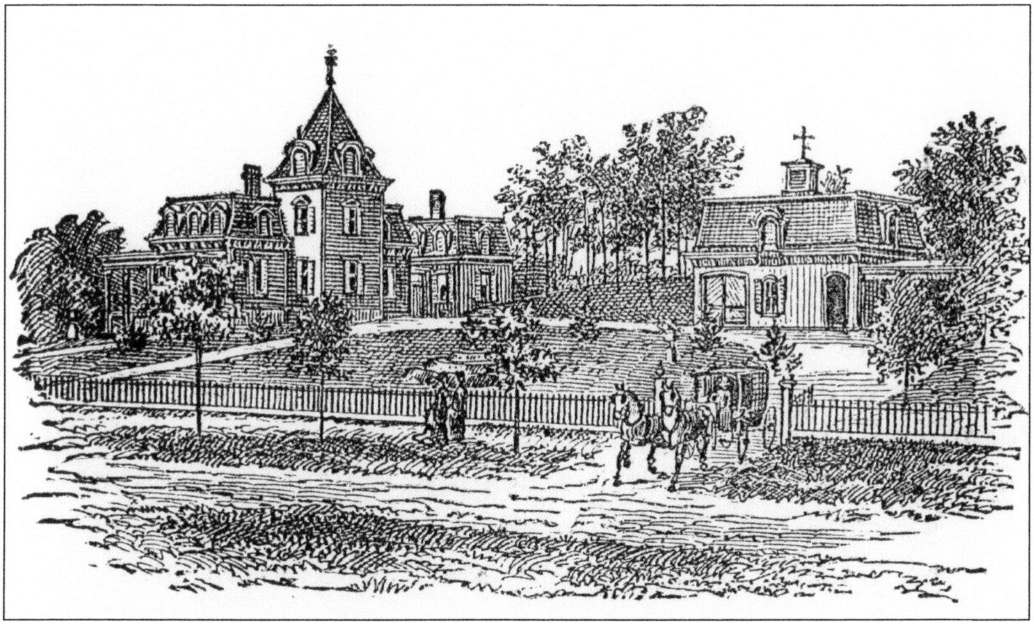

Joseph Lyman, agricultural editor of the *Tribune*, started construction of this house on the northwest corner of Metropolitan Avenue and Church Street (118th Street) in 1871. At the time of its construction, the home was in Richmond Hill, but this section is now in Kew Gardens. It was one of the earliest homes to be constructed in the area. On January 29, 1872, the *Brooklyn Union* announced, "Mr. Joseph H. Lyman died at his residence of small pox."

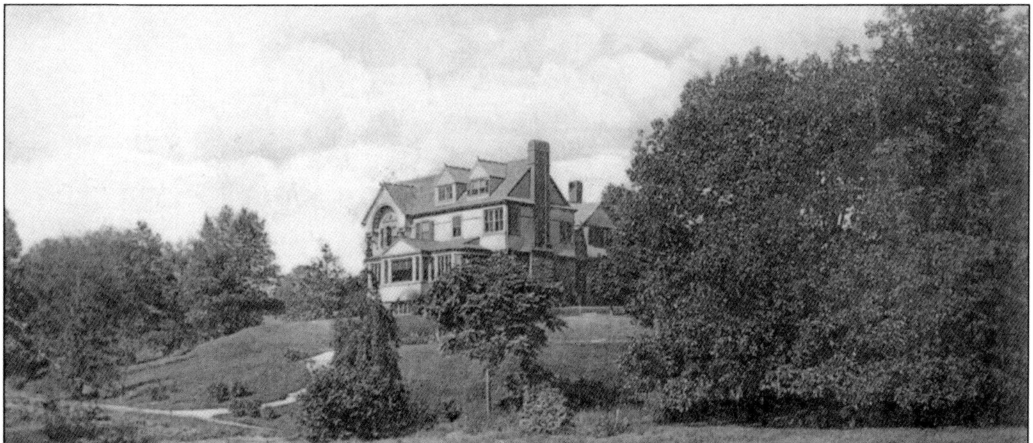

This palatial house was built in 1886 by Lt. William Cowles and was located between 116th and 118th Streets, above Curzon Road in what is now Kew Gardens. On October 10, 1891, Cowles was at the helm of the presidential yacht the *Despatch*, a schooner-rigged steamship that had been the official yacht of Presidents Hayes, Garfield, Arthur, Cleveland, and Harrison, when it ran into a storm and sank.

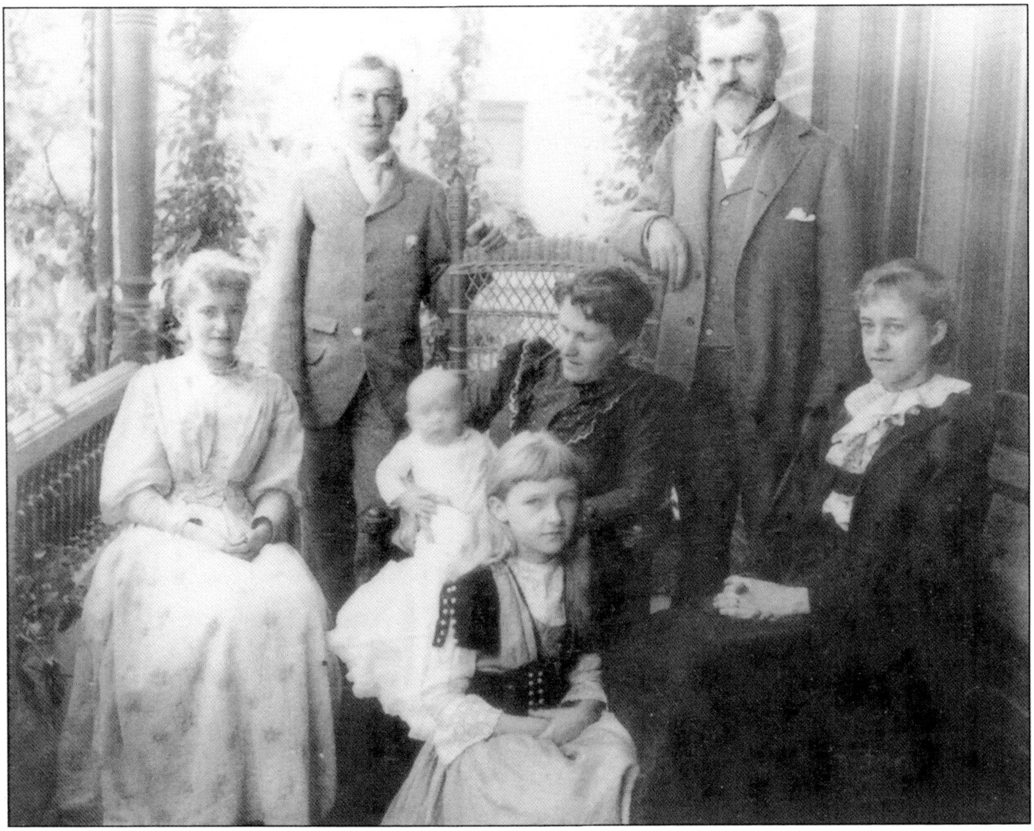

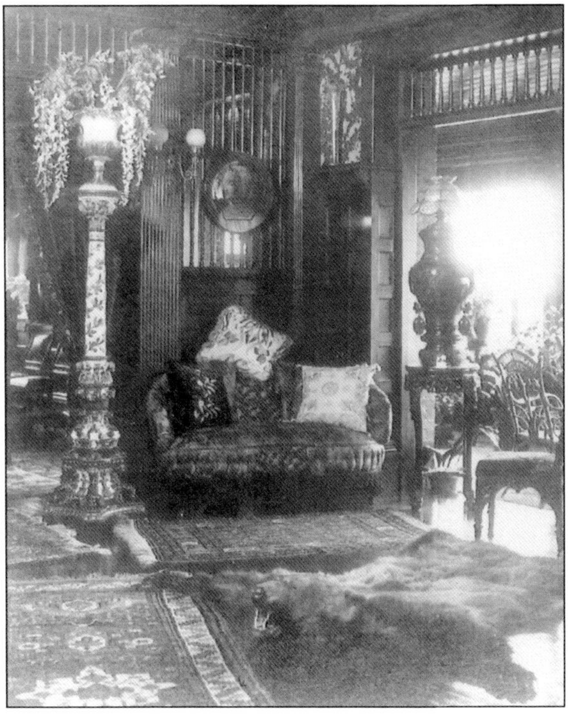

The Lang family purchased the grand Cowles mansion in 1892. Julius Lang founded the Fuchs & Lang Manufacturing Company in 1871. He is shown here with his wife, Mathilde, and their three daughters and two sons. The Fuchs & Lang Company was well regarded in the lithograph trade. In 1912, it filed suit against the White Star Line when cases of the firm's merchandise sank in the cargo hold of the *Titanic*.

The interior of the Lang home displays high Victorian elegance. The home was surrounded by beautiful gardens and contained a conservatory. The home's south side had large bay windows. Former owner Mary Cowles was the daughter of Sen. Allen Thurman. When he visited, the senator sat in his rocking chair by the bay window. He could see the sea by day and, at night, the lights of the Fire Island lighthouse.

The Broadway play *Dear Ruth*, by the noted playwright Norman Krasna, opened on December 13, 1944, at the Henry Miller Theatre. It is a lightweight romantic comedy set in Kew Gardens, Queens. A teenage girl has a pen-pal romance with a soldier during World War II. She signs her older sister's name to the letters, causing a number of complications. The play was a success and stayed open for two years. This is a cast photograph from the play.

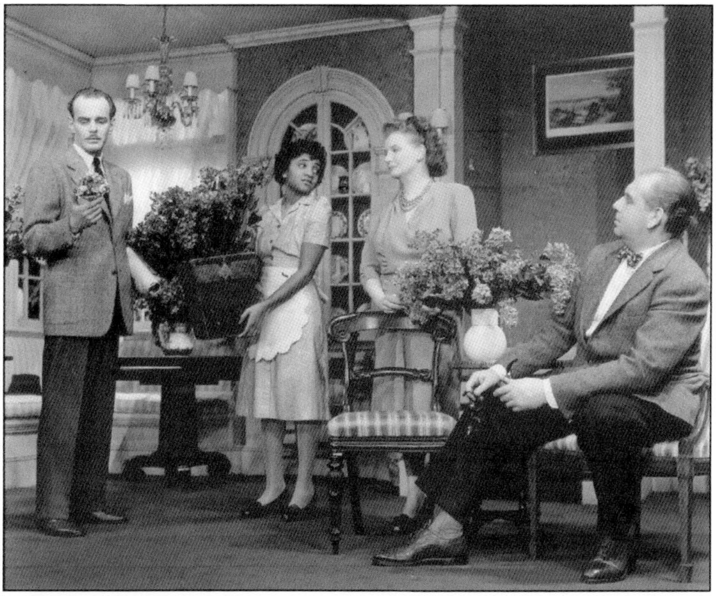

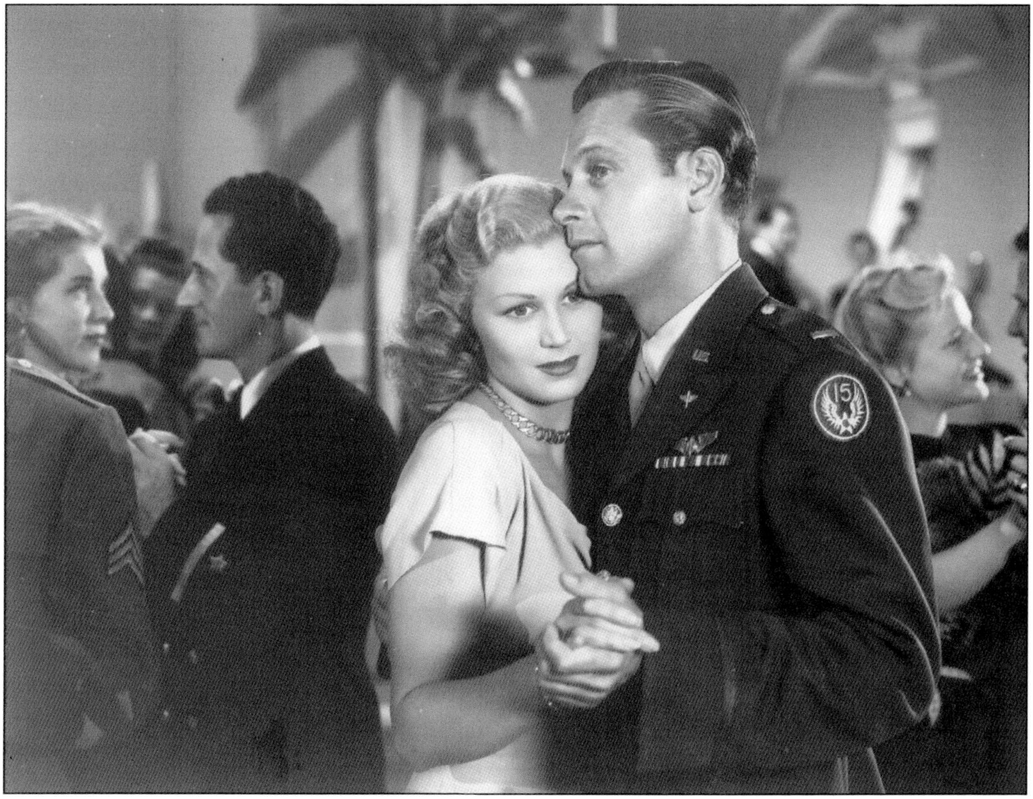

Dear Ruth was made into a film by Paramount Pictures in 1947. Its lead stars were Joan Caulfield and William Holden. Norman Krasna also worked on the movie's screenplay. He was born in Corona, Queens, and worked as a screenwriter, playwright, producer, and film director. Krasna garnered four Academy Award screenwriting nominations, winning for 1943's *Princess O'Rourke*. He wrote the perennial family favorite film *White Christmas* (1954).

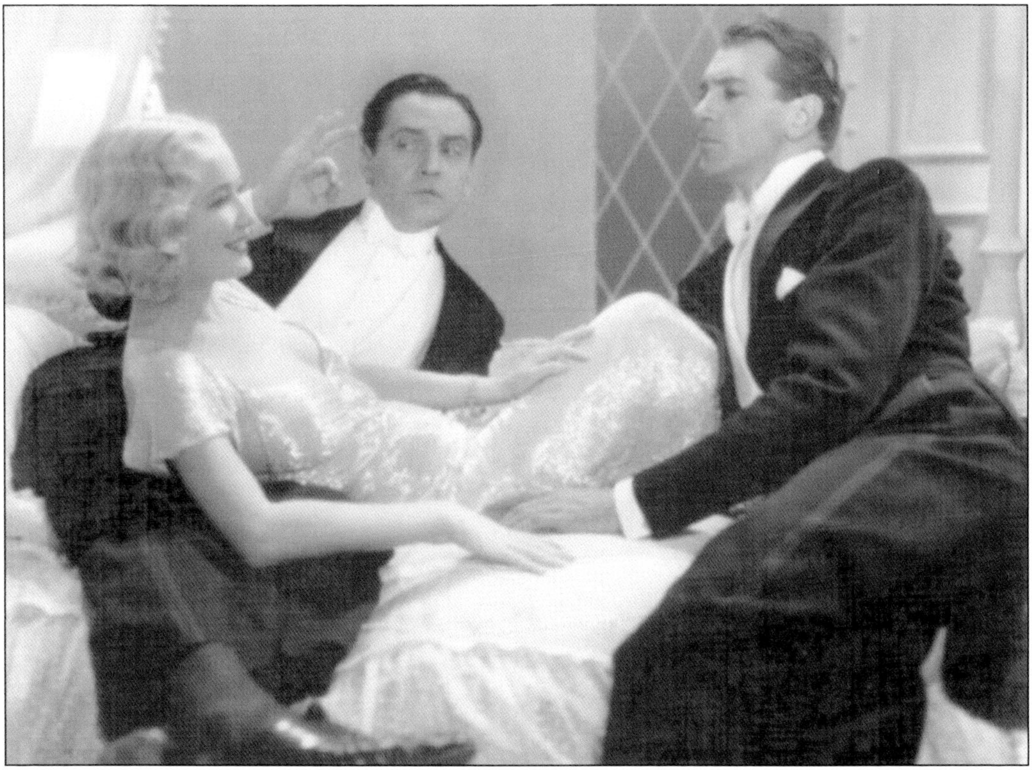

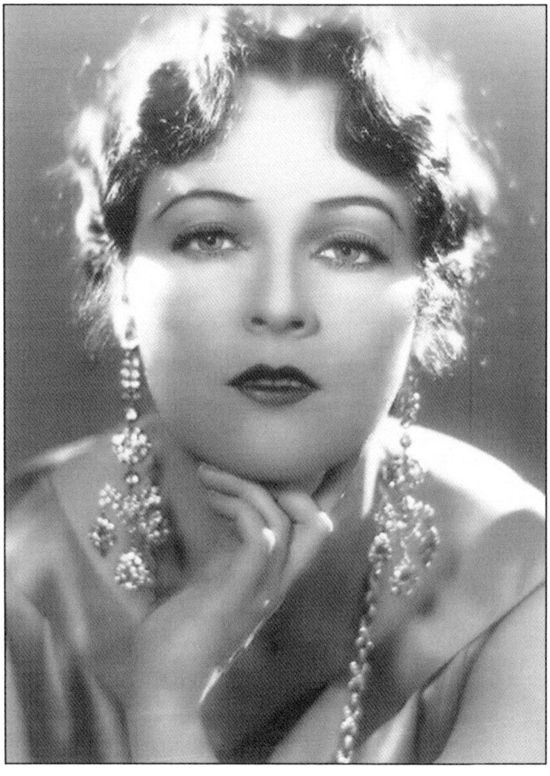

Miriam Hopkins (1902–1972) appears with Fredric March (center) and Gary Cooper in the 1933 film *Design for Living.* After 10 successful years on the stage, she joined Paramount in 1930 and became one of Hollywood's top-ranking stars. The *Brooklyn Daily Eagle* of November 15, 1931, said of Hopkins: "Seated in her mother's apartment in Kew Gardens at 83-46 118th Street she talked of her impressions of Hollywood, her love of New York and its theaters and concerts."

Jacqueline Logan (1901–1983) lived in Kew Gardens when Florenz Ziegfeld hired her as a dancer. After winning a screen test, she became a star of silent films, appearing in Cecil B. DeMille's *King of Kings* in the role of Mary Magdalene. She was on board William Randolph Hearst's yacht with such guests as Charlie Chaplin and Marion Davies in 1924 when film director Thomas Ince died under mysterious circumstances.

Will Rogers (1879–1935) was an American cowboy, vaudeville performer, humorist, social commentator, and motion-picture actor. He traveled around the world three times, acted in 71 movies, wrote more than 4,000 nationally syndicated newspaper columns, and became a world-famous personality for his earthy anecdotes and folksy style. By the mid-1930s, Rogers was adored by the American people. He died in 1935 in an airplane crash in Alaska.

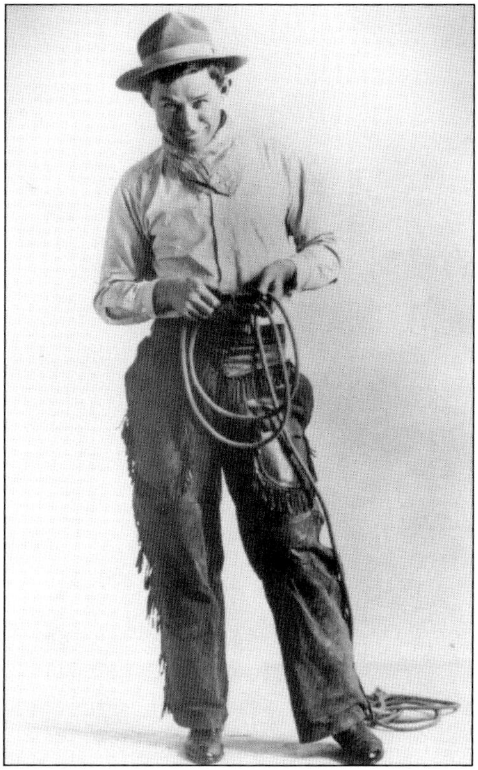

Will Rogers lived in Kew Gardens from 1917 to 1919 at this house. During his time there, the address was listed as 124 Onslow Place, Kew Gardens, Long Island, New York. The address was later changed to 124 Eighty-second Avenue, Kew Gardens, New York.

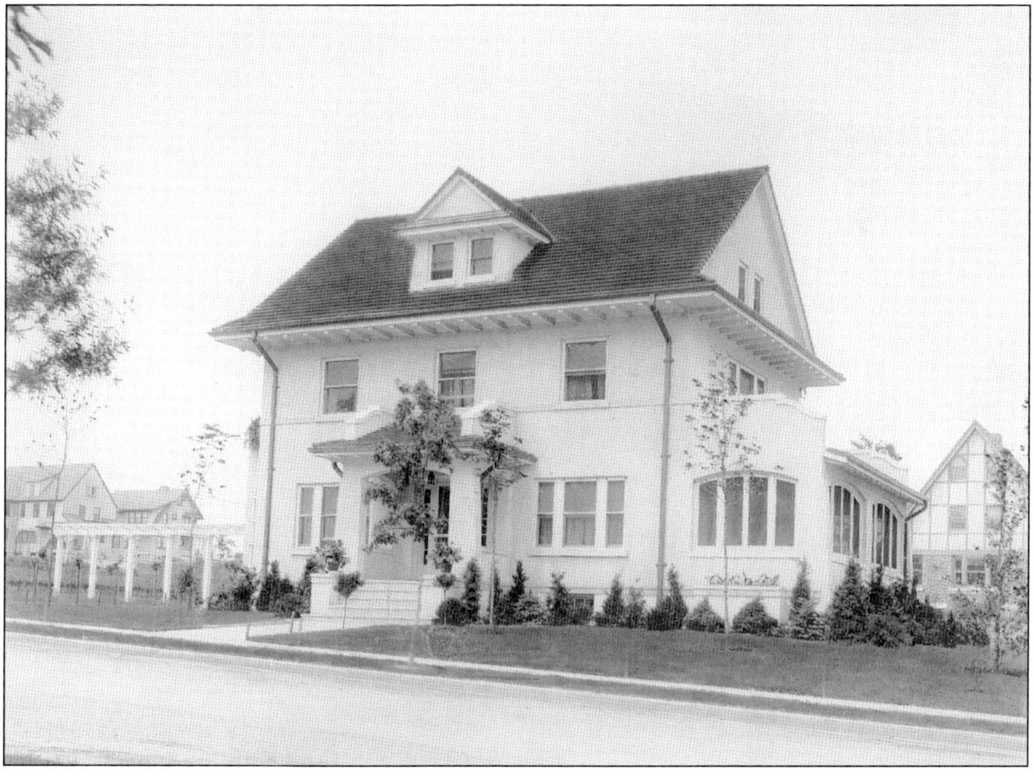

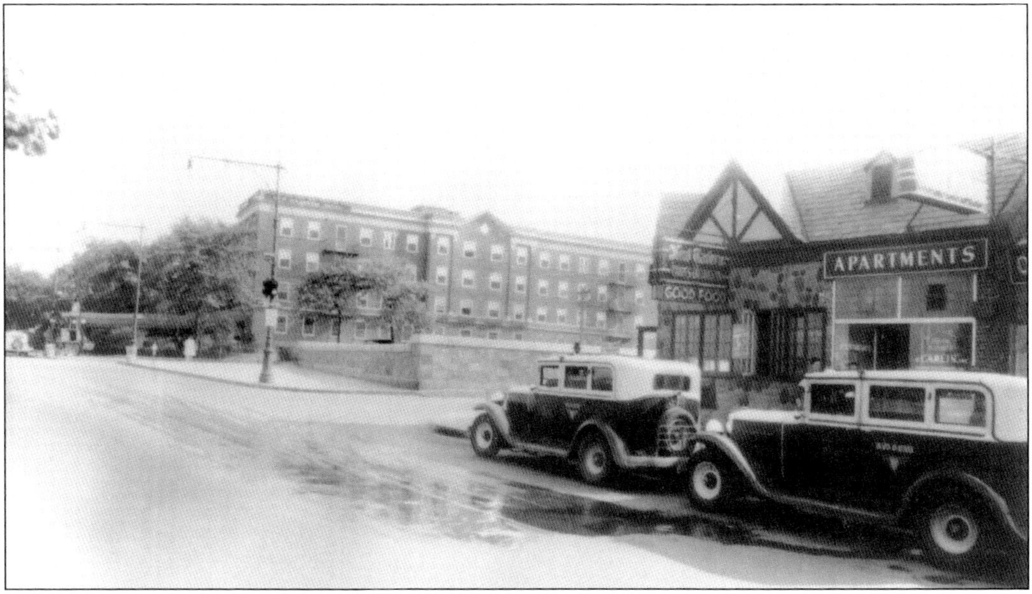

Gene Fowler (1890–1960) was a journalist, author, and dramatist. He interviewed Wild West Show promoter Buffalo Bill. Fowler worked for the *New York Daily Mirror* and King Features. He wrote a dozen screenplays as well as books, including biographies and memoirs. He was friends with W.C. Fields, whose hostility toward children was legendary. Fields claimed that Fowler's sons were the only children he could stand. This is a view from Queens Boulevard, with the Kew Gardens Inn in the distance.

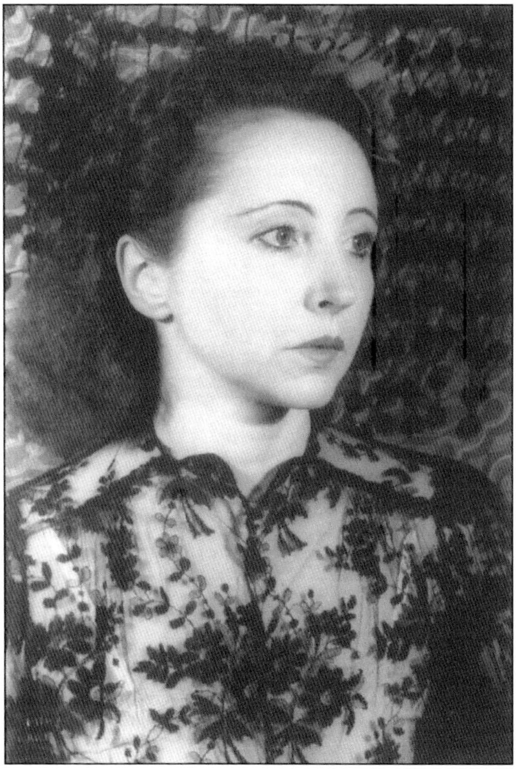

The author Anaïs Nin (1903–1977) published journals, novels, critical studies, essays, and short stories. Her August 13, 1914, diary entry expresses her feelings about her home: "Description of heaven on earth. Green lawns strewn with flowers, tiny houses, little white roads neatly designed, a few trees, bright sunshine, small gardens full of flowers. . . . I have to say hurrah for Kew Gardens . . . hurrah for the God who has sent us to this earthly paradise."

"Lefty" Gomez (1908–1989) was a professional baseball player. A left-handed pitcher, Gomez played in Major League Baseball for the New York Yankees (1930–1942) and for the Washington Senators (1943). Gomez, a seven-time all-star and a five-time World Series champion with the Yankees, was elected to the National Baseball Hall of Fame in 1972. He lived on Metropolitan Avenue and 122nd Street.

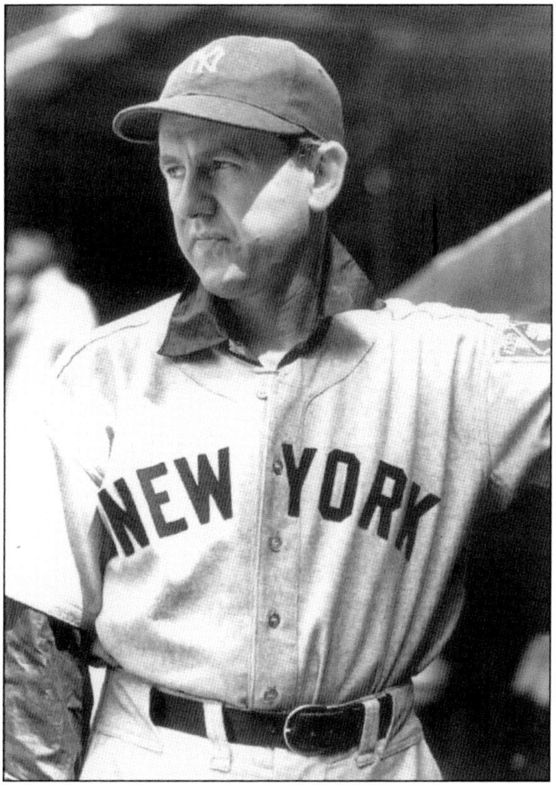

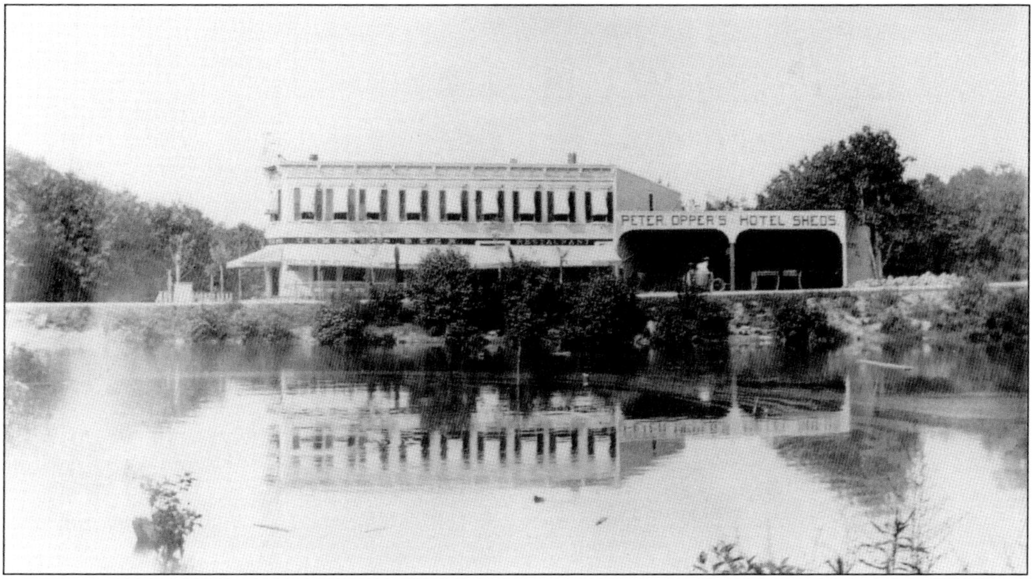

This 1897 photograph shows Peter Opper's Road House, on Eighty-second Avenue between Kew Gardens Road and Queens Boulevard. In front is Muller's Goldfish Pond, drained after 1932, when two young boys drowned. This triangular section, which bordered Maple Grove Cemetery, was part of the Timothy Jackson farm. It was purchased by August Muller, who turned it into Maple Hill Park. The site had a number of saloons, a beer garden, and picnic grounds, and it is now part of Kew Gardens.

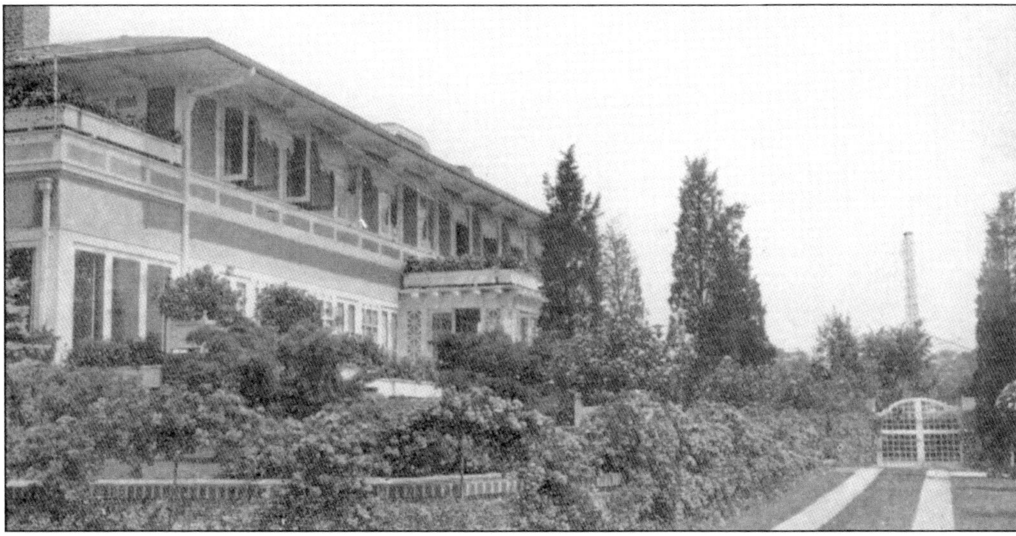

Joseph Fleischman (1863–1938), one of the leading florists in the world, built this mansion at 78 Beverly Road. At the age of 15, he rose at 3:00 a.m., picked lilies growing in a pond near his home, and peddled them on the sidewalks of New York. He became a millionaire florist with shops in New York, Chicago, and Washington. He went on to build the Hotel Le Marquis on Thirty-first Street in 1903.

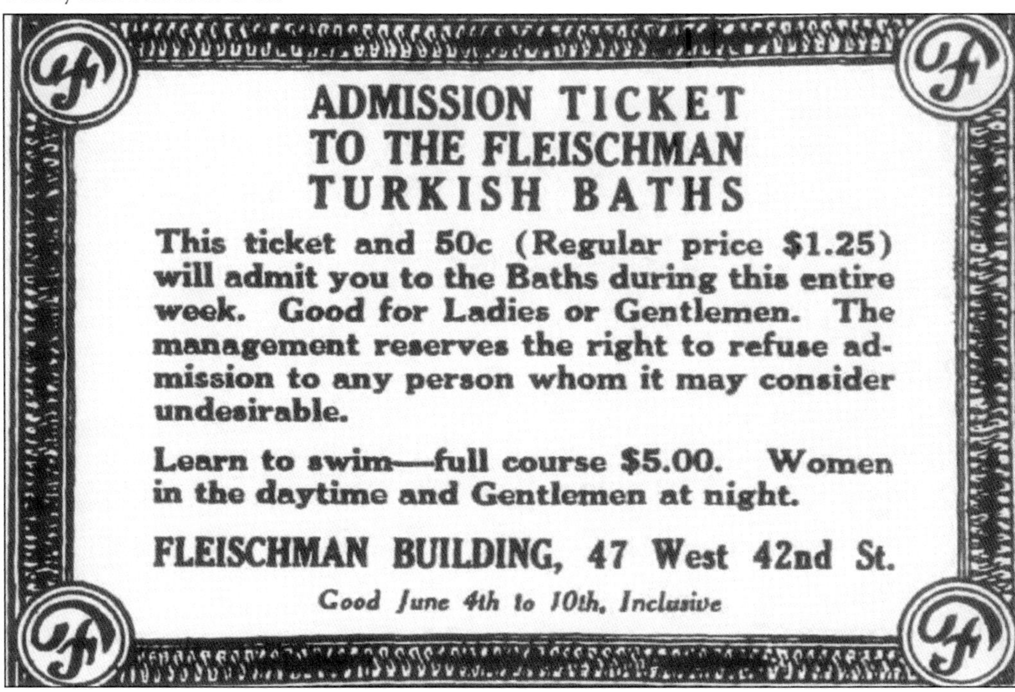

In 1907, Joseph Fleischman opened an elaborate Turkish bath called Fleischman Baths, located in the top three floors of the Bryant Park Building on Sixth Avenue in Manhattan. The facility contained a porcelain-lined swimming pool, dormitories, glass-domed solarium with tropical gardens, art marbles, fountains, live peacocks, and a lavish restaurant and bar. In 1938, he died at his mansion, which was torn down the following year. The Beverly House apartments stand on the site today.

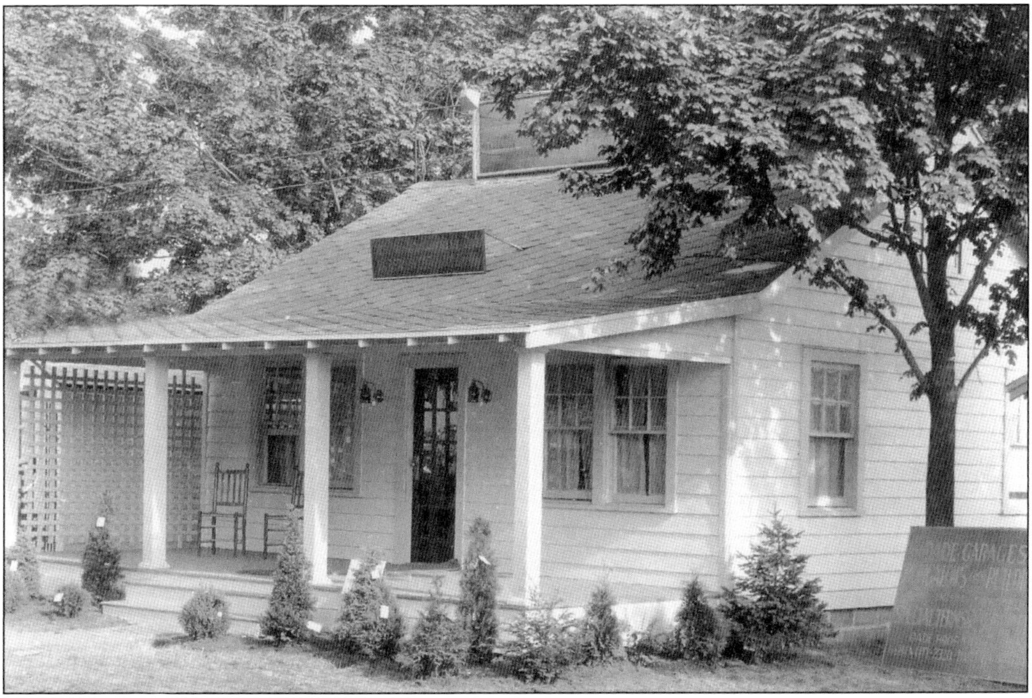

The Kew Forest Coach Company waiting room was built on a small, triangle-shaped traffic island on Queens Boulevard between Kew Gardens and Eightieth Roads. The coach company leased the property in 1928 to build a waiting room for its passengers. The wooden structure was surrounded by shrubbery and had wicker chairs for the waiting passengers. The porch facade entrance faced the Kew Gardens Inn. (Courtesy Ron Marzlock.)

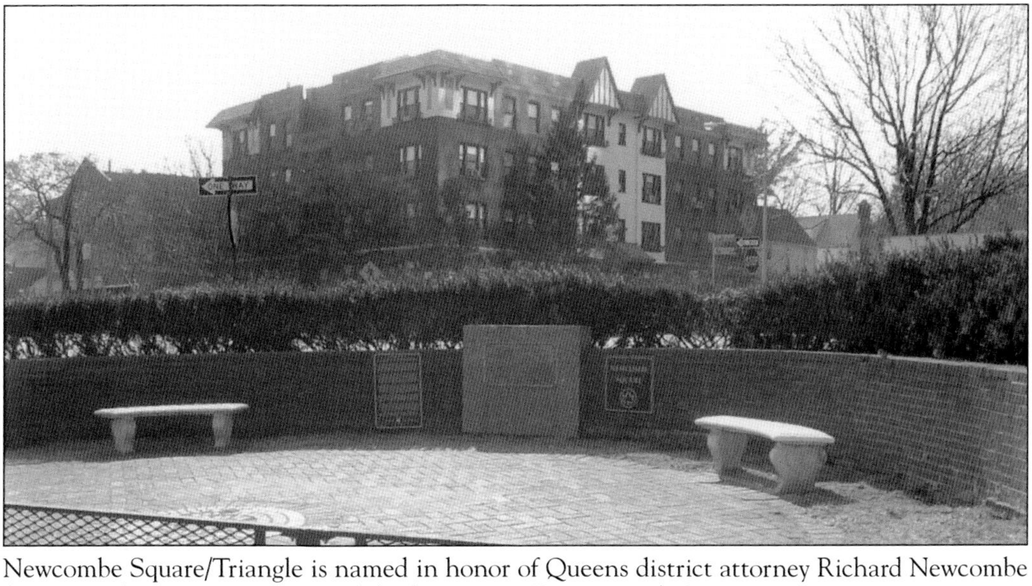

Newcombe Square/Triangle is named in honor of Queens district attorney Richard Newcombe (1880–1930). It occupies the site of the former Kew Forest Coach Company waiting room structure. Newcombe prosecuted some of the most famous cases of the 1920s. He was the prosecuting attorney for the Snyder-Gray murder trial. He also made the notable decision not to prosecute millionaire Edward Browning during the 1926 scandal.

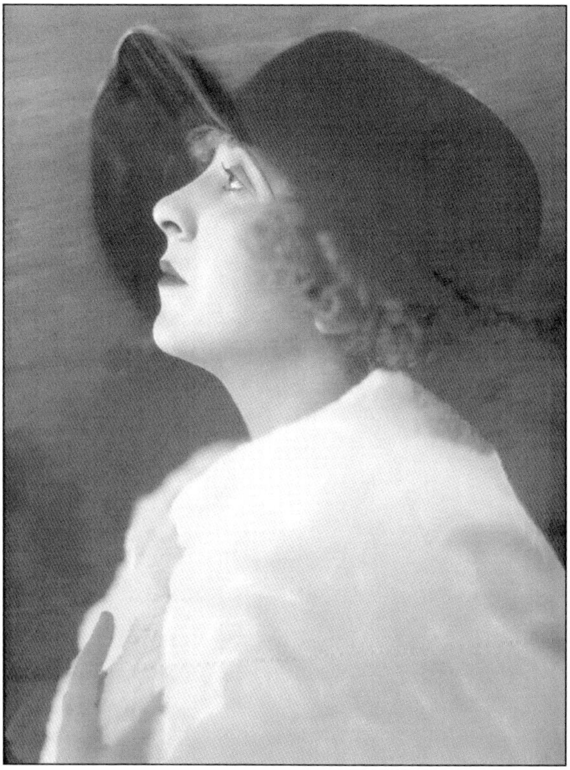

Vaudeville star Nan Halperin (1898–1963) lived in Kew Gardens. Early in her career, she toured throughout the United States, performing with stock companies. Her first appearance on the Broadway stage was in 1914, and by 1915, she was a headliner at New York's legendary Palace Theater. In 1916, she became the first performer to secure a three-year contract with the booking agency of B.F. Keith and E.F. Albee.

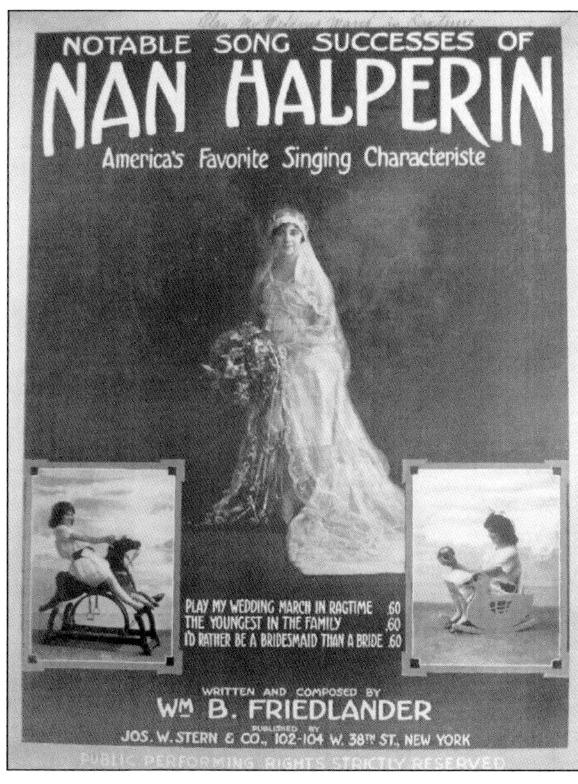

Halperin's most famous musical pieces were school cycles first performed in 1916. She depicted five stages of girlhood, her character growing before the eyes of her audience, from a young child to a mischievous teen, a comical bridesmaid, a bride, and a divorcée. She continued her career in films in the 1930s and retired in 1934. Her husband, William Friedlander, a composer, wrote many of the songs for her acts.

The actor Dick Van Patten was born in 1928 and raised in Kew Gardens. He worked as a model and actor, making his Broadway debut at the age of seven. Successful on the New York stage, he moved to Hollywood and enjoyed a lengthy career in film and television. He is best known for his role of Tom Bradford on the television sitcom *Eight Is Enough*. He has appeared in such films as Mel Brooks's *Robin Hood: Men in Tights* and the Academy Award winner *Charly*.

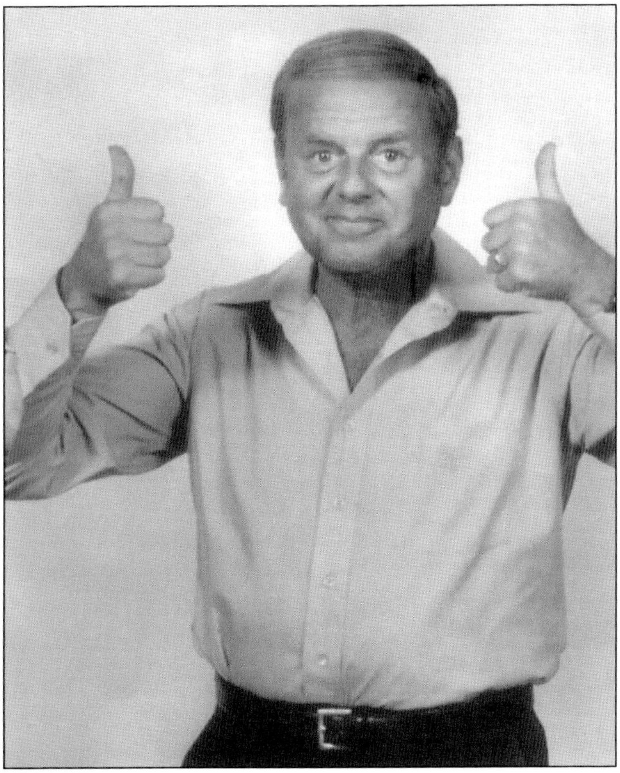

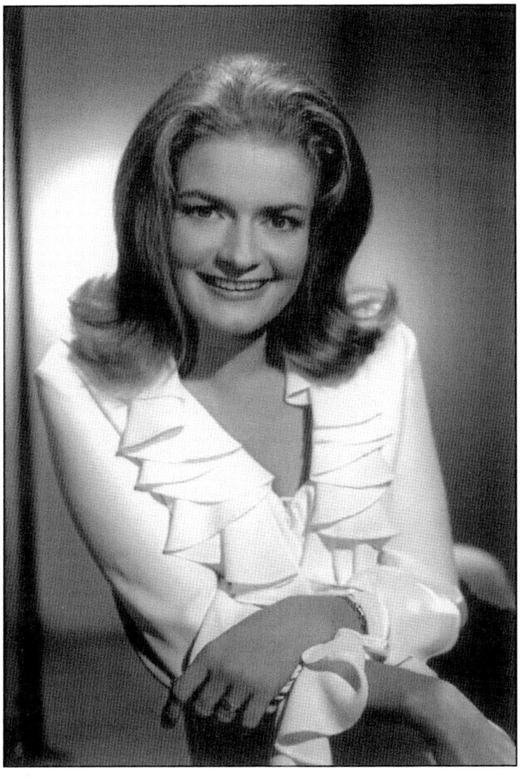

Joyce Van Patten, born in 1934, is the younger sister of Dick Van Patten. She began auditioning for modeling roles as a young child. By the age of eight, Van Patten was appearing on radio and on Broadway. She acted in a number of popular plays, including *The Desk Set* (1955) and *A Hole in the Head* (1957). She appeared in numerous television shows, including the soap drama *As the World Turns*.

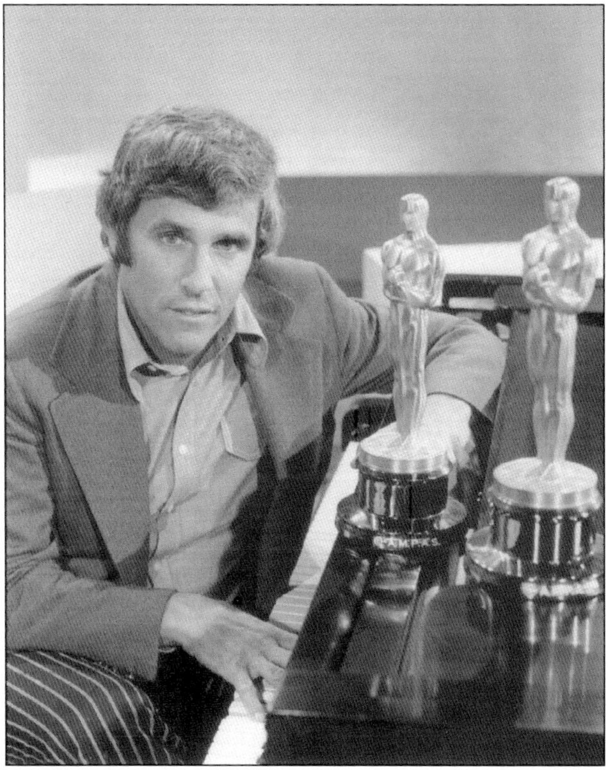

The musician and composer Burt Bacharach was born in Missouri in 1928. In 1932, he moved to Kew Gardens, where he studied cello, drums, and piano. He is known for his popular hit songs from the late 1950s through the 1980s, many with lyrics by Hal David. He wrote hits for Dionne Warwick, Dusty Springfield, Bobbie Gentry, Jackie DeShannon, Tom Jones, Herb Alpert, The Carpenters, B.J. Thomas, and others. Bacharach has written 73 Top 40 hits.

Jerry Springer is a television presenter, news anchor, actor, and musician. He was born in England in 1944 and moved to Kew Gardens. He lived at the Roger Williams Apartment and attended P.S. 99. He is best known as the host of a tabloid talk show, *The Jerry Springer Show*, which debuted in 1991.

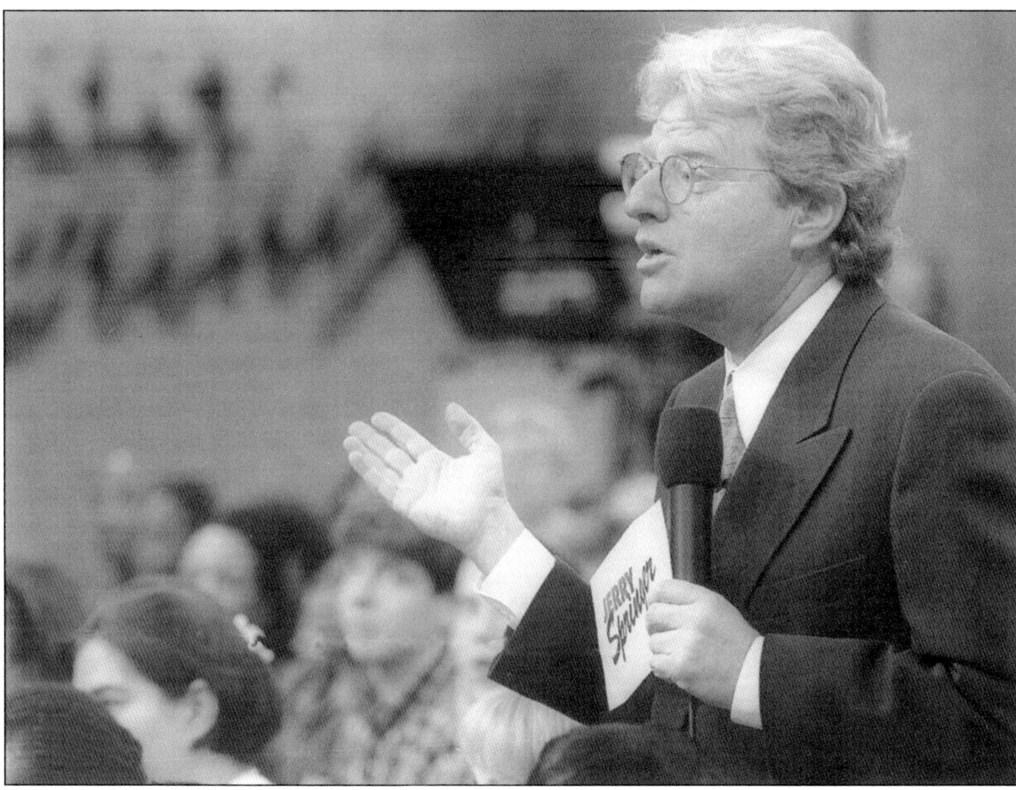

Rodney Dangerfield (1921–2004) was a comedian and actor known for the catchphrase, "I don't get no respect!" At the age of 10, his family moved to an apartment above the present-day Austin's Ale House in Kew Gardens. In the 1960s, he created the luckless, neurotic character that was to make him famous. He is also remembered for his 1980s films, especially *Easy Money*, *Caddyshack*, and *Back to School*.

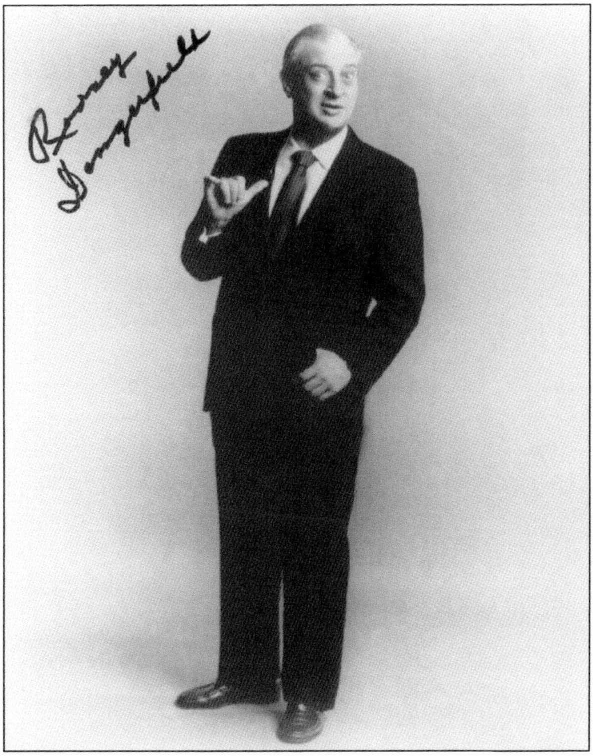

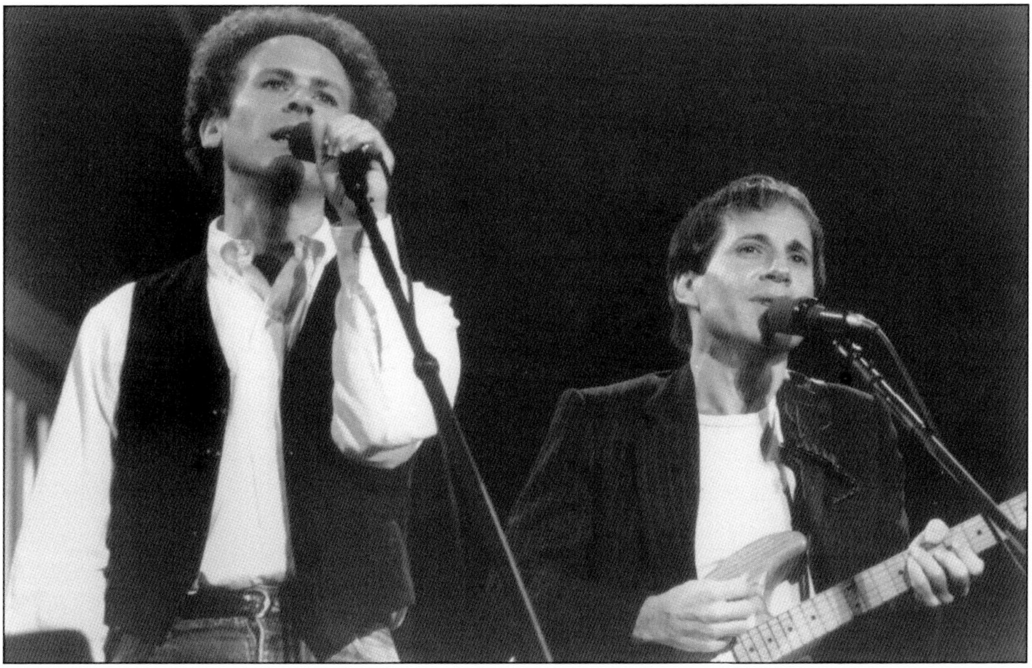

Art Garfunkel (left), half of the music duo Simon & Garfunkel, was born at the Kew Gardens Hospital in 1941. He and Paul Simon, childhood friends, grew up in Kew Gardens Hills and attended Forest Hills High School. They rose to fame in the 1960s. One of their first hit songs was "The Sound of Silence." Their music was featured in the 1967 landmark film *The Graduate*.

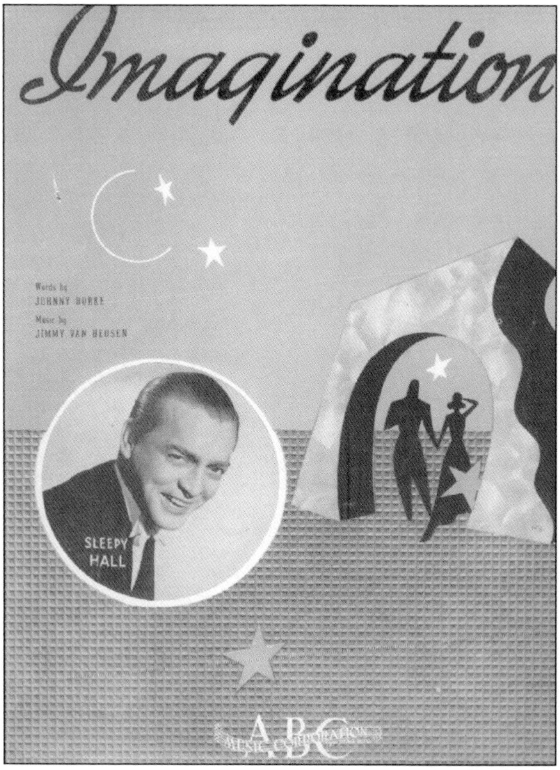

Charles "Chick" Bullock (1898–1981) was a popular American jazz and dance band vocalist, most active in the 1930s. He recorded some 500 tunes over the course of his career. He sang with musicians such as Duke Ellington, Luis Russell, Cab Calloway, Tommy Dorsey, and Jimmy Dorsey. Bullock's recordings proved so popular that he used pseudonyms for some recordings, including the name Sleepy Hall. He performed many times at the Homestead Hotel.

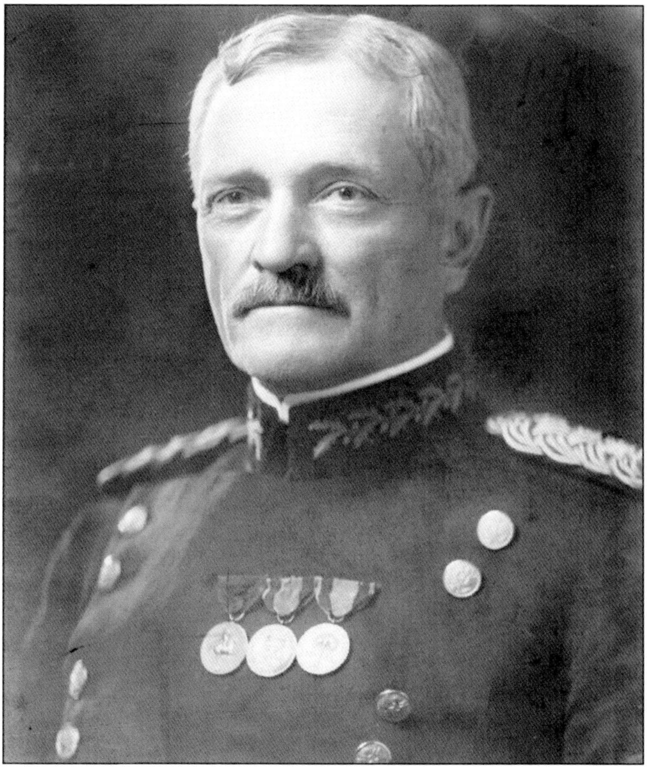

US Army general John Pershing (1860–1948) led the American Expeditionary Forces in World War I. During his lifetime, he achieved the highest rank in the Army, General of the Armies. The *Richmond Hill Record* of October 12, 1925, reported the following on his visit to the area: "General Pershing visiting in Kew Gardens, the guest of his nephew, Fred Pershing. General Pershing is frequently a visitor, and is always welcomed and honored here."

The scandal of the 1920s began at a sorority dance, where 14-year-old Frances Bell "Peaches" Heenan caught the eye of 51-year-old millionaire Edward West Browning. Their relationship drew the attention of New York City officials, which prompted Browning to marry Heenan in 1926, with her mother's consent. Their wedding portrait is shown here. They moved into the luxurious Kew Gardens Inn with her mother and occupied a number of rooms.

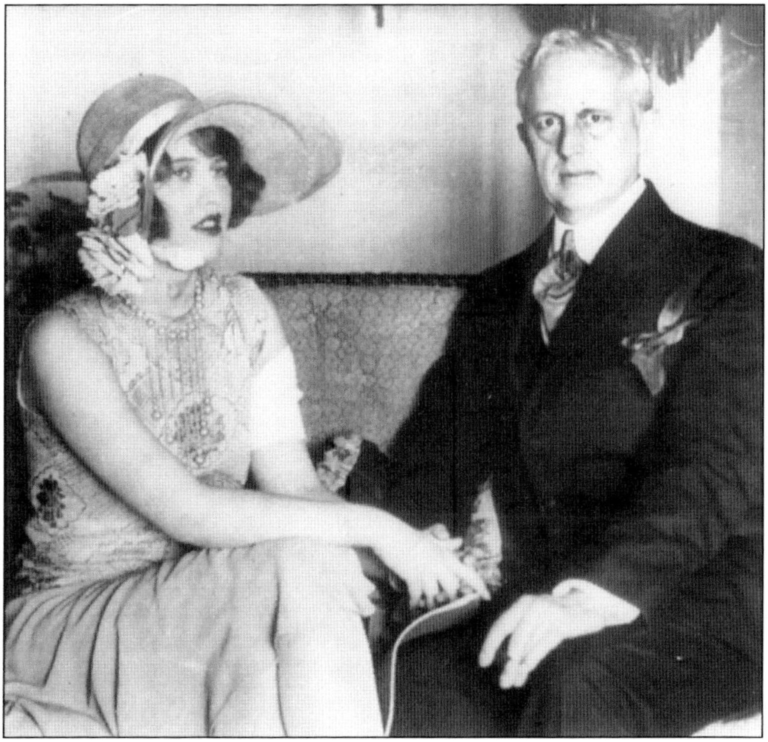

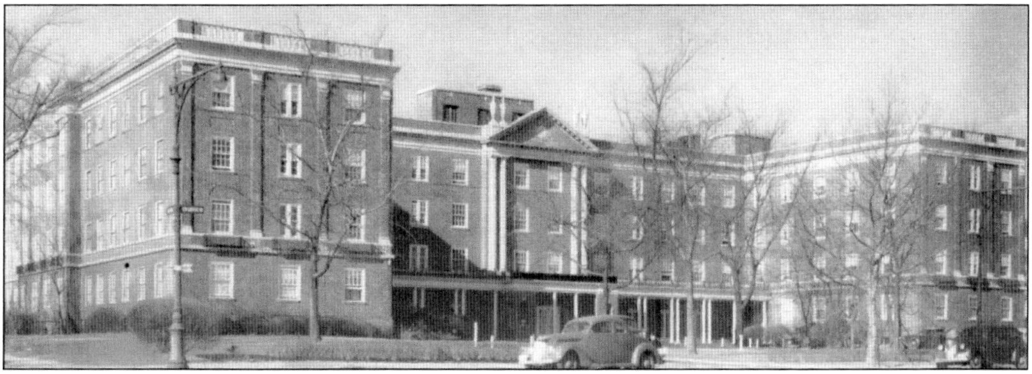

This is the Kew Gardens Inn, where the Brownings lived in harmony, while Peaches Heenan racked up $1,000 shopping bills. The marriage did not last; six months later, Browning found an empty apartment, cleared of all possessions. Browning sued Heenan for abandonment, and she countersued for mental cruelty, with pretty absurd claims. She had the public in her favor but lost the case. The judge claimed that she falsified evidence.

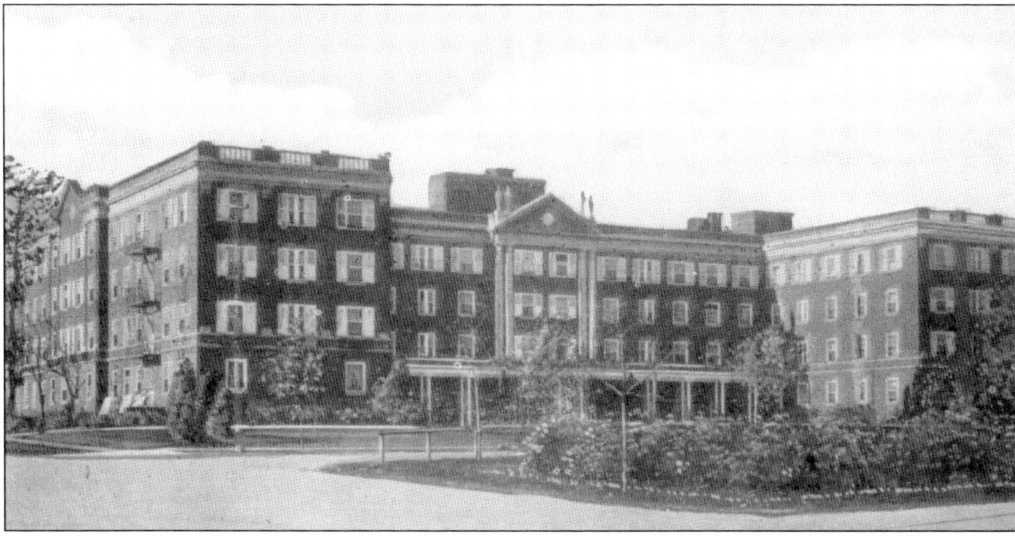

In 1927, Ruth Snyder was accused of conspiring with her lover, Judd Gray, in the murder of her husband. The trial attracted huge attention. Found guilty, they were executed by electric chair, Snyder becoming the first woman executed in New York State. A reporter secretly strapped a camera to his leg and took an infamous photograph of her execution. The jury stayed at the Kew Gardens Inn (shown here) at a cost of $1,879.

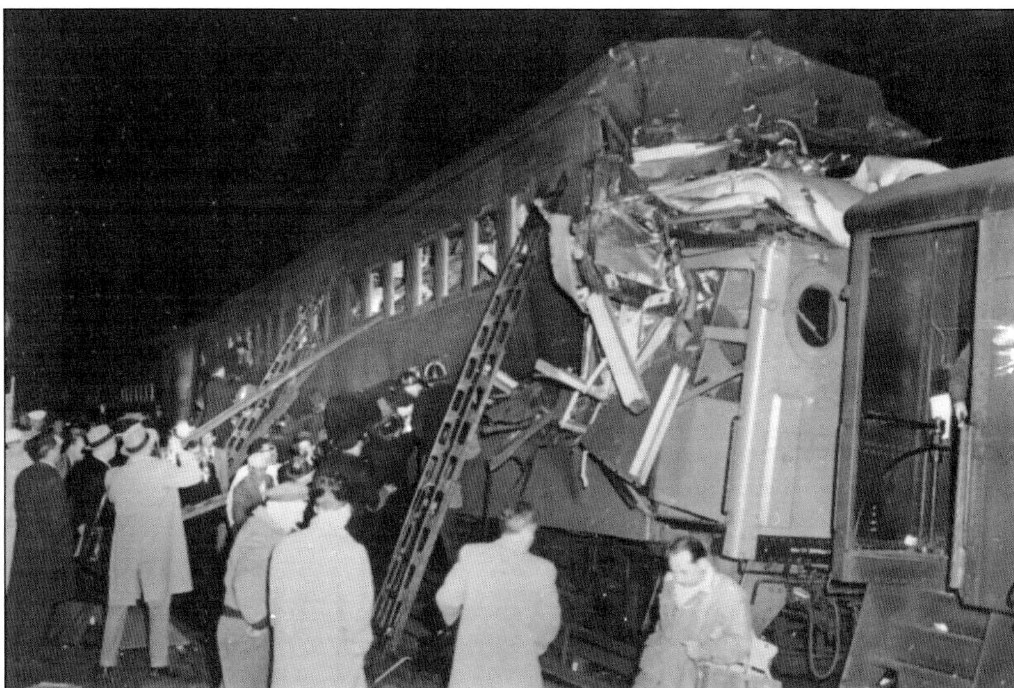

The worst train wreck in Long Island Rail Road history happened on November 22, 1950. A Hempstead train had left the Kew Gardens Station, headed to Jamaica, when it stalled. A Babylon train struck it, pushing the Hempstead train 75 feet, lifting its last car 15 feet into the air, and splitting it lengthwise. The first car of the Babylon train was sheared off to the floor and demolished. The collision left 78 dead and 363 injured.

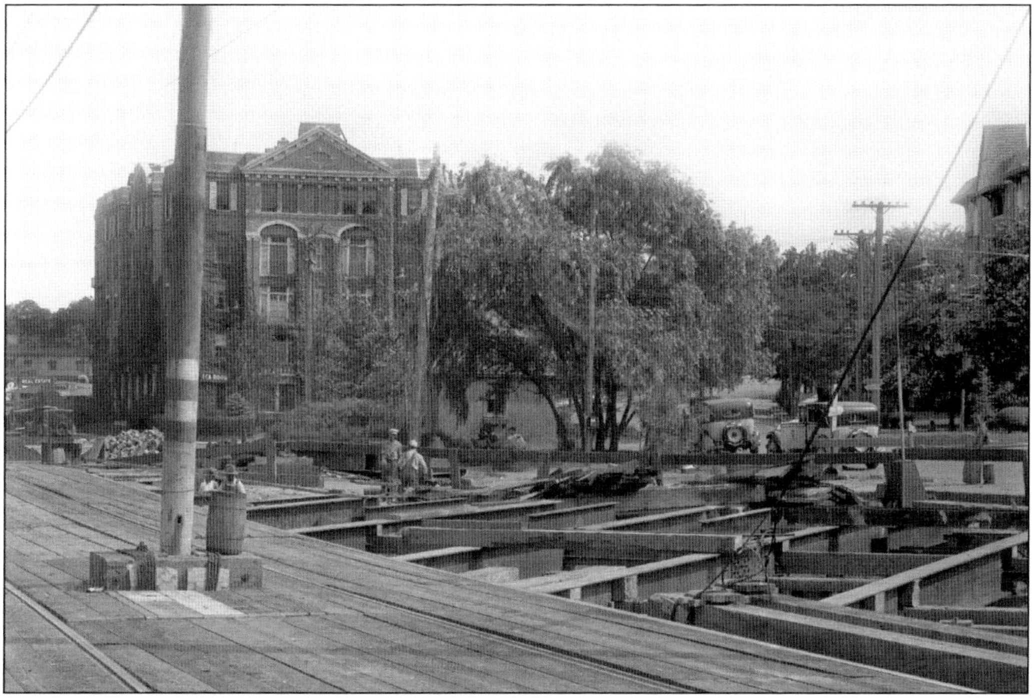

The Independent Subway (IND), constructed under Queens Boulevard, was a major project in the 1930s. In this view of the fork in the road, Kew Bolmer Apartment is at center, Kew Gardens Road is at right, and Queens Boulevard is on the left. *Kew-Forest Life* described the construction on March 29, 1930: "At present they are using pile drivers to drive steel beams along each side of the excavation." The Union Turnpike–Kew Gardens Station opened on December 31, 1936. (Courtesy Ron Marzlock.)

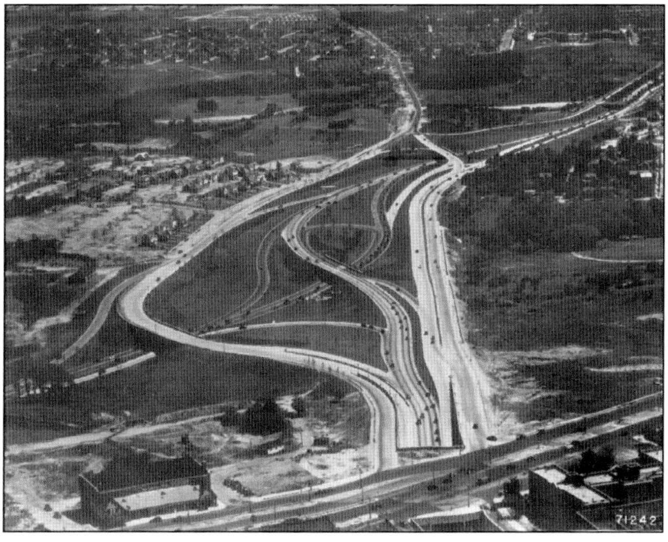

Construction of Grand Central Parkway began in 1931. The initial section of the parkway, a nine-mile-long, four-lane section between Kew Gardens and Glen Oaks, opened in 1933. Shown here is the Kew Gardens Loop at the junction for the Interborough (Jackie Robinson) Parkway in 1939. Queens Boulevard is at the bottom, with the Kew Gardens Inn at the right next to Union Turnpike and the Interborough underpass. The lone building at lower left is the Kew Garden Theater.

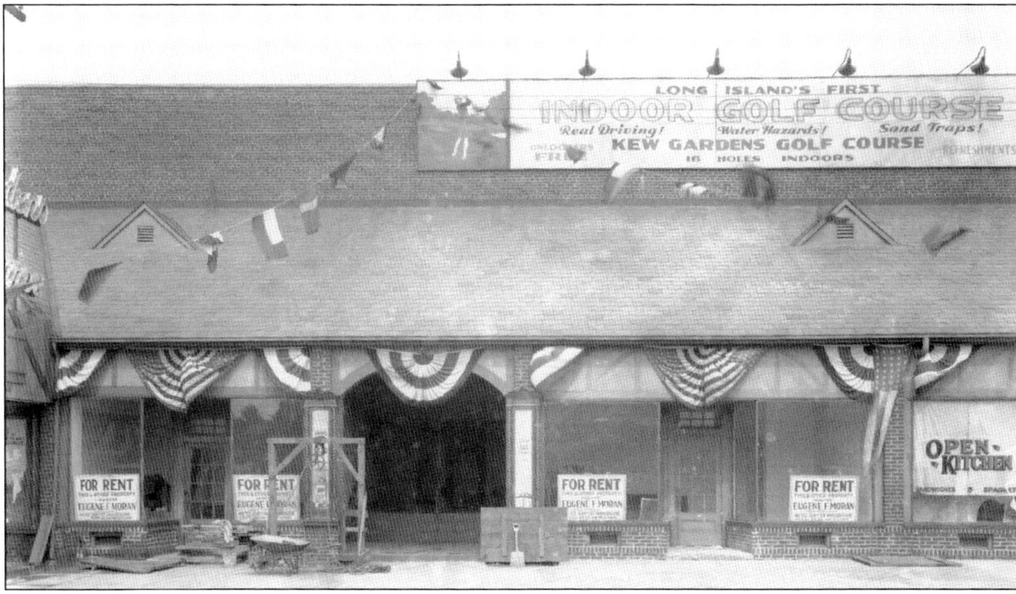

The Kew Gardens Theater, constructed in 1927, was located at the corner of Seventy-eighth Avenue and Queens Boulevard. The theater did not prosper, and it was turned into an indoor miniature golf course in 1930. The *Daily Star* said this of the new facility on August 7, 1930: "One of the outstanding attractions of the Kew Gardens course is a spectators' gallery seating more than 200 persons and affording a perfect view of all the holes." (Courtesy Ron Mazlock.)

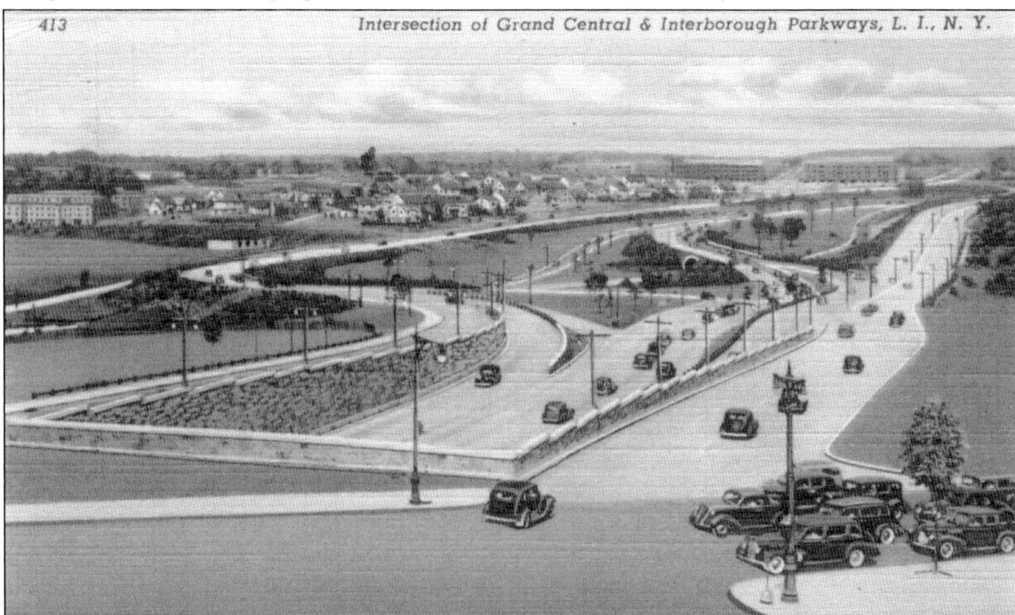

In the foreground, cars stop at an intersection on Queens Boulevard. The Grand Central and Interborough (Jackie Robinson) Parkways and the Union Turnpike pass Kew Gardens Hills in the distance. The underpass goes below Queens Boulevard in the foreground. Construction on the Interborough started in 1933. This traffic intersection became known as the "pretzel" by local residents.

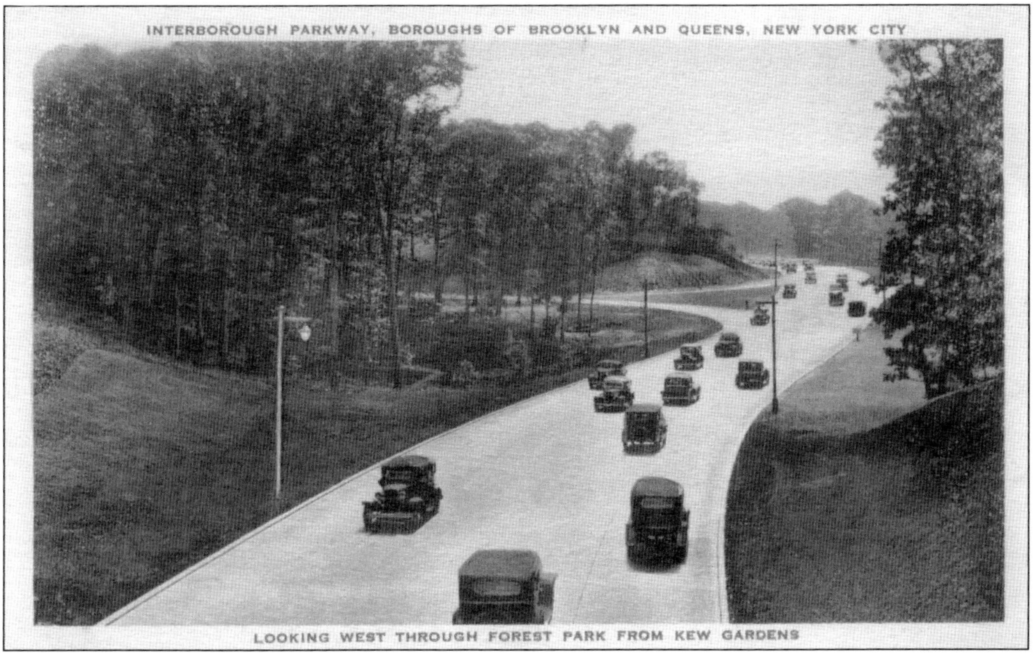

This postcard image looks west on the Interborough Parkway from Kew Gardens. The parkway's name was changed to honor Jackie Robinson in May 1997, marking the 50th anniversary of his breaking baseball's color line. In addition to playing for the Brooklyn Dodgers, Robinson owned property and lived in the area along the parkway.

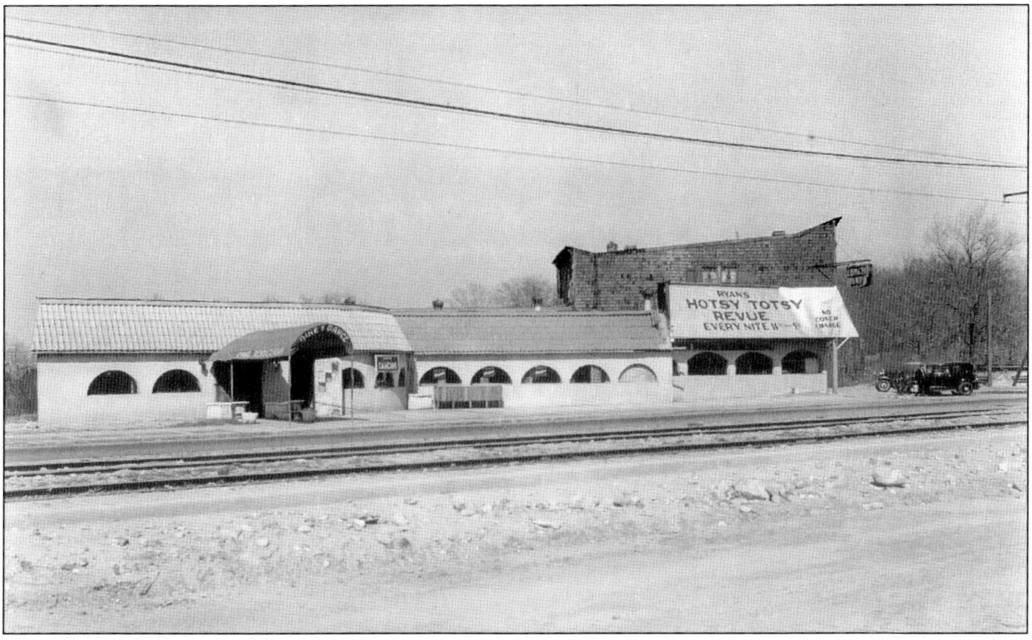

Ryan's Rendezvous was a cabaret located on Queens Boulevard at Eighty-third Avenue, near the site of the present-day criminal court. Its patrons wined, dined, and danced the night away in the years after Prohibition was repealed. In 1943, the Rendezvous was destroyed by a fire of unknown origin.

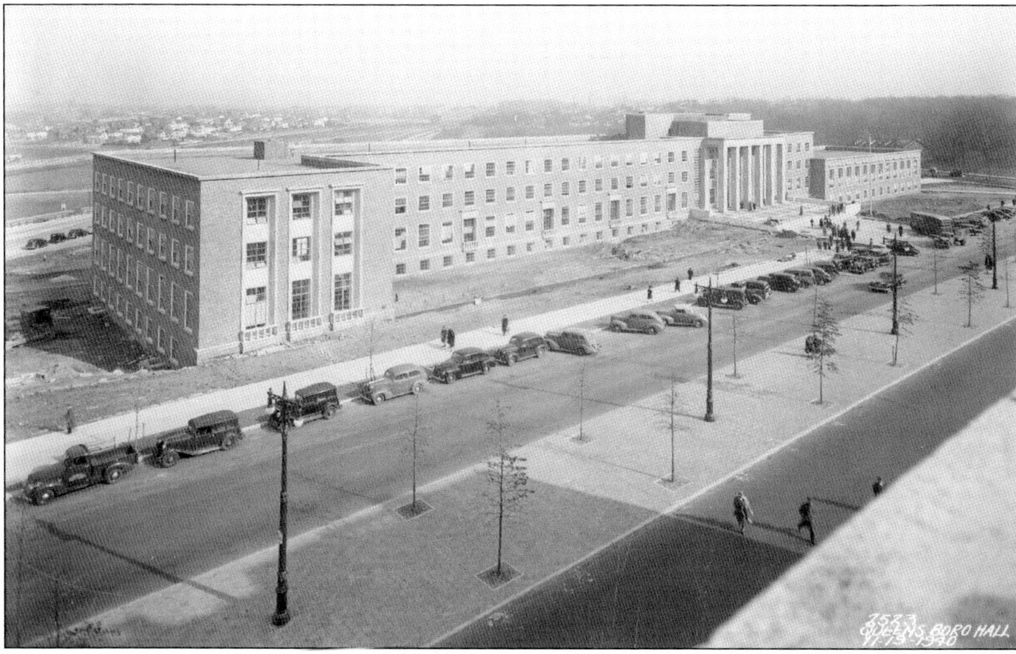

Queens Borough Hall in Kew Gardens houses the office of the Queens Borough president and other city offices. It is located on Queens Boulevard. Designed by architects William Gehron and Andrew J. Thomas in the austere Classical style, it was constructed in 1940 for $1.8 million. The red brick facade is 580 feet long and four stories high. It was opened on December 4, 1940, with Mayor Fiorello H. La Guardia officiating. (Courtesy QBPL Archives, Queens Chamber of Commerce.)

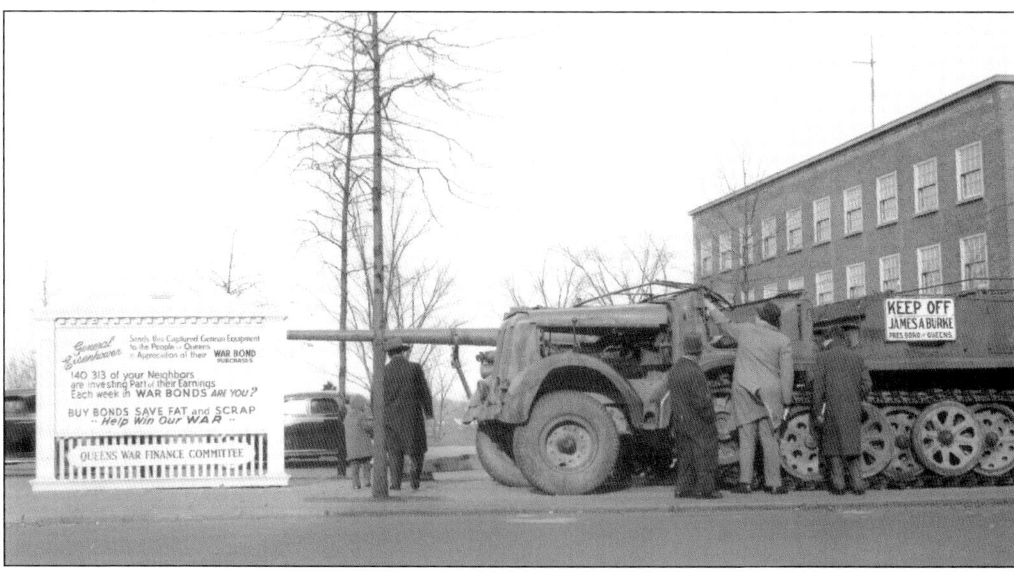

A captured World War II German vehicle is displayed at Queens Borough Hall in 1944. It was set up as a promotional prop by the Queens Finance Committee. The sign reads, "General Eisenhower sends this captured German Equipment to the people of Queens in appreciation of their War Bond purchases. 140,313 of your neighbors are investing part of their earnings each week in War Bonds are you? Buy Bonds, save fat and scrap. Help win the war."

This statue, titled *Civic Virtue*, was commissioned by the New York City Municipal Art Commission to artist Frederick Macmonnies in 1915. It was completed in the year 1919 at a cost of $60,000. The statue was carved from a single marble block by the world renowned Piccirilli Brothers. The 15-foot-tall statue, depicting a heroically posed man stepping over two serpentine women, symbolizes the conquest of virtue over vice and corruption.

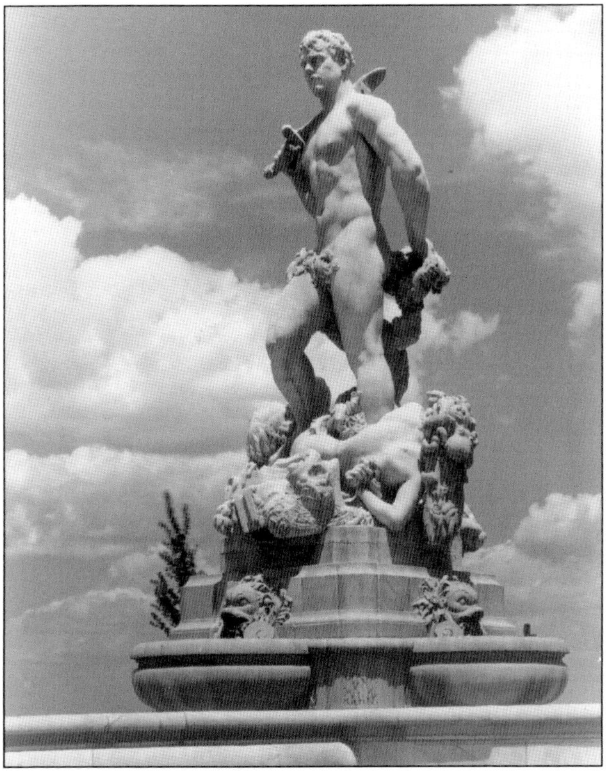

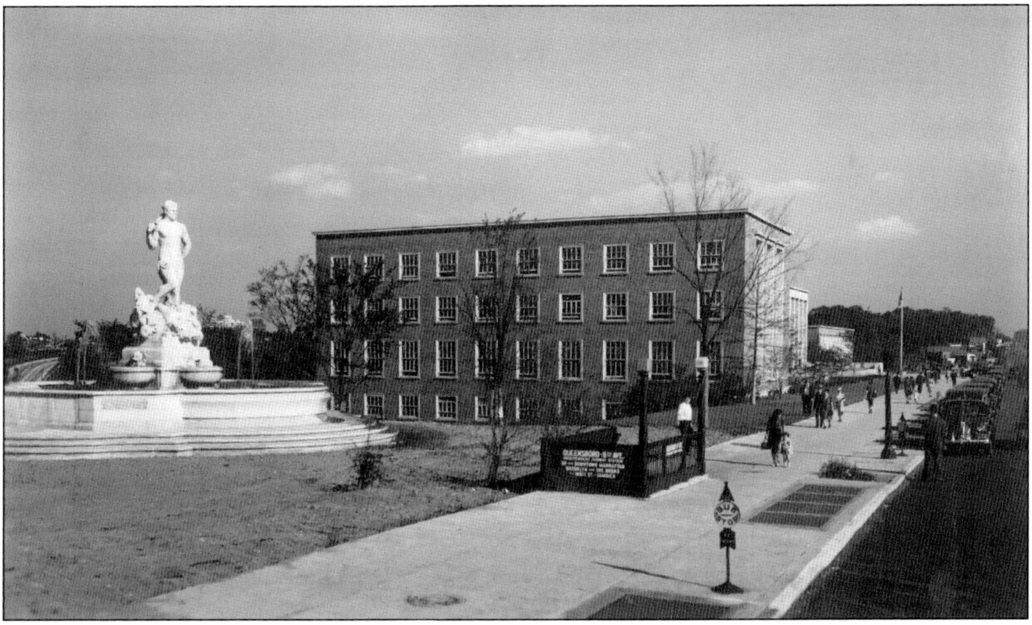

Controversy followed the statue's installation, as feminists protested the work, calling it degrading and chauvinistic. The statue stood at Manhattan City Hall Park until it was moved in 1941, given as a gift to Queens, to stand in front of its newly erected borough hall (seen here). Today, the statue stands in Green Wood Cemetery, next to the tomb of its talented creator, Frederick Macmonnies. (Courtesy QBPL Archives, Queens Chamber of Commerce.)

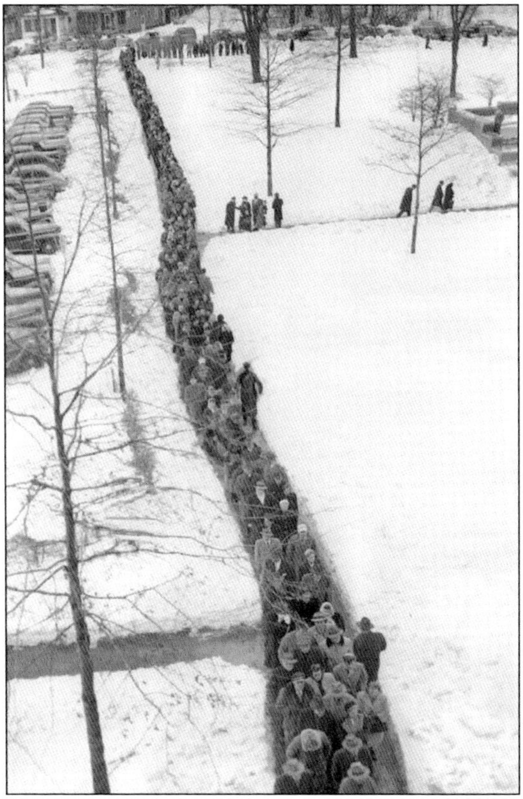

This photograph was taken on December 31, 1947, during the great December 26–27 snowstorm, when everything stopped. The Department of Taxation and Finance was once housed in Borough Hall, and these are people lined up to renew their license plates. They are picking up their 1948 New York license plates, trying to beat the December 31 deadline. Today, drivers keep the plates and just change the window sticker. (Courtesy Ron Marzlock.)

Pictured here are the 1925 Field Day Celebrations, led by the Richmond Hill High School, at the Overlook in Forest Park. Behind the building is a large grassy area called Horseshoe Fields, after its shape. The fields were used for various activities, including May pole dancing and picnics. In the winter, the field was sprayed with water to create a skating rink.

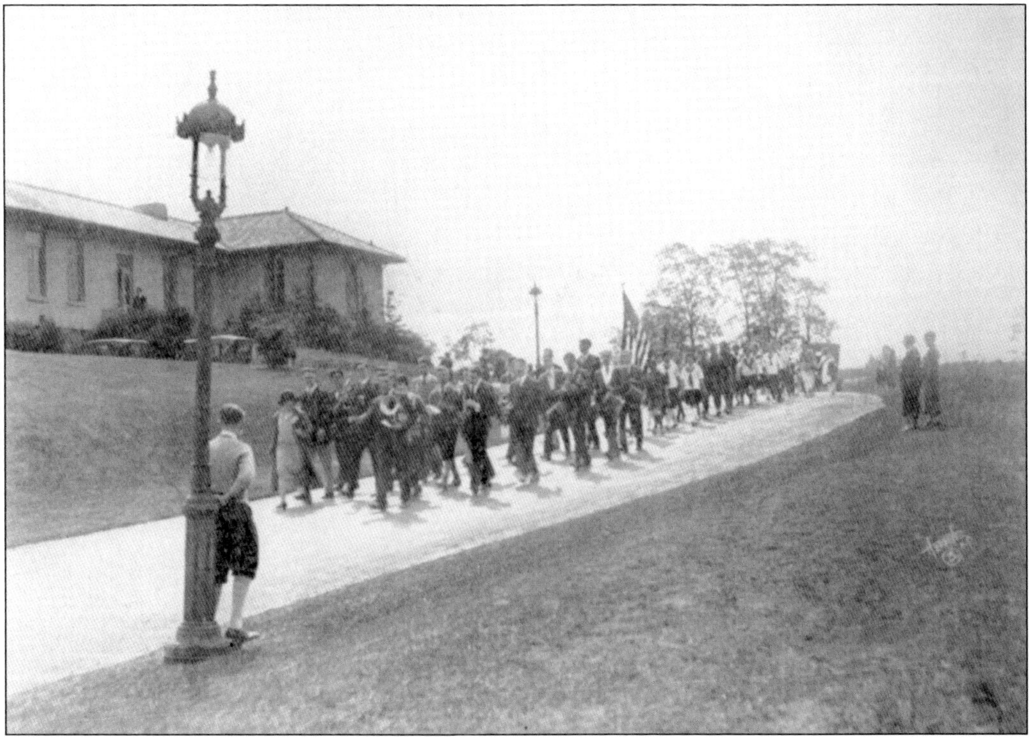

The Kew Gardens Country Club was not only a community center; it housed a police booth, a newsstand, and the neighborhood's first post office. In 1930, the Kew Gardens US Post Office (shown here) opened on Austin Street near Lefferts Boulevard. It was moved in 1957 to the other side of Lefferts Boulevard on Austin Street. (Courtesy Ron Marzlock.)

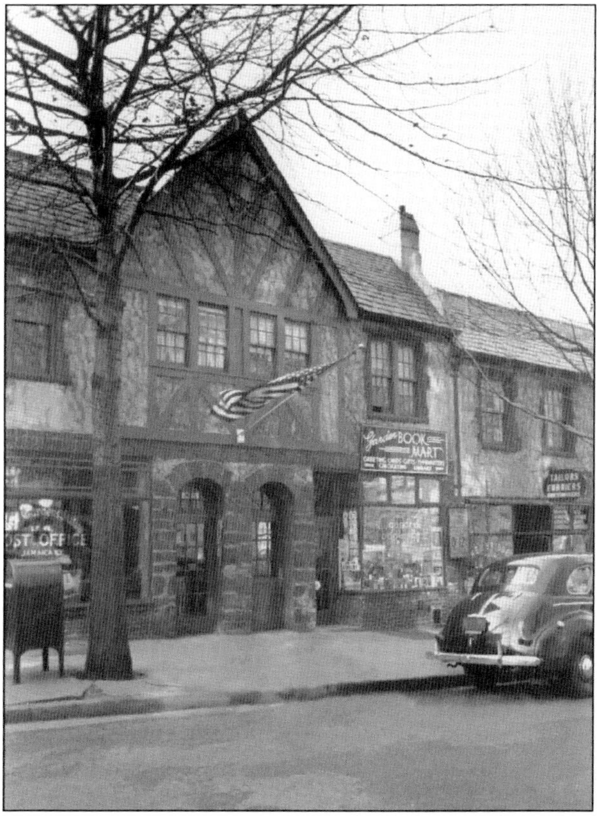

The *Brooklyn Daily Eagle* reported on September 5, 1936, "Kew Gardens will get a brand new theater on September 19 at Austin St. and Lefferts Boulevard. The Austin is operated by Edward N. Rugoff and Herman Becker. It will be operated under a single-feature policy, with diversified short subjects." After years of operation, the theater closed. New owners bought it and restored it to its Art Deco origins. It is now called the Kew Gardens Cinema.

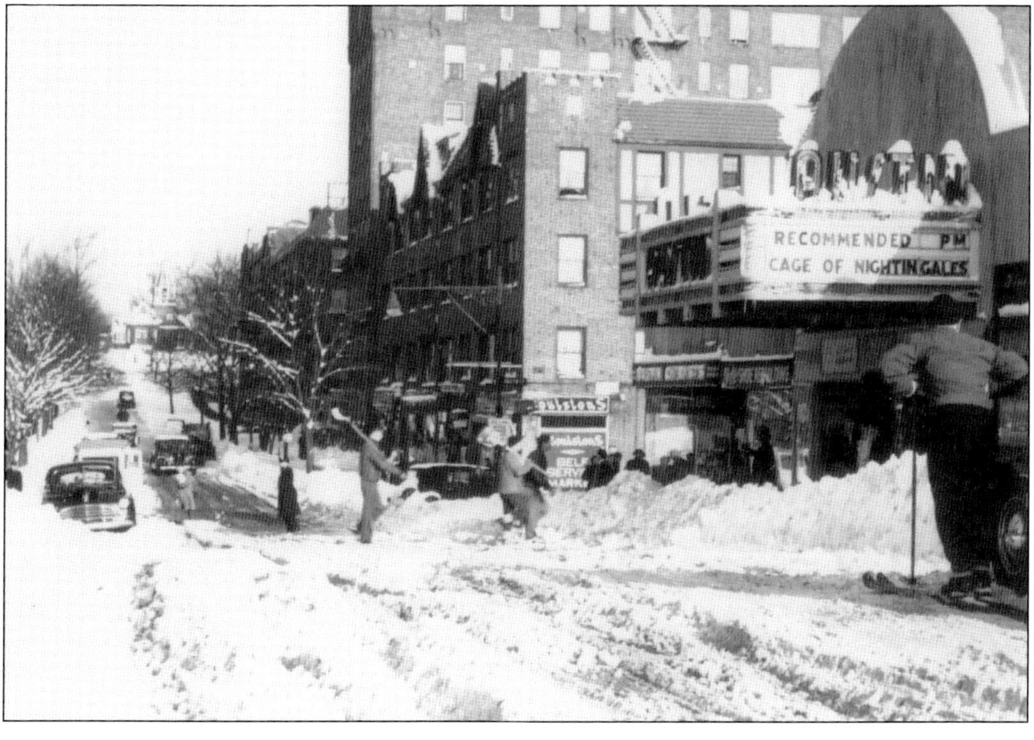

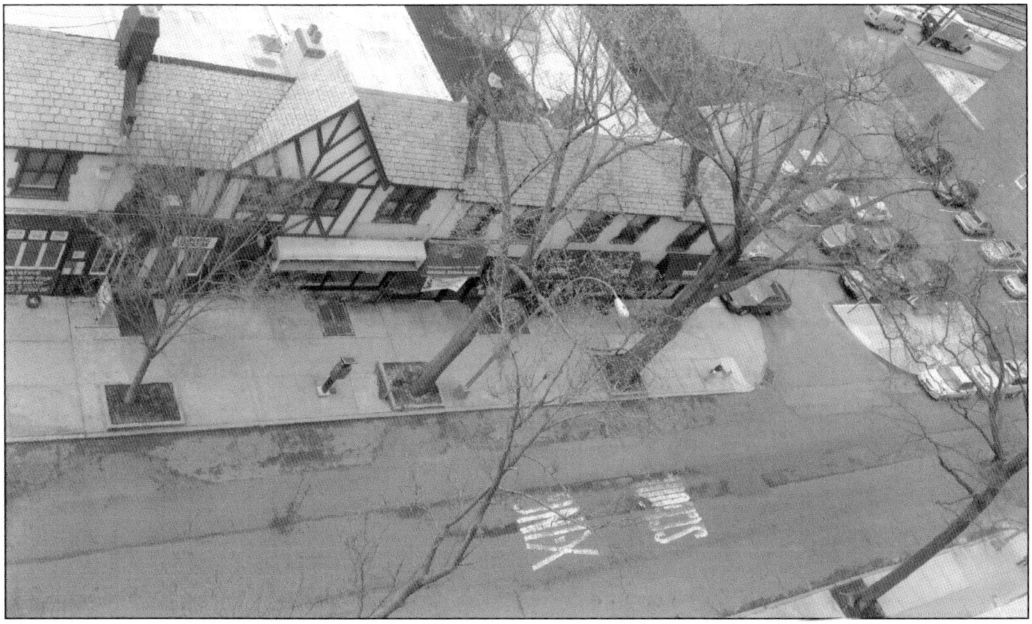

On March 13, 1964, Catherine "Kitty" Genovese was chased and stabbed by a man named Winston Moseley while walking to her apartment on Austin Street in Kew Gardens (pictured here). She screamed for help. One man in a nearby apartment building shouted at the attacker, who then fled. Wounded, Genovese tried to make her way to her apartment. She staggered to the back of the building, collapsing in a hallway a few doors from her own. (Courtesy of Howard Sydell.)

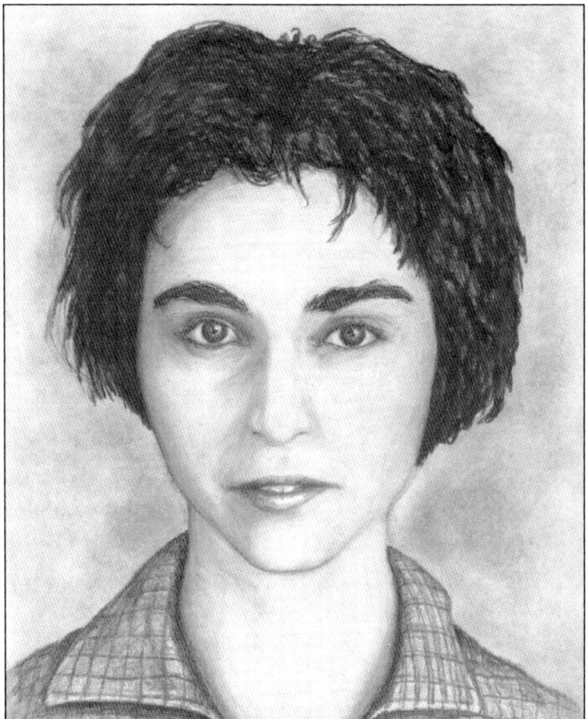

This sketch shows Kitty Genovese. Winston Moseley returned, sought out Genovese, and attacked her again, fatally. A neighbor called police after Moseley fled the second time. Newspapers reported that 38 neighbors had watched the killer stalk and stab Genovese for half an hour. In initial reports, the neighbors were described as being apathetic. Later reports questioned whether the neighbors' inaction could have been due to drowsiness and confusion rather than apathy.

Seven

Past Memories

The Place We Call Home

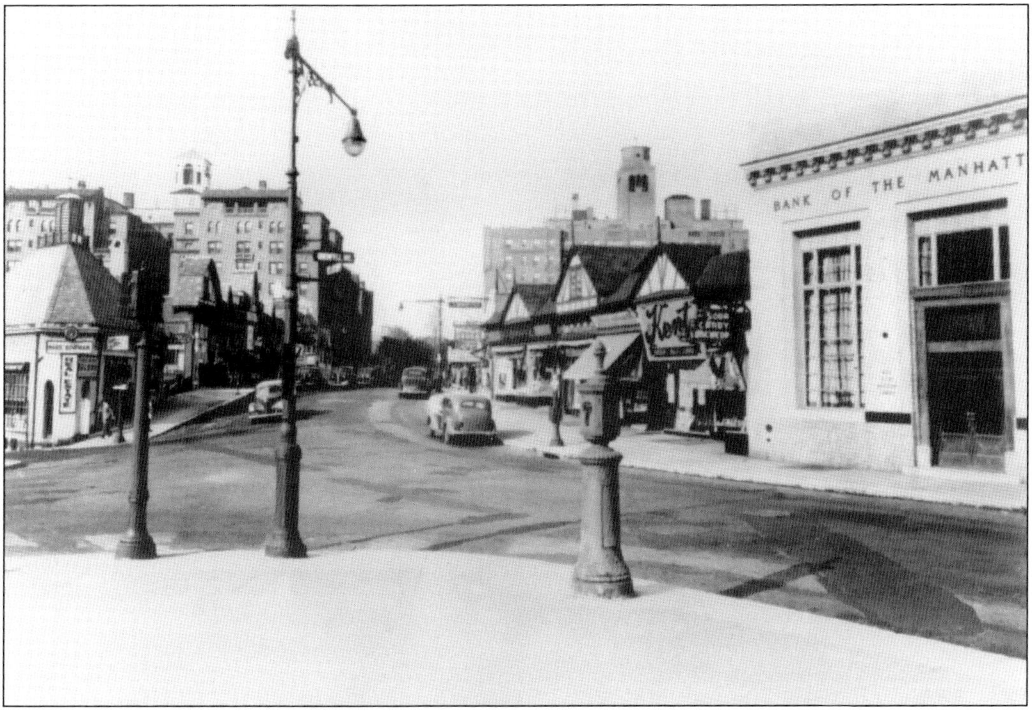

This is a 1940 view of Lefferts Boulevard Bridge crossing over the Long Island Rail Road tracks. This unique bridge, called the Ponte Vecchio (Italian for "old bridge"), refers to the famed bridge in Florence, Italy, with gold shops built on both sides of it. The Mowbrary Apartments are in the distance on the left, and the Shellball Apartments are on the right.

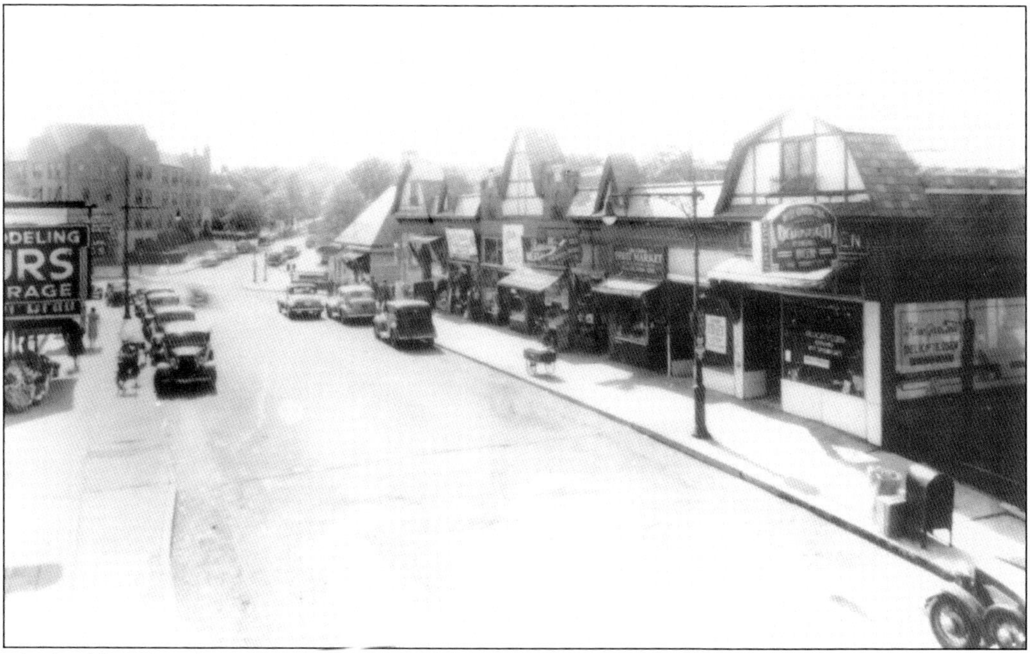

The building facade on the right has a neo-Tudor design. "The Lefferts Boulevard Bridge was built in 1910. The stores on either side have their own bridge which went up, with the stores, in the early 1930s. The stores' principal bridges actually run through the 'roofs,' not under their floors. The storefronts are then 'hung' from the bridges like a curtain hanging from a rod," according to Barry Lewis.

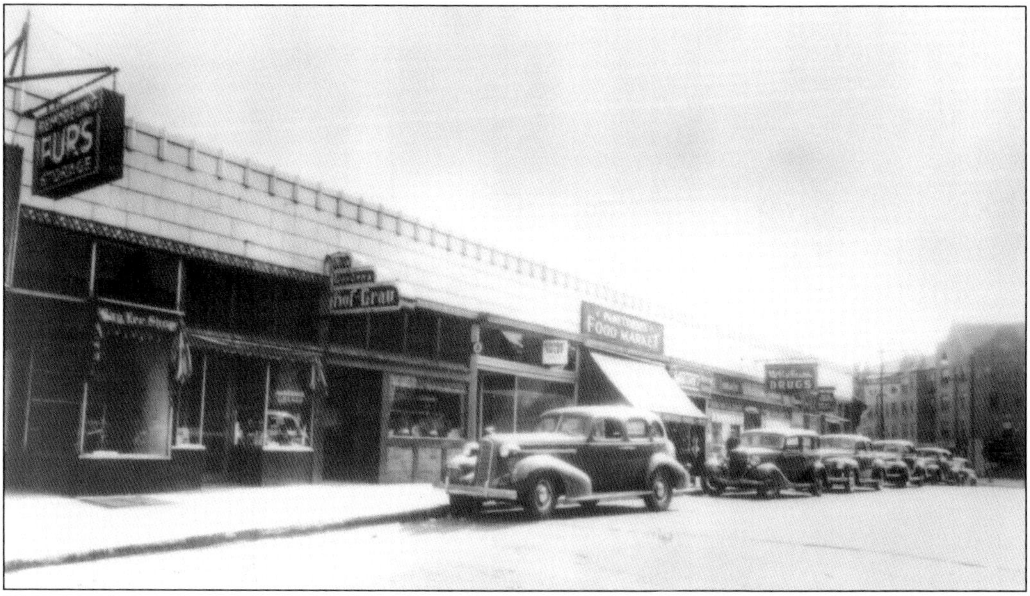

The facade on this building on the Lefferts Boulevard Bridge has an Art Deco pattern. "Kew Gardens became my home as a young bride in 1945. I moved into the Dale Gardens, a charming oasis. Old fashioned lamp lights lit the slate walks. I watched the community grow and change. Gone are the tennis courts on Austin Street, but essentially the feeling of a 'small' town community still remains," remembered Jacqueline Byron.

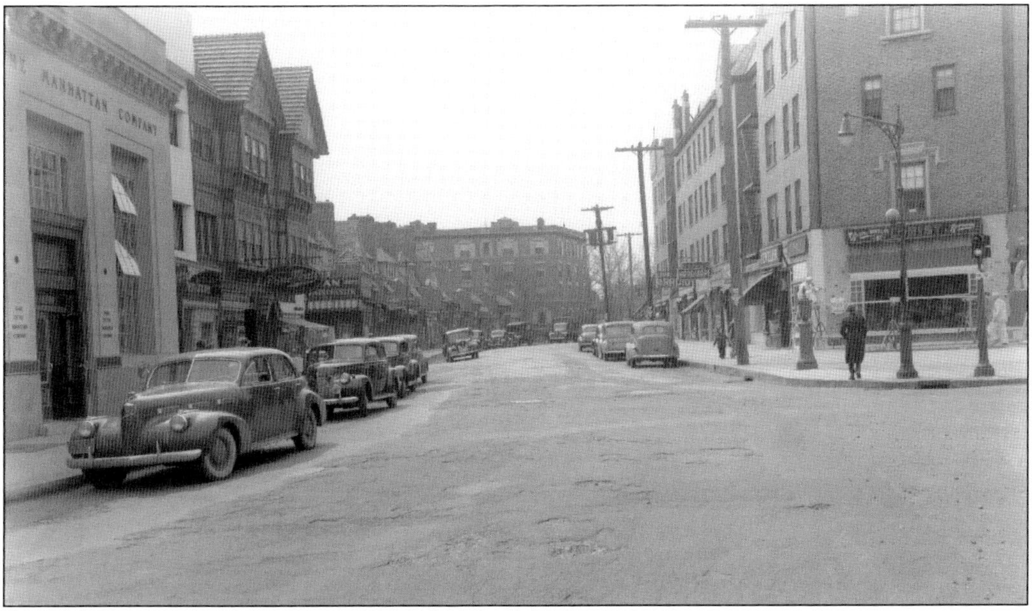

The 1912 Homestead Building (at left) on Lefferts Boulevard lost half of its structure in 1928, when it was ravaged by fire. Dawn McGee remembers "walking up Lefferts to the subway to school and passing the Homestead on the way home, with its exotic food smells. I also remember the snowstorm of '76 when Lefferts did not get plowed for a week (or so it seemed), and we rode our sleds right on Lefferts!"

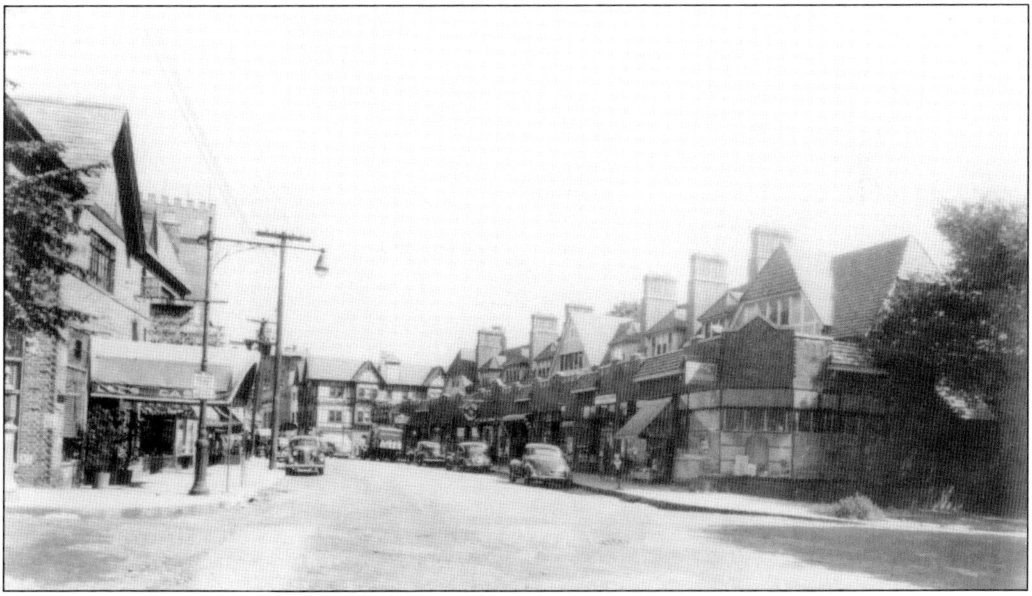

This is Lefferts Boulevard between Beverly and Cuthbert Roads. John Mihoulides recounts, "We had a wonderful time growing up in Kew Gardens. Fifty years before, we pledged to meet on New Year's Eve 1999, at Duffy's Bar. We had a bottle of champagne but Duffy's was gone. Eight of us, standing on the corner of Beverly and Lefferts across from where my father's shoe repair store was. At midnight, we toasted a new century. We kept our pledge!"

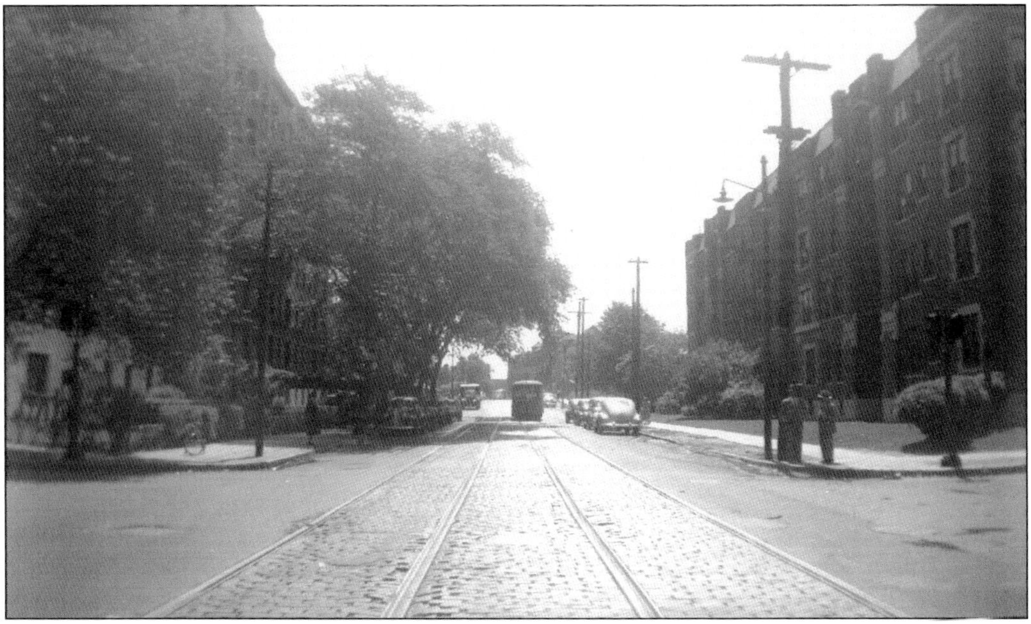

This trolley on Metropolitan Avenue is coming to Park Lane South. The McDonald family has lived here since 1972. Malini Singh McDonald recalls, "In 1997, Ian and I looked out our apartment window at Wallenberg Square. We said, 'Wallenberg would be an awesome spot for Shakespeare.' Thirteen years later, our dreams became a reality when our company, Black Henna Productions, produced *Much Ado About Nothing* there for the community. Dreams do come true!"

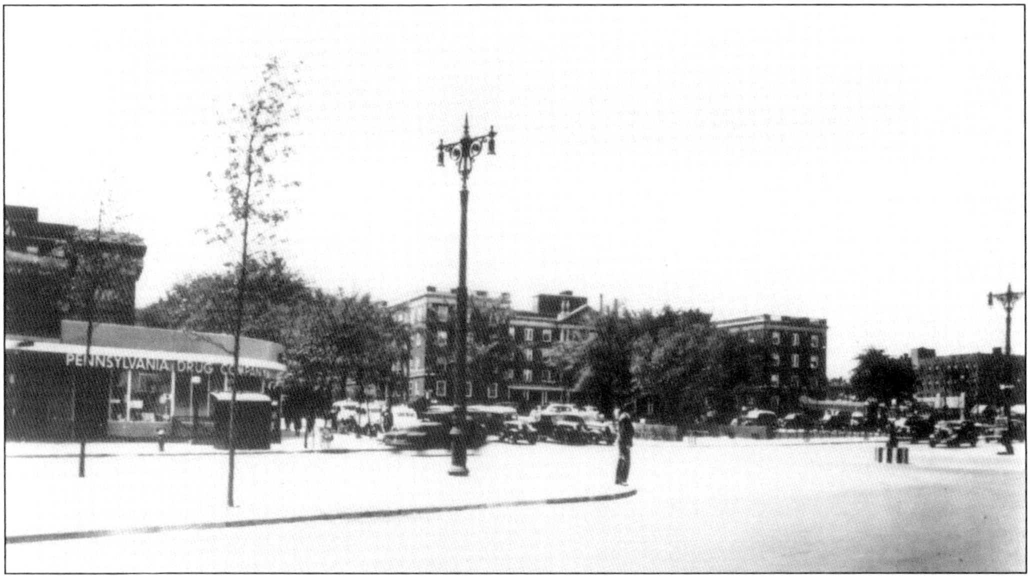

Queens Boulevard is seen here, with Kew Gardens in the background. In 1932, to honor the 200th birthday of Pres. George Washington, 200 memorial trees were planted on the Queens Boulevard malls from Union Turnpike, Kew Gardens, to Hillside Avenue. Visible on the left are two of these trees.

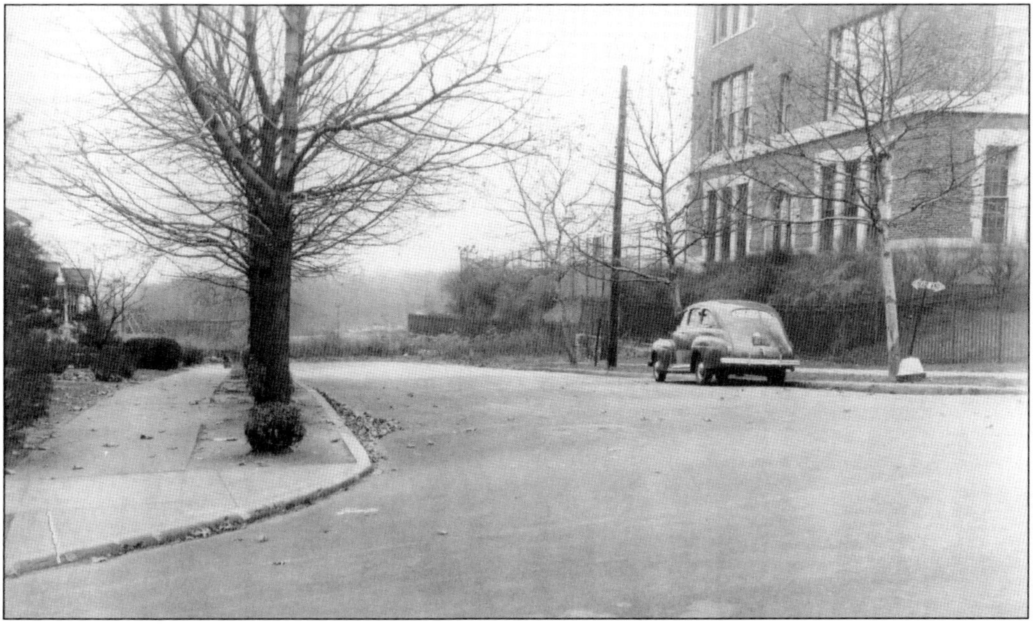

This photograph looks onto Eighty-second Road from Kew Gardens Road, past P.S. 99. "In 1970, galvanized by the City's plans to widen Lefferts Boulevard and cut down the old established trees, the Kew Gardens Improvement Association (KGIA) was formed and successfully fought off that proposal. The KGIA, with the Kew Gardens Civic Association, have worked on many community issues; the LIRR Kew Gardens station renovation and establishing an Early Childhood Center as part of P.S. 99," said Sylvia Hack.

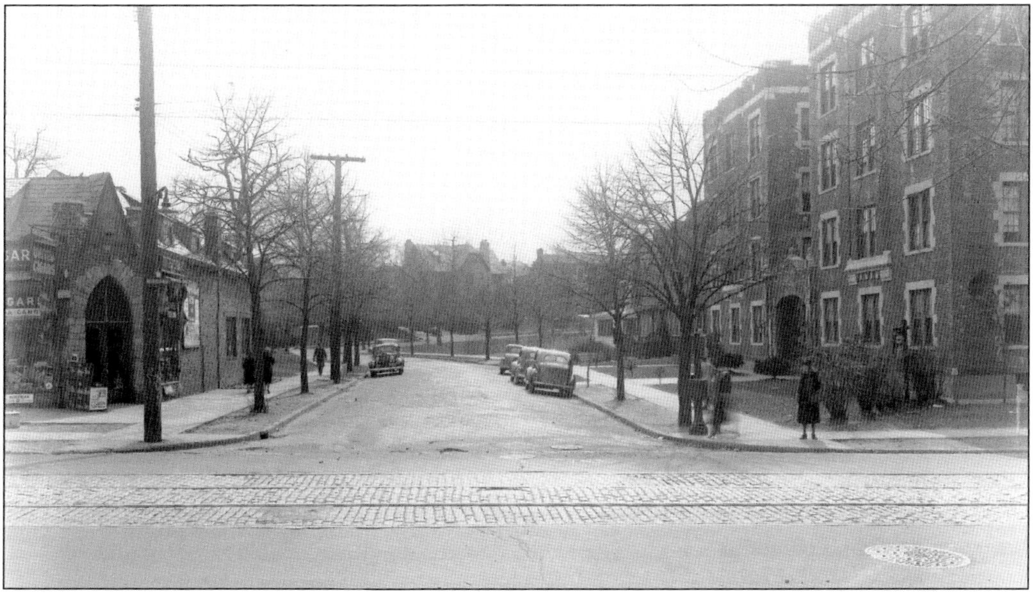

This photograph is looking south on 116th Street from Metropolitan Avenue. "My earliest memories of Kew Gardens, was coming to see the European art films at the Austin Movie Theater. We'd go to the Austin if we didn't want to go down to 'the Village' to the Bleecker St. Cinema or the 8th Street Playhouse, both known for their revivals and European art films. The Austin was our local version of a 'Village' art house," remembers Barry Lewis.

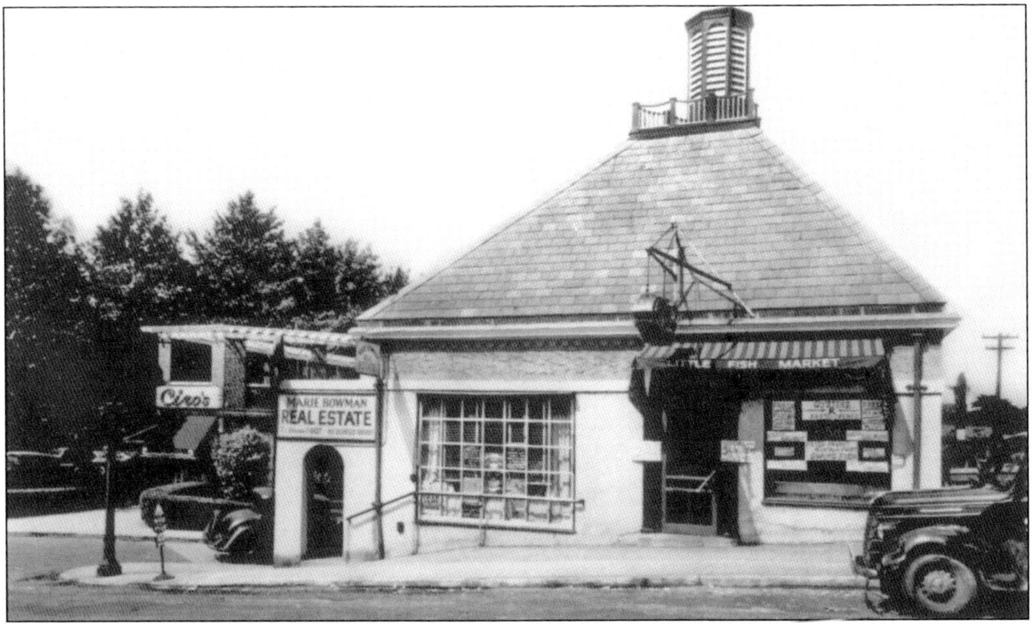

Marie Bowman Real Estate is pictured on the Lefferts Boulevard "Ponte Vecchio." Today, Dani's House of Pizza, founded by Ramiz Dani in 1959, occupies this building. "I remember 25 cents for a slice and a coke at the best pizza place in the world. Dani was friends with all the neighborhood kids and he knew all of them by name. If you didn't have a quarter, he gave you credit," remembers Linda Widder Wiesner.

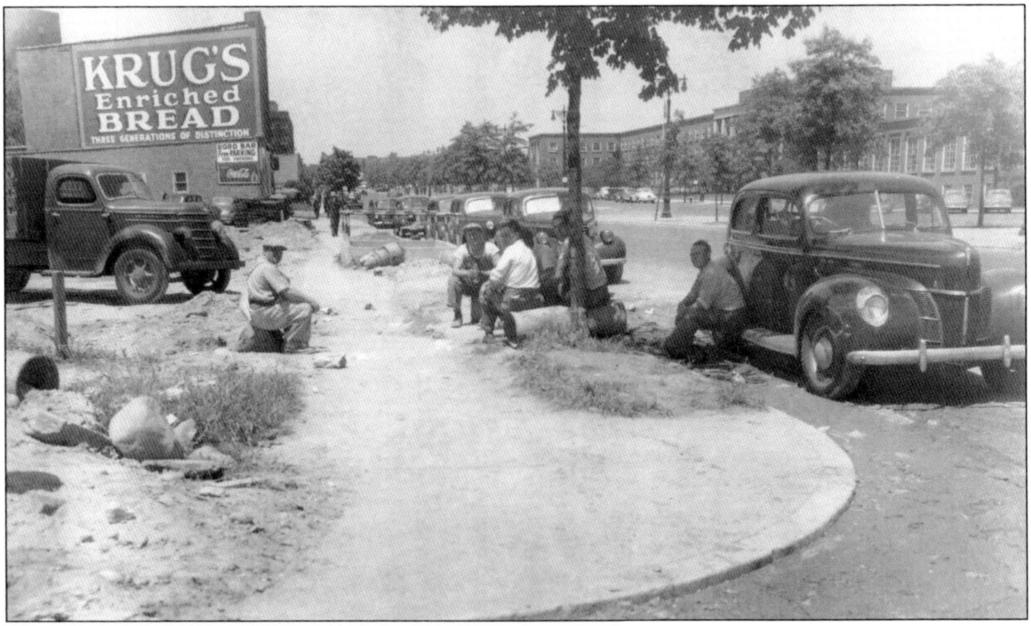

This 1942 photograph looks northwest onto Queens Boulevard from Eighty-second Avenue, with Borough Hall in the background. Founded in 1914, the Kew Gardens Civic Association has been the prime guardian of the community, preserving much of its character through constant vigilance and extraordinary dedication. Its 1915 foresighted agreement with the electric utility resulted in the electric wires going underground or in rear yards, rather than on the streets.

INDEX

Consistent with our mission to preserve history on a local level, this book was printed in South Carolina on American-made paper and manufactured entirely in the United States. Products carrying the accredited Forest Stewardship Council (FSC) label are printed on 100 percent FSC-certified paper.

MADE IN THE USA